Beginner

Teacher's Book

New Headway

English Course

Amanda Maris

Liz and John Soars

OXFORD

UNIVERSITY PRESS

OXFORD
UNIVERSITY PRESS

Great Clarendon Street, Oxford OX2 6DP

Oxford University Press is a department of the University of Oxford.
It furthers the University's objective of excellence in research, scholarship,
and education by publishing worldwide in

Oxford New York

Auckland Bangkok Buenos Aires Cape Town Chennai
Dar es Salaam Delhi Hong Kong Istanbul Karachi Kolkata
Kuala Lumpur Madrid Melbourne Mexico City Mumbai
Nairobi São Paulo Shanghai Taipei Tokyo Toronto

Oxford and Oxford English are registered trade marks of
Oxford University Press in the UK and in certain other countries

First published 2002
Fourth impression 2004

Any websites referred to in this publication are in the public domain and
their addresses are provided by Oxford University Press for information only.
Oxford University Press disclaims any responsibility for the content.

ISBN 0 19 437634 6

Printed and bound in Spain by Unigraf S.l. (Madrid)

Acknowledgements

Illustrations by:
Adrian Barclay pp14, 118
Chris Paveley pp113, 114, 124

Contents

New Headway Beginner

Introduction

New Headway Beginner is a foundation course for adult and young adult absolute beginners. It is also suitable for students who have already learned a little English, perhaps some years ago, but who don't yet feel confident enough to move on. They want to go back before they move forward.

New language is introduced gradually and methodically, in measured amounts, and in a logical order. Vocabulary has been selected carefully to avoid overloading. There are many controlled practice activities which aim to give beginners the confidence to proceed, but there is also some simple skills work, which incorporates manageable communicative activities appropriate for the low level. In the *Everyday English* section, we deal with social and functional language, and survival skills.

Organization of the course

The organization of *New Headway Beginner* is similar to *New Headway Elementary* and *New Headway Pre-Intermediate*. Each unit has these components:

- Starter
- Presentation of new language
- Practice
- Vocabulary
- Skills work – always speaking, combined with reading and/or listening and/or writing
- Everyday English

STARTER

The *Starter* section is designed to be a warmer to the lesson and has a direct link with the unit to come. This link might be topical or grammatical, or it might revise input from a previous unit.

PRESENTATION OF NEW LANGUAGE

New language items are presented through texts, mainly dialogues, which students can read and listen to at the same time. This enables students to relate the spelling to the sounds of English, and helps with pronunciation, as well as form and use. Sometimes there are two presentation sections. This is to break up what would otherwise be too large a 'chunk' of new language.

The main verb forms taught are:
- *to be*
- Present Simple
- *there is/are*
- Past Simple
- *can/can't*
- *I'd like*
- Present Continuous for now and future

We have chosen not to teach *have got*, for two reasons. Firstly, its Present Perfect form (*have* + the past participle) is confusing as *have got* refers to the present, not the past; secondly, *have* with its *do/does/did* forms is perfectly acceptable. This pattern has the advantage of fitting in with all the other verbs that students are learning.

There are *Grammar Spots* in the presentation sections. These aim to focus students' attention on the language of the unit. There are questions to answer, charts to complete, and short exercises. The *Grammar Spot* ends by cueing a section of the Grammar Reference at the back of the book.

PRACTICE

This section contains a variety of controlled and freer practice exercises. The primary skills used are speaking and listening, but there is also some reading and writing.

There are information gap exercises, mingle activities, information transfer listening exercises, questionnaires, and a lot of personalized activities. There are exercises where the aim is overt analysis of the grammar, such as *Check it*.

VOCABULARY

There is a strong lexical syllabus in *New Headway Beginner*. The vocabulary is carefully graded and recycled throughout, so that students don't suffer from overloading. Lexical sets are selected according to two criteria. They complement the grammatical input, for example, daily activities with the Present Simple; or members of the family with apostrophe *'s*. However, they are mainly chosen for their usefulness. Low-level students need to know the words of everyday life – food, sports, numbers, dates, travel, time, jobs, describing people and places, shopping, sightseeing, saying how you feel.

Skills work

LISTENING

Regular unseen listening sections, in dialogue or monologue form, provide further practice of the language of the unit and, later in the course, help to develop students' ability to understand the main message of a text.

READING

At the beginning of the course, the language in the readings is tightly controlled and graded, and only one or two words will be unknown to the students. As the course progresses, the readings become longer, with slightly more unfamiliar vocabulary in the texts. This gives students practice in dealing with new words and prepares them for the longer texts in *New Headway Elementary*.

SPEAKING

In the presentation sections, students have the opportunity to practise the pronunciation and intonation of new language. In the practice sections, less controlled exercises lead to freer speaking practice.

There are many speaking exercises based around the listening and reading activities. There is speaking to do *before* a text, to launch the topic and make students interested; and there are speaking activities *after* a text, often in the form of discussion.

WRITING

Writing exercises are usually, but not always, small in scope. Students are invited to write about their best friend, a postcard, a short introduction to their home town, and a description of a holiday.

EVERYDAY ENGLISH

This is a very important part of the syllabus of *New Headway Beginner*. There is language input and practice of several kinds:

- survival skills, such as numbers, saying dates, the alphabet, saying prices, filling in forms, and asking for directions
- social skills, such as social expressions and greetings
- functional areas, such as making requests, going shopping, and saying how you feel

There is sometimes an element of 'phrasebook language' in these sections. We are not asking students to analyse too deeply how a piece of language operates. For example, in Unit 7 we introduce *Can I ...?* in a variety of situations. We don't want teachers or students to worry too much about a modal verb that inverts in the question and doesn't take *do/does*. We merely want students to see how this phrase can be used to get what you want in a polite manner.

GRAMMAR REFERENCE

This is at the back of the Student's Book, and it is intended for use at home. It can be used for revision or for reference.

REVISION

There are four Stop and check tests on pp130–139 of the Teacher's Book. There are also three Progress tests, on pp121–127.

Workbook

All the language input – grammatical, lexical, and functional – is revisited and practised. There are also vocabulary, pronunciation, and listening exercises.

A Student's Workbook Cassette/CD accompanies the Workbook. There are listen and repeat exercises, and also unseen listenings. The cassette/CD is particularly beneficial to students who lack confidence in speaking and who have listening and/or pronunciation problems.

⚠ Most of the exercises in the Workbook can be completed without the cassette/CD. However, a small number (e.g. the unseen listenings) will require students to listen to the recording. Students for whom this is not possible can refer to the tapescripts on p81.

Teacher's Resource Book

This contains photocopiable games and activities to supplement the main course material.

Video

A *New Headway Beginner* Video, Video Guide, and Activity Book are available to accompany the course. The video takes the form of six episodes centred around four people sharing a house in Oxford. The first episode can be shown after Unit 4, and subsequent episodes after Units 6, 8, 10, 12, and 14.

Finally!

The basic criterion for selection of every activity in *New Headway Beginner* is its usefulness for the survival of a low-level student in an English-speaking environment. The book provides a package that will fit neatly in the suitcase! We are trying to lay the foundations for what we hope will be a successful and enjoyable language-learning future.

A step-by-step approach

Beginners require a very careful, staged approach with plenty of repetition, practice, and revision to help them internalize new language and to give them confidence. Suggested stages are as follows:

STARTER

This short warmer to the lesson must not be allowed to go on too long. Generally speaking, five minutes is the maximum.

PRESENTATION OF LANGUAGE POINT

You can vary the presentations if you like. Sometimes it is useful to play a recording first while the students look at the picture with the text covered. Then, after that, they can read and listen. This method may be helpful for some non-European students who are not very familiar with Roman script.

LISTENING AND REPEATING (DRILLING)

When introducing a new item of language, stop and practise pronunciation when students have grasped the meaning. You can use the recording as a model, or provide the model yourself. There are short pauses on the recording; you will need to stop the tape/CD to give students time to repeat at an appropriate pace. Allow students to listen to the word, phrase, or sentence two or three times before you ask them to repeat it. For example, to drill the sentence *How are you?* Play the recording and/or model the sentence yourself two or three times using the same pronunciation and intonation, then ask the students as a class to repeat the phrase, i.e. *choral drilling*. Don't say it with them, but instead listen to what they are saying. Say *Again* for them to repeat a second time. If it sounds as if they have got it right, ask one or two students individually to say it again for you to check, i.e. *individual drilling*. If the choral repetition *doesn't* sound right, remodel the phrase for students to listen to again, then have them repeat chorally again, before moving on to individual drilling.

PRACTICE

Move carefully from controlled to freer practice. Beginners require plenty of practice in order both to get their mouths round new language and vocabulary, and also to internalize and remember it. Don't stint on practice or revision, but equally do not spend too long on any one thing, or the students may get bored and switch off. You can always come back later and do more work on it.

The following techniques ensure enough practice as well as variety.

Pairwork

A lot of work can be done in pairs. Open and closed pairwork are often referred to in the teaching notes.

Open pairwork

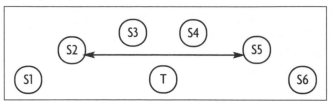

As a stage after drilling and before closed pairwork, you can call on two students at a time to practise the lines of a dialogue, ask and answer a question, etc. across the room, with the rest of the class listening.

Do open pairwork:
- to set up and demonstrate a closed pairwork activity
- to check understanding of a task
- to check students' grammar, pronunciation, and intonation before they go on to closed pairwork
- after a closed pairwork activity or a written exercise to check performance of the task.

Don't call on the whole class to perform open pairwork. Two or three pairs of students, each performing one or two exchanges, should be sufficient to check language. More than this may make the activity drag and become boring.

Closed pairwork

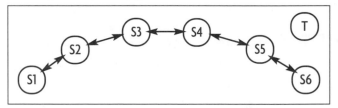

With closed pairwork, students talk and listen only to each other. This gives them more speaking time and a chance to practise with a peer without having to 'perform' in front of you and the class. It is important, though, for you to monitor students' performances unobtrusively. This will help you to identify persistent errors and misunderstandings. Do not interrupt and correct students while you monitor unless absolutely necessary, as this inhibits fluency. Instead, make a note of persistent errors and put some of them on the board for students to correct afterwards. (It is probably not necessary to identify the culprits!)

Chain practice

This is a good way of using flashcards in a practice speaking activity. It offers variety, a change of pace, and a lot of speaking practice of the language point without becoming boring. The following example describes a way of using flashcards of famous people.

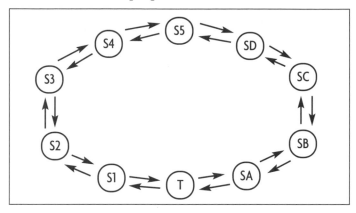

1 Stand in a circle with the students, with the flashcards in your hand.
2 Turn to S1 on your left, show the first card, and ask a question, e.g. *What's his/her name?* S1 answers, and receives the flashcard from you.
3 S1 then turns to S2 and asks the same question. S2 answers, and receives the card.
4 While S1 is asking S2, turn to SA on your right, show the second card, and ask the question *What's his/her name?* SA answers, receives the card, and turns to ask SB.
5 While SA is asking SB, turn back to S1 with the third flashcard, and ask the same question.
6 Continue the process until all the flashcards are in circulation and the students are asking and answering. There will be a bottleneck when the student opposite you starts getting questions from both sides at once, but it's part of the fun. Eventually the flashcards should all come back to you. This practise game can get fast and furious!

Classroom practices

Whether you have a monolingual or a multilingual class, it will save a great deal of time and effort if, at the beginning, you set up clear classroom practices and establish familiar routines. This will quickly provide comfort and reassurance for beginners who can find it nerve-racking to deal with a new and alien language. Also, many complete beginners are adults who haven't been in the classroom for a long time, and whose previous experience of learning a language was probably very different.

CLASSROOM LANGUAGE

Numbers 1–30 and the alphabet will have been introduced by Unit 4 so that you can refer students to page and exercise numbers in English, and spell words for them. You could also spend a little time at the beginning pre-teaching some useful

classroom language, e.g. *Sorry, I don't understand.*, *Can you spell it, please?* and instructions, e.g. *Work with a partner, Read, Listen, Repeat, All together, Again, Homework*, etc. All of this will enable you to keep an 'English' atmosphere.

When having to give instructions for an activity, rehearse them beforehand so that they are simple, clear, and concise, and *demonstrate* rather than explain wherever possible. Avoid repeating yourself or over-explaining, as it tends only to create further confusion.

EXPLAINING NEW VOCABULARY

Explanation of new vocabulary to beginners can be problematic, particularly in multilingual classes, and/or where you have no knowledge of the students' mother tongue. Make sure that students have a simple bilingual dictionary. Use pictures and/or draw on the board whenever possible. Do not worry if you are not a brilliant artist – simple line drawings are very quick and effective. Start collecting flashcards, posters, photos, etc. to help you.

Example sentences with the new word in context are often better than explanations. Giving a similar word or the opposite can also be useful, e.g. *finish = stop, get up ≠ go to bed.*

PRONUNCIATION OF NEW VOCABULARY

When you introduce new vocabulary, make sure you drill the pronunciation of the words as well. This should be done after the meaning has been established so that students are not mouthing words that they do not understand. It is also a good idea to get yourself into the habit of highlighting and marking up on the board the main stress of new words, and having students copy this down, e.g. *teacher* or *teacher*.

USE OF MOTHER TONGUE

There can be no doubt that it is useful to *know* the students' own language (L1), especially if you have a monolingual class. How much you *use* it is another matter. It is probably best to use it sparingly:

- Perhaps in the first lesson talk to students in L1 about the course, how they will work, etc. and explain that you will be using English with them.
- Perhaps use L1 to check instructions for a new and unfamiliar activity, or to check understanding of a new language point, but only after using English.
- You can use L1 for translation of new vocabulary (where there is a one-to-one direct translation) and to deal with students' queries, particularly when it would waste a lot of time trying to explain in English.

Otherwise, you may find that if beginners feel that it is acceptable to use their own language freely in the classroom, they are inhibited from taking the plunge and speaking English to you and to each other, and it becomes more difficult for them to make that important leap.

am/are/is, my/your • This is . . .
How are you? • What's this in English?
Numbers 1–10 and plurals

Hello!

Introduction to the unit

Starting Unit 1 of *New Headway Beginner* probably marks the beginning of a new course with a new group of students. The title of Unit 1 is 'Hello!' and aims to let the students get to know each other and you, and for you to get to know them of course! The context of greetings and introductions in different settings allows students to do this and shows them how they can communicate in English in a meaningful way with even quite basic language.

Key language aims are also fulfilled with the introduction of parts of *to be*, the introduction of some basic vocabulary (including some international words), numbers 1–10, and *-s/-es* plural endings.

Language aims

Grammar – *am/are/is* The verb *to be* is introduced in the singular with the subjects *I, you, this*, and *it* (*he/she/they* are introduced in Unit 2). The focus is on the positive and on questions with the question words *what* and *how*. (The question words are introduced through the functions of meeting people and greeting: *What's your name?*, *How are you?*, and talking about objects: *What's this in English?* Other question words are introduced and reviewed systematically throughout the course.)

Possessive adjectives *My* and *your* are introduced in the unit, with the other possessive adjectives being presented across the first four units of the course.

Vocabulary A set of key everyday words is introduced, some of which are international words, e.g. *camera*. There is an opportunity to extend this basic set via the classroom context.

Everyday English Numbers 1–10 and *-s/-es* noun plurals are introduced and practised. Students are introduced to the pronunciation of the *-s/-es* plural endings:

/s/	/z/	/ɪz/
books	cars	houses

Workbook *To be* and *my/your* are consolidated through further practice on greetings and introductions; key vocabulary, numbers 1–10 and *-s/-es* plurals are also practised.

Notes on the unit

STARTER (SB p6)

T 1.1 Smile, greet the class, and say your own name – *Hello, I'm (Liz)*. Point to yourself to make the meaning clear. Point to the speech bubbles and play the recording.

Invite students to say their own name, including the greeting *Hello*. If you have a very large group, you could ask a few students to say their name and then get students to continue in pairs. Keep this stage brief as students will have the opportunity to introduce themselves and each other in the next section.

WHAT'S YOUR NAME? (SB p6)

am/are/is, my/your

1 **T 1.2** Focus attention on the photos of Sandra and Hiro. Point to the conversation on p6 and ask students to read and listen. Play the recording through once.

Play the recording twice more, first pausing at the end of each line and getting the students to repeat as a class. Students then repeat lines individually before practising the conversation in open and then in closed pairs (see Teaching Beginners Tips and Techniques, TB p6). Encourage an accurate voice range – the amount by which pitch of the voice changes. (Many languages do not use such a wide voice range as English so this needs to be actively encouraged.) Also make sure students can accurately reproduce the contracted forms *I'm* and *name's*. If necessary, model the sentences again yourself to help emphasize the pronunciation in a visual way.

GRAMMAR SPOT

Focus attention on the contractions. Ask students to circle the contracted forms in exercise 1. Demonstrate this by writing the conversation on the board and puttting a circle round the first contraction *I'm*.

---

2   This is a mingle activity. Demonstrate the conversation with one student for the rest of the class. Then ask another two students to repeat the conversation in open pairs (see Teaching Beginners Tips and Techniques, TB p6). Demonstrate the meaning of 'stand up' and get the students to move around the class practising the conversation. You may like to encourage them to shake hands as they introduce themselves, particularly if they don't know each other. Monitor and check for pronunciation.

This is . . .

3   This section focuses on introducing people in a slightly more formal context, giving surnames as well as first names. Give your first name again: *I'm Liz.* Write it on the board: *Liz is my first name.* Then say your surname and write it on the board: *My surname is Brown.* Repeat *I'm Liz Brown – Liz is my **first** name, Brown is my **surname**.* Then ask a student whose first name you know: *Mayumi – Mayumi is your first name, what's your surname?* Elicit surnames from other students.

T 1.3 Focus attention on the photo of Sandra, Hiro, and John on p7. Point to the conversation and ask students to read and listen. Play the recording through once. Play the recording again and get students to point to the correct characters as they are referred to in the conversation.

Play the recording twice more, first pausing at the end of each line and getting the students to repeat as a class. Students then repeat lines individually before practising the conversation in open and then in closed pairs.

Encourage accurate pronunciation of the short sound /ɪ/ and of the linking:

/ɪ/ /ɪ/
this is John Mason

4   Point to the gapped conversation. Choose two confident students to demonstrate the conversation with you for the rest of the class. Introduce the students to each other and encourage them to shake hands when they say *Hello.* Choose two more groups of three to practise the conversation in front of the class.

Divide the class into groups of three and get each student take it in turns to introduce the other two. Monitor and check for pronunciation and intonation. Depending on the class, when the activity is over, you may like to ask one or two groups to go through the conversation again while the whole class listens.

SUGGESTION

If appropriate, you can play a memory game based on the students' names. Ask one student to go round the class saying everyone's name while the other students help if necessary. Encourage students in a multilingual group to pronounce everyone's name as accurately as possible. (You might want to do the memory game yourself, too, to make sure you have remembered all the students' names!)

How are you?

5   **T 1.4** Focus attention on the photo of Sandra and John on p8. Check students can remember the names of the characters by asking *Who's this?* Point to the speech bubbles in the photo and ask students to read and listen. Play the recording through once.

Play the recording twice more, first pausing at the end of each line and getting the students to repeat as a class. Students then repeat lines individually before practising the conversation in open and then in closed pairs. Encourage accurate stress and intonation on the questions:

How are you?

And you?

6   **T 1.5** Focus attention on the photo of John and Hiro on p8. Check students can remember the names of the characters. Follow the same procedure as for exercise 1.

7   Ask individual students *How are you?* to elicit the answer *Fine, / Very well, thanks. And you?* Reply to each student in turn. Make sure students realize that *And you?* requires an answer *Fine, / Very well, thanks.*

Then get students to ask and answer you and each other in open pairs across the class. It may be helpful to gesture to your partner when you say *And you?* to aid comprehension.

8 This is another mingle activity. (You may like to develop a gesture which means 'mingle'.) Focus attention on the speech bubbles. If necessary, check comprehension of *OK, fine, very well* with simple board drawings of faces – a straight face for *OK* ☺, a half smile for *fine* ☺, and a full smile for *very well* ☺. Demonstrate the conversation with one student for the rest of the class. Then ask another two students to repeat the conversation in open pairs. Get the students to move around the class practising the conversation. Monitor and check for pronunciation and intonation.

GRAMMAR SPOT

Focus attention on the gapped sentences. Elicit the word to complete the first sentence with the whole class as an example (*am*). Then ask students to complete the other sentences.

Answers
I **am** Sandra.
How **are** you?
This **is** John.

Read Grammar Reference 1.1 and 1.2 on p121 together in class, and/or ask students to read it at home. Encourage them to ask you questions about it, in L1 if appropriate.

PRACTICE (SB p9)

Introductions

1 Focus attention on the photos and conversations. Give students 30 seconds to read. Hold up the book so the class can see the photos. Read out the first line of the first conversation and point to the female character in the photo. Ask *Anna or Ben?* Point to the male and ask *Who's this?* Elicit the identities of Carla·and David for the second photo.

It is a good idea to write the first conversation gap-fill on the board and do it with the whole class, as students may not be familiar with this kind of exercise. Write students' suggestions (right or wrong) in the gaps.

T 1.6 Play the conversations for students to listen and check. See if they can hear and correct any mistakes themselves before you offer correction. Then check the answers with the whole class.

Answers and tapescript
1 A Hello. **My** name's Anna. **What's** your name?
  B Ben.
2 C Hello. My **name's** Carla. What's **your** name?
  D **My** name's David.

Get students to practise the conversations first in open pairs and then in closed pairs. Monitor and check for accurate pronunciation. If necessary, model the conversations again, either yourself or from the tape, and get students to practise again.

2 If students had few problems with the gap-fills in exercise 1, you could put them in pairs to try to complete the conversations in exercise 2 together. Go round and monitor, but don't correct any mistakes yet.

T 1.7 Play the conversations for students to listen and check before you check the answers with the whole class.

Answers and tapescript
1 B **Hello**, Anna. **How** are you?
  A Fine, thanks, Ben. **And you?**
  B **Very** well, thanks.
2 D Hi, Carla. **How are** you?
  C **Fine**, thanks. **And you?**
  D OK, **thanks**.

Get students to practise the conversations first in open pairs and then in closed pairs. Monitor and check for accurate pronunciation. If necessary, model the conversations again, either yourself or from the tape, and get students to practise again.

3 **T 1.8** Focus attention on the conversation and play the recording. Make it clear that students should just listen the first few times and not try to fill in the answers. Play the recording twice more, then write the first line up on the board and elicit what the second should be. Get them to fill in the number 2 on the correct line in their books, then finish the exercise individually or in pairs. Play the recording again for them to check their answers. Elicit the whole conversation in the correct order from the class and put it on the board for the practice stage which follows.

As this is a longer conversation than the students have practised up to now, play the recording two or three times and get the students to repeat chorally and individually. Then get them to continue in groups of three. (If appropriate, get them to stand up as this often encourages a more dynamic performance!) Let students refer to the correct order on the board, but discourage them from reading it word for word, as they will lose the correct intonation and not make eye contact with the other students. Monitor and check for accurate pronunciation and intonation. If you think more practice is needed at this stage, get students to repeat the conversation using their own names.

Answers and tapescript
R Hello. My name's Rita. What's your name?
T I'm Tina, and this is Mary.
R Hello, Tina. Hello, Mary.
M Hello, Rita. How are you?
B I'm OK, thanks. And you?
M Fine, thanks.

Read Grammar Reference 1.3 on p121 together.

ADDITIONAL MATERIAL

Workbook Unit 1
Exercises 1–5 These provide further practice on greetings and introductions.

VOCABULARY (SB p10)

What's this in English?

1 Many of the words in the lexical set may be known to the students as they are 'international' words or may be similar in their own language. Focus on the example and then get students to work individually or in pairs or groups of three to match the rest of the words to the photos. Monitor and check for correct spelling.

Check the answers with the whole class.

Answers
2 a camera
3 a television
4 a sandwich
5 a hamburger
6 a book
7 a computer
8 a bag
9 a house
10 a car

2 **T 1.9** Play the recording and get students to listen and repeat the words. Check for accurate word stress and, if necessary, explain the system of stress marks used in *New Headway* by writing the words with more than one syllable on the board and highlighting the stress:

•
photograph

•
sandwich

•
television

•
hamburger

•
computer

•
camera

3 **T 1.10** Focus attention on the speech bubbles. Demonstrate the conversation by pointing to the example in 1 and asking *What's this in English?* Elicit the reply *It's a photograph.* Play the recording and get students to repeat. Point to different pictures on p10 and get students to ask and answer in open pairs. Check for accurate pronunciation of *It's a* and if students produce **Is a*, repeat the drill.

Students then continue asking and answering about the objects in exercise 1, working in closed pairs.

GRAMMAR SPOT

Focus attention on the contracted form. Ask students to circle the same form in the conversation.

4 Pick up a book and ask *What's this in English?* Elicit the reply *It's a book.* Pick up another object that students don't know how to say in English and elicit the question *What's this in English?* Give the answer *It's a (dictionary).* Students then continue picking up or going to objects in the classroom and asking and answering. Write up the words on the board and highlight the word stress if necessary. (Try to avoid words beginning with a vowel and the need for students to use *an.* Also, try to limit students' questions to vocabulary that will be useful to them at this stage in their learning, e.g. *pen, dictionary,* and try not to let the activity go on too long!)

SUGGESTION
You can ask students for more examples of 'international' words or cognates with the students' own language (e.g. *supermarket, cinema, hospital, telephone, video, cassette, radio, tennis, golf, football*). Put the words on the board and practise the pronunciation.

ADDITIONAL MATERIAL

Workbook Unit 1
Exercises 6 and 7 These provide further practice on vocabulary and pronunciation.
Exercise 8 In this exercise students translate sentences containing the main grammar points presented in the unit.

Numbers 1–10 and plurals

> **SUGGESTION**
>
> Students need a lot of practice with numbers, so from now on, use numbers as much as possible when referring to pages and exercises. Continue to do quick number revisions in future lessons, especially as more numbers are introduced. This can include number dictations, either with you dictating or with the students working in pairs:
>
> **Teacher dictation:** Say numbers at random, writing them down yourself so that you have a means of checking. Students write the figures, not the words, as you say them. Have one student read their list of numbers out to check.
>
> **Pairs dictation:** Students prepare a list of random figures to dictate to their partner. They take it in turns to dictate their list. The student who is taking down the dictated numbers writes the figures, not the words, and then reads the list back to their partner to check the answers.
>
> Make sure you limit the range of numbers to those covered at any stage in the course, e.g. Unit 1: numbers 1–10.

1 **T 1.11** Play the recording once and get students to read and listen to the numbers. Write *two* and *eight* on the board and put a stroke through the *w* and the *gh* to show that they are silent. Play the recording again and get students to repeat. Get students to say the numbers round the class, starting again at *one* once they reach *ten*. You can also get students to say the numbers in reverse order if appropriate. If students need more practice, write figures at random on the board and get students to say the numbers as you write.

ADDITIONAL MATERIAL

Workbook Unit 1
Exercises 9–11 These provide further practice on numbers.

2 This exercise presents and practises formation of plurals with *-s/-es*, and reviews the vocabulary from this unit and numbers 1–10. Focus attention on the pictures and get students to count the objects/people and say the correct number, e.g. 1 *ten*.

Look at the example with the whole class. Then get students to complete the rest of the exercise, referring back to the list of numerals and words at the top of the page. Monitor and check for correct spelling.

T 1.12 Play the recording and get students to check their answers. Get students to write the words on the board as a final check.

Answers and tapescript
1 **ten** sandwiches
2 **two** books
3 **six** bags
4 **five** computers
5 **four** houses
6 **seven** hamburgers
7 **eight** cameras
8 **nine** photographs
9 **three** cars
10 **ten** students

> **GRAMMAR SPOT**
>
> Focus attention on the singular nouns and the plural noun endings. Ask students to underline the plural endings in exercise 1.
>
> Refer students to Grammar Reference 1.4 on p121.

3 **T 1.13** Play the recording through once and let students just listen. Play the recording again and get the students to repeat chorally and individually.

Refer students to Grammar Reference 1.4 on p121 and highlight the use of the *-ies* plural, e.g. *city – cities*.

ADDITIONAL MATERIAL

Workbook Unit 1
Exercises 12 and 13 These exercises provide further practice on plurals. Exercise 13 recycles numbers.

Don't forget!

Word list
Ask the students to turn to p128 and look at the word list for Unit 1. Explain that this contains important words from the unit. Go through the words in class and then ask students to learn the words for homework. Test them on a few of the words in the following lesson.

2

Countries
Where are you from? • *he/she/they*
his/her • Numbers 11–30

Your world

Introduction to the unit

The title of Unit 2 is 'Your world' and it focuses on countries and cities, and talking about where people are from. The characters introduced in Unit 1 are shown again in a different context. The syllabus of *Wh-* question words is reviewed and extended, and students continue with numbers 11–30. In terms of skills, students meet their first unseen listening task and also a short reading text. These are important first steps in developing listening and reading skills and help to prepare students for handling progressively longer listening and reading texts across the course.

Language aims

Grammar – Where are you from?; *he/she/they* Students build on the *Wh-* questions introduced in Unit 1 with the introduction of *Where are you from?* The verb *to be* with *I* and *you* is consolidated and also extended to include *he/she/they*.

Possessive adjectives *His* and *her* are introduced and *my* and *your* are reviewed from Unit 1.

Vocabulary A set of common cities and countries are introduced.

Everyday English The numbers syllabus is extended to cover 11–30.

Workbook The key lexical set of countries and cities is reviewed, including focuses on spelling and pronunciation.

He/she and *his/her* is consolidated through gap-fill activities.

Talking about where people are from is further practised through gap-fill activities, and reading and listening tasks.

Numbers 11–30 are practised in a range of activities.

POSSIBLE PROBLEMS

- Beginners often make mistakes with *he/she* and *his/her* (especially if subject pronouns are not used and/or if the possessives are expressed differently in their own language). The course provides a lot of practice on this possible area of confusion, but be prepared to monitor and check the use of *he/she* and *his/her* and go over these points whenever problems occur. Further confusion is possible with the contracted form *he's*. It's worth taking the time to drill the pronunciation of *his* /hɪz/ and *he's* /hi:z/ to help students perceive and produce the difference.

- Students often have problems distinguishing 'teen' numbers (13–19) from 'ten' numbers (30, 40, 50, etc.). Highlight the different word stress:

| ● | ● | ● | ● |
| *thirteen* | *thirty* | *fourteen* | *forty* |

Notes on the unit

SUGGESTION
Take the opportunity to review the greetings covered in Unit 1 at the beginning of each class. Greet each student as they arrive in class and ask how they are. Encourage students to greet each other in English so that they get into the habit of using the language they have learnt in a meaningful way.

STARTER (SB p12)

1 Focus attention on the countries in the box and on the map on p13. Demonstrate the activity by getting students to locate Australia on the map. Students continue locating the countries in exercise 1 on the map, working in pairs. If there is any disagreement, check the answers with the whole class.

Answers

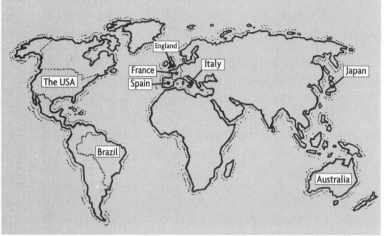

Get students to write their own country on the map. Remind them of the question *What's … in English?* from Unit 1 so that they can ask you for the name of their country, e.g. *What's (Belgique) in English?* (If you do not recognize the name of the country in the students' mother tongue, then ask them to point it out on the map.) Write up the names of the countries on the board and drill the pronunciation as necessary.

2 **T 2.1** Play the recording and get the students to repeat chorally and individually. Pay particular attention to stress. If you have a lot of students from other countries, get them to say the name of their country and check their pronunciation.

WHERE ARE YOU FROM? (SB p12)

he/she, his/her

1 **T 2.2** This conversation introduces the second person question form. Focus attention on the photos of Sandra and Hiro, who appeared in Unit 1. Point to the conversation and ask students to read and listen. Play the recording through once. Play the recording again and then ask *Where's Spain? Where's Japan?* Get students to point to the correct part of the map.

Play the recording again, pausing at the end of each line and getting the students to repeat as a class. Students then repeat lines individually before practising the conversation in open and then in closed pairs.

Encourage accurate reproduction of the contrastive stress in the questions, and of the falling intonation:

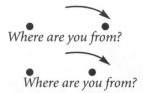

Where are you from?

Where are you from?

2 This is another mingle activity. If you have a multilingual class, make sure that all the students' countries are written on the board and practised beforehand. If you have a monolingual class, you might like to teach them *I'm from* (town/city) *in* (country) to vary the answers. Demonstrate the conversation with one student for the rest of the class. Then ask another two students to repeat the conversation in open pairs. Get the students to move around the class practising the conversation. Monitor and check for pronunciation.

3 **T 2.3** Focus attention on the photos of Hiro and Sandra. Point to the sentences and ask students to read and listen. Play the recording through once. Play the recording again and get students to repeat. Encourage students to reproduce the long and short sounds in *his* and *he's*:

/ɪ/   /iː/
His name's Hiro. He's from Japan.

Write the sentences about Hiro on the board. Circle *his* and *he*. Repeat ***His name's Hiro, he's from Japan*** and model the sentence on another male class member: ***His name's Erdi, he's from Turkey.*** Now contrast with a female student: *BUT **Her name's Ali, she's from Indonesia**.* Write up the sentences about Sandra and circle *Her* and *She*. Elicit more examples from the class to consolidate the use of *he/she* and *his/her*.

GRAMMAR SPOT

Focus attention on the contractions. Ask students to circle the contracted forms in exercise 3.
Read Grammar Reference 2.1 and 2.2 on p121 together in class, and/or ask students to read it at home. Encourage them to ask you questions about it.

4 Focus attention on the passport photos on p13. Read sentence 1 with the whole class. Students continue working individually and then check their answers in pairs.

T 2.4 Play the recording through once and let students check their answers. Play the recording again and get students to repeat chorally and individually.

Answers and tapescript
1 **His** name's Rick. He's **from the United States**.
2 **Her** name's Sonia. She's **from Brazil**.
3 **His** name's Jack. He's **from England**.
4 **His** name's Sergio. He's **from Italy**.
5 **Her** name's Marie. She's **from France**.
6 **Her** name's Kim. She's **from Australia**.

ADDITIONAL MATERIAL

Workbook Unit 2
Exercises 1–3 These provide further practice of the
countries introduced in the Student's Book.
Exercise 5 This introduces the countries in the United
Kingdom.

Questions

5 **T 2.5** This exercise introduces third person question
forms. Play the recording and get the students to repeat
chorally and individually. Check students can reproduce
the falling intonation of the *wh-* questions.

GRAMMAR SPOT

Focus attention on the contraction *where's*. Ask
students to circle the contraction *where's* in exercise 5.
Check students recognize *What's* in exercise 5 as the
contraction of *What is*.
Focus attention on the gapped sentences. Complete the
first sentence with the whole class as an example (*is*).
Then ask students to complete the other sentences.

Answers
Where **is** she from?
Where **is** he from?
Where **are** you from?

Refer students to Grammar Reference 2.3 on p121.

---

6 Go through the photographs on p13 yourself first asking
What's his/her name? and *Where's he/she from?* and
eliciting the answers, before getting students to do the
same in pairs. Monitor and check for correct use of
he/she and *his/her*.

SUGGESTIONS

• If students need further practice with *I/you, my/your,
he/she*, and *his/her*, make a photocopy of TB p106 and
cut out the role cards. This exercise provides further
practice by giving students a new name and country.
The cards provide a male and a female name from
each of the countries in the Student's Book and also
from the countries introduced in exercise 5 in Unit 2
of the Workbook (*Wales, Scotland,* and *Northern*

Ireland). *Canada* is also included from later in the
unit. You can either just use the cards with the
countries introduced in the Student's Book, or
pre-teach/check the other countries.

• Review the exchanges *What's your name? My name's
(Robert). Where are you from? I'm from (the United
States)*, writing them on the board if necessary. Also
review when to use *he/she*.

• Give the role cards out to the students, telling them
this is their new name and country. Ask students to
stand up and go round the class asking and
answering the question. Tell them they must try to
remember everyone's new name and country.

• When students have finished, point to various
students and ask the class *What's his/her name?* and
Where's he/she from? If the class is good, you can also
check with the student in question whether the class
has remembered correctly, asking *Is that right?*, and
having them answer *Yes* or *No*.

• Alternatively, or in addition to the above suggestion,
you could bring in pictures of famous people for
further practice. You could use them for open
pairwork, or you could try a question and answer
chain as follows:

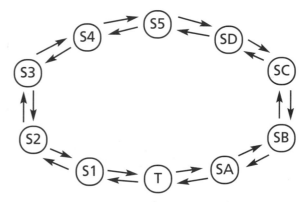

1 Stand in a circle with the students, with the pictures
in your hand.
2 Turn to S1 on your left, show the first card and ask
What's his/her name? and *Where's he/she from?* S1
answers, and receives the picture from you.
3 S1 then turns to S2 and asks the same question. S2
answers, and receives the picture.
4 While S1 is asking S2, turn to SA on your right,
show the second picture, and ask the question
What's his/her name? and *Where's he/she from?* SA
answers, receives the picture, and turns and asks SB.
5 While SA is asking SB, turn back to S1 again with
the third picture, and ask the question.
6 Continue the process until all the pictures are in
circulation and the students are asking and

answering. There will probably be a bottleneck when the student opposite you starts getting questions from both sides at once, but that's part of the fun. Eventually the pictures should all come back to you.

ADDITIONAL MATERIAL

Workbook Unit 2
Exercise 6 This consolidates *he/she – his/her*.
Exercise 7 This focuses on *Where are you from?* and also reviews the greetings from Unit 1.

PRACTICE (SB p14)

Cities and countries

1 Focus attention on the names of the cities on p14 and drill the pronunciation chorally and individually. Model the conversation and get students to repeat chorally. Students repeat the conversation with a different city, e.g. Paris, in open pairs. Students continue working in closed pairs.

   T 2.6 Play the recording and let students check their answers.

Answers and tapescript	
Where's Tokyo?	It's in Japan.
Where's Paris?	It's in France.
Where's Barcelona?	It's in Spain.
Where's Milan?	It's in Italy.
Where's Oxford?	It's in England.
Where's Rio de Janeiro?	It's in Brazil.
Where's Boston?	It's in the United States.
Where's Sydney?	It's in Australia.

2 This is the first information gap exercise that students have encountered in the book, and it therefore needs careful setting up. Make sure students understand that they shouldn't look at each other's pages until the end of the activity. Each student has the name and country/city of four of the eight people in the photos. The aim is for each student to find out about the other four by asking their partner. If possible, explain this using the students' own language and demonstrate a couple of question and answer exchanges with a good student yourself first. Remind students of the forms they will need to talk about the men and women in the photos (*What's his/her name?* and *Where's he/she from?*). Drill all four questions again if necessary.

   Divide the class into pairs and make sure students know if they are Student A or B. Student A should look at p14 in the unit and Student B at p138 at the end of the book. Students can refer to each photo by saying the number. They should write their answers in the spaces provided.

While the students are asking and answering about the people in the photos, go round monitoring and helping out. If the names cause problems, get students to write them on a separate piece of paper and show it to their partner. When they have finished, you can check by asking individual students to tell you about one of the people in the photos. Say *Tell me about number one*, etc.

Answers	
Tell students to look at each other's pages.	

Talking about you

3 Point to a few students and ask the class *What's his/her name?* and *Where's he/she from?* Focus attention on the speech bubbles and get students to practise the questions and answers in open pairs across the class. Then get students to replace the examples in exercise 3 with students' names and countries and to include the name of a city/town if appropriate. Students continue working in closed pairs.

ADDITIONAL MATERIAL

Workbook Unit 2
Exercise 4 This reviews towns and countries.

Questions and answers

4 **T 2.7** Focus attention on the photo of Sandra and Luis on p15. Ask students *What's her name?* about Sandra and elicit the answer. Ask *What's his name?* about Luis and use the opportunity to elicit/teach *I don't know.*

   Play the conversation through once and get students to complete as many gaps as possible. (With a weaker group, you may want to let them listen through once before they fill in the gaps.) Play the conversation again and get students to complete their answers. Check the answers with the whole class.

   Answers and tapescript
   S Hello, I'm Sandra. What's **your** name?
   L **My** name's Luis.
   S Hello, Luis. Where are you **from**?
   L **I'm** from Spain. Where are *you* from?
   S Oh, I'm from Spain, too. **I'm** from Madrid.

   Play the recording again, pausing at the end of each line and getting the students to repeat as a class. Get a couple of pairs of students to practise the conversation in open pairs and then get the class to continue in closed pairs.

   SUGGESTION
   If you have pictures of famous people of different nationalities, you can use these for further practice. If not, you can write on the board the names of some famous people whose nationalities students will know, for further question and answer practice.

5 **T 2.8** This exercise consists of three short conversations with people from different countries and it is the students' first unseen listening. They should be well prepared for the language by now, but some students tend to panic without the support of the written word. Explain that they only have to listen for two countries in conversations 1 and 2, and one country in conversation 3. Tell them not to worry if they don't understand every word!

Play the first conversation and elicit where Akemi is from (Japan). Play the rest of the recording and let students compare their answers in pairs. Play the recording again as many times as is necessary to let students complete their answers.

> **Answers**
> 1 Gérard: **France**
>   Akemi: **Japan**
> 2 Bud: **the United States**
>   Charles: **England**
> 3 Loretta and Jason: **Australia**
>
> **T 2.8**
> 1 **G** Hello, I'm Gérard. I'm from France.
>   **A** Hello, Gérard. I'm Akemi from Japan.
> 2 **C** Hello. My name's Charles. What's your name?
>   **B** Hi, Charles. I'm Bud. I'm from the United States. Where are *you* from?
>   **C** I'm from Oxford, in England.
>   **B** Oh, yeah. I'm from Chicago.
> 3 **L** Hi, I'm Loretta. I'm from Sydney, Australia.
>   **J** Hi, Loretta. I'm Jason. I'm from Australia, too.
>   **L** Wow! Are you from Sydney?
>   **J** No. I'm from Melbourne.

> **SUGGESTION**
> Allowing students to tell you other details that they have understood from a listening can help build their confidence, so you can ask extra questions within the students' language range, e.g. *What's his/her name? Where in (England)?*

6 Look at the example with the whole class. Elicit the match for question 2 (Her name's Irena) and then get students to continue working individually before checking their answers in pairs.

T 2.9 Play the recording and let students check their answers.

> **Answers and tapescript**
> 1 Where are you from? I'm from Brazil.
> 2 What's her name? Her name's Irena.
> 3 What's his name? His name's Luis.
> 4 Where's he from? He's from Madrid.
> 5 What's this in English? It's a computer.

> 6 How are you? Fine, thanks.
> 7 Where's Toronto? It's in Canada.

Check it

7 Focus attention on the first pair of sentences as an example. Check students understand that the convention of ticking (✔) indicates that something is correct. Students continue working individually to choose the correct sentence.

Get students to check their answers in pairs before checking with the whole class.

> **Answers**
> 2 What's his name?
> 3 'What's his name?' 'Luis.'
> 4 He's from Spain.
> 5 Where's she from?
> 6 What's her name?

READING AND LISTENING (SB p16)

Where are they from?

1 This is the first reading text that the students have encountered in the book. It presents the subject pronoun *they*. Focus attention on the photo and get students to guess where Miguel and Glenna are from. Get students to read the text through quickly and check (Miguel – Brazil, Glenna – Canada). Check comprehension of *Canada* by getting students to locate it on the map on p13.

T 2.10 Play the recording and ask students to read and listen. Then explain any new words. Words and phrases not previously introduced are *married, doctor, hospital, teacher, school,* and *in the centre of. Married* can be explained by referring to a famous married couple. To explain *doctor,* you can turn to p18 of the Student's Book (the start of Unit 3), where there is a picture of a doctor. Ask students *Where?* about the doctor to elicit/explain *hospital. Teacher* and *school* should be easy to explain in the context of the classroom. *In the centre of* can be illustrated on the board.

GRAMMAR SPOT

Focus attention on the gapped sentences. Complete the first sentence with the whole class as an example (*is*). Then ask students to complete the other sentences.

> **Answers**
> She **is** a doctor.
> He **is** a teacher.
> They **are** from Brazil.

If necessary, highlight the use of *he/she/they*, by pointing to a male student and saying *he*, a female student and saying *she*, a pair of students and a group of students and saying *they*.

Refer students to Grammar Reference 2.4 on p121.

2 Students work in pairs to complete the sentences about the text. Make sure they understand they can give the country or city as the answer to number 1. Go over the answers by asking individual students to read out their completed sentences.

> **Answers**
> 1 Miguel is from **Brazil/Rio**.
> 2 He's a **teacher**.
> 3 His school is in the **centre** of Rio.
> 4 Glenna is from **Toronto** in Canada.
> 5 She's a **doctor**.
> 6 Her **hospital** is in the centre of Rio.
> 7 They **are** in New York.
> 8 They are **married**.

3 Focus attention on the questions in the speech bubbles in exercise 3. Highlight the use of the contraction *'s*. Get students to ask and answer in open pairs. Students then work individually to write questions about Miguel and Glenna, using the prompts. Then get students to write other questions using *What … ?* and *Where … ?* Monitor and help as necessary. Students ask and answer in closed pairs. Monitor and check for correct use of *he/she* and *his/her*, and for falling intonation on the *wh-* questions.

ADDITIONAL MATERIAL

Workbook Unit 2
Exercises 8 and 9 These provide further reading and sentence completion practice.
Exercise 10 This is an exercise to practise listening for correct information.
Exercise 11 In this exercise students translate sentences containing the main grammar points presented in the unit.

EVERYDAY ENGLISH (SB p17)

Numbers 11–30

1 Get students to say numbers 1–10 round the class, repeating as many times as necessary until students can say them without hesitation.

2 **T 2.11** Focus attention on numbers 11–20. Remind students of the system used in the book for highlighting word stress. Play the recording and get students to listen, read, and repeat chorally. Play the recording again and get students to repeat individually. If necessary, remind students that the *gh* in *eighteen* is silent by writing the

word on the board and crossing out the letters.

Get students to say numbers 1–20 round the class. Again, get them to repeat as many times as necessary until they can say the numbers without hesitation.

3 Give students a number dictation. (See Unit 1 *Everyday English* Suggestion TB p12.) Then write a random selection of numbers 1–20 (as figures) on the board and get students to say the numbers first chorally, then individually.

4 Focus attention on the example. Then get students to continue matching in pairs.

   T 2.12 Play the recording through once and get students to check their answers. Play the recording again and get them to repeat, first chorally then individually. Check students can distinguish the word stress on *thirteen* and *thirty*:

   ●   ●
   thirteen   *thirty*

   Get students to say numbers 1–30 round the class. Get them to repeat as many times as necessary until they can say the numbers without hesitation.

5 **T 2.13** Focus attention on the panel of numbers in exercise 5. Play the first number as an example and focus on the answer (*12*). Play the recording through once and get students to tick the numbers. Let students check their answers in pairs and then play the recording again if necessary. Check the answers with the whole class.

> **Answers and tapescript**
> 1 twelve
> 2 sixteen
> 3 twenty-one
> 4 seventeen
> 5 thirty

6 Get students to do a number dictation in pairs using numbers 1–30 (See Unit 1 *Everyday English* Suggestion TB p12). Student A should say the numbers and Student B write. Then get students to change roles. Monitor and check for accurate pronunciation and comprehension of the numbers. Note any common errors, and drill and practise the numbers again in the next lesson.

ADDITIONAL MATERIAL

Workbook Unit 2
Exercises 12–16 These exercises review and consolidate numbers 11–30.

Don't forget!

Word list
Ask the students to turn to p128 and go through the words with them. Ask them to learn the words for homework, and test them on a few in the following lesson.

Jobs

am/are/is – negatives and questions

Address, phone number • Social expressions

Personal information

Introduction to the unit

The title of Unit 3 is 'Personal information' and the main aim of the unit is to allow students to exchange more information about themselves. This includes job, age, address, phone number, and whether students are married or not. The grammar of the verb *to be* is recycled and extended to include the *we* form, negatives, *wh-* and *Yes/No* questions and short answers. In terms of skills, students get practice in listening and speaking, and reading and speaking.

The lexical set of jobs is presented and the *Everyday English* syllabus is extended to include social expressions.

Language aims

Grammar – *am/are/is* The verb *to be* is recycled and extended to include the subject pronoun *we* in the negative and positive, negative forms *'m not, isn't*, questions with question words including *How old* and *Who*, *Yes/No* questions and short answers.

Possessive adjectives *My*, *your*, *his*, and *her* are reviewed from Units 1 and 2.

Vocabulary A set of common jobs is presented and there is an opportunity to extend this set with students' own jobs.

Everyday English This section focuses on social expressions including greetings at different parts of the day (*Good morning*, etc.) and key situational language like *Pardon?*, *Sorry*, etc.

Workbook The lexical set of jobs is recycled.

The forms of *to be* are fully reviewed with exercises on the negative, questions, and short answers.

Students are given extra practice in listening and reading.

There is an exercise on word stress.

The social expressions from *Everyday English* are reviewed.

Notes on the unit

STARTER (SB p18)

> **NOTE**
> In this section, students are asked to give their own job. If you have a multilingual group or you don't speak the students' own language, ask them to look up the name of their job in a dictionary before the lesson. Briefly check the pronunciation with the students so that they are prepared for exercise 2.

1 This section introduces some job vocabulary and practises the question *What's your job?* Students will already be familiar with *doctor* and *teacher* from the Reading in Unit 2, so use these as examples to demonstrate the activity.

If you think students might know some of the jobs, put them in pairs and ask them to match any jobs they know and guess the others. Then check answers with the class. If you think students won't know any of the vocabulary or won't want to guess the answers, then do the matching activity as a whole-class exercise.

T 3.1 Play the recording and get students to listen and repeat the words, first chorally and then individually. Concentrate on correct pronunciation and word stress. Make sure students don't get confused by the spelling of *nurse* and *businessman* and pronounce the *u* incorrectly:

nurse   /nɜːs/
businessman   /'bɪznɪsmən/

2 Focus attention on the speech bubbles. Write the sentences up on the board and circle the *a* in each answer to emphasize that we use an article before jobs. Drill the question and answers chorally and individually. Quickly check if students have jobs which are different from those in the Student's Book. If students want to use a job beginning with a vowel, e.g. *engineer,* point out they will have to use *an – I'm an engineer.*

WHAT'S HER JOB? (SB p18)

Negatives – *isn't*

1 **T 3.2** Briefly review *his* and *her* by pointing to a man and a woman in the Starter pictures and eliciting *What's his job?* and *What's her job?* Play the recording, pausing at the end of each line and getting the students to repeat chorally and individually. Make sure students include the article *a* each time. Students practise talking about the people in the pictures in open and then in closed pairs. Monitor and check for correct intonation and use of *his/her* and *a.*

> **SUGGESTION**
> If you think students need more practice, you can use flashcards of the same jobs that appear in the Student's Book. Get students to ask and answer *What's his/her job?* in pairs, swapping the flashcards as they finish with them.

2 Point to the teacher in the Student's Book and say *He isn't a student. He's a teacher.* Shake your head as you say the negative sentence to make the meaning clear. Point to the doctor and say *She isn't a nurse. She's a doctor.*

> **GRAMMAR SPOT**
> Focus attention on the negative sentence and what the contracted form is in full. Make sure students understand that the sentence is negative. Ask students to circle the negative forms in exercise 2.

T 3.3 Play the recording, pausing at the end of each line and getting the students to repeat chorally and individually. Make sure students can reproduce the negative form correctly and that they include the article *a* each time.

Write the following cues on the board to demonstrate the activity:

Number 2   He / shop assistant ✘ / taxi driver ✔
Number 3   She / teacher ✘ / police officer ✔

Get students to give the above sentences in full (*He isn't a shop assistant. He's a taxi driver* and *She isn't a teacher. She's a police officer.*). Students then continue talking about the pictures in closed pairs. Monitor and check for correct intonation, pronunciation of *isn't,* and use of *a.*

> **SUGGESTION**
> If you think students need more practice with *is/isn't,* you can get them to produce sentences with information about each other. You can talk about jobs and also review the language from Unit 2, e.g.
> *Ana isn't a student. She's a teacher.*
> *Juan isn't a teacher. He's a doctor.*
> *Yoshi isn't from Tokyo. He's from Osaka.*
> *Her name isn't Helen. It's Elena.*

ADDITIONAL MATERIAL

Workbook Unit 3
Exercises 1–3 These exercises review jobs, the questions *What's his/her job?,* and *is/isn't.*

Questions and short answers

3 Focus attention on the website file details. Read through the information with the class. Check comprehension of *address, phone number,* and *age* and drill the pronunciation of these words. Remind students of *married* from the Reading in Unit 2.

4 Focus attention on the example in number 1. Put students into pairs to complete the questions and answers. Note that students will have to generate the question *Where's she from?* for the *Country* category on the website file. This question should not be a problem for them, as they have already practised it several times. The question *How old is she?* is also new and is given in full so that students can familiarize themselves with it before they practise it. The short answer *No, she isn't* is included in this exercise. Again, students will be able to

generate the question (*Is she married?*) for this answer, and *Yes/No* questions and short answers are covered in the following exercise. (With a weaker group, you could complete the questions and answers with the whole class first and use the 'Listen and check' phase for repetition.)

T 3.4 Play the recording, pausing after each question and answer and get students to check their answers.

Answers and tapescript
1 What's her **name**? Amy Roberts.
2 Where's she **from**? England.
3 What's her **address**? 18, Market Street, Manchester.
4 What's her **phone number**? 0161 929 5837.
5 How old is she? She's **twenty**.
6 What's **her job? She's a student**.
7 Is she **married**? No, she isn't.

Play the recording again and get students to repeat all the questions and answers. Do this chorally and individually. Point out that in English we give our phone numbers using single figures 0–9, and that 0 is pronounced 'oh'.

Get students to ask and answer about Amy, working in open and then closed pairs.

SUGGESTION
For further practice, cut out a picture of a man from a magazine (or draw one on the board) and provide similar ID information about him. Students then practise asking and answering the questions with *he/him*.

GRAMMAR SPOT
Focus attention on the questions and short answers. Make sure students understand that we don't repeat the key word from the question in the short answer. Ask students to circle the short answer in exercise 4.

5 *Yes/No* questions and short answers, which appeared in exercise 4, are covered in full here.

T 3.5 Focus attention on the speech bubbles. Ask students to read and listen. Play the recording through once. Play the recording again, pausing at the end of each line and getting the students to repeat as a class. Check for accurate reproduction of the rising intonation on the question and falling intonation on the answer:

Is Amy from America? No, she isn't.

Focus on the question cues in number 1 and demonstrate the first question and answer exchange with a confident student – *Is she from London? No, she isn't.* Students continue to ask and answer about the other cities in question 1, working in open pairs. Students

continue asking and answering the other questions in closed pairs. Monitor and check for correct intonation and correct use of short answers.

Answers
1 Is she from London? — No, she isn't.
 Is she from Liverpool? — No, she isn't.
 Is she from Manchester? — Yes, she is.
2 Is she 16? — No, she isn't.
 Is she 18? — No, she isn't.
 Is she 20? — Yes, she is.
3 Is she a teacher? — No, she isn't.
 Is she a nurse? — No, she isn't.
 Is she a student? — Yes, she is.
4 Is she married? — No, she isn't.

6 This exercise practises the positive and negative forms in sentences. Focus attention on the two examples in number 1. Students complete the sentences with the information about Amy. Get students to check their answers in pairs before checking with the whole class.

Answers
2 Her phone number **isn't** 0171 929 5837. It's 0161 929 5837.
3 She **isn't** 18. She's 20.
4 She **isn't** married.

ADDITIONAL MATERIAL

Workbook Unit 3
Exercise 4 An identity card exercise to practise personal information.
Exercise 5 A third person question formation exercise.
Exercise 6 An exercise to practise third person short answers.

WHAT'S YOUR JOB? (SB p20)

Negatives and short answers

1 *Yes/No* questions in the second person and short answers in the first person are presented here. Focus attention on the information about Jeff. Give students time to read it through.

T 3.6 Play the recording through once and ask students just to listen. Play the recording again and get students to complete as many questions and answers as they can while they listen. Get them to compare their answers in pairs and help each other to complete the conversation, using the information about Jeff.

Play the recording again and get students to check their answers and/or complete any they missed. Check the answers with the whole class.

GRAMMAR SPOT

1 Focus attention on the negative sentence and what the contracted form is in full. Make sure students understand that the sentence is negative. Ask students to circle the negative forms in exercise 1.

2 Focus attention on the short answers. Make sure students understand that we use the full form in the third person affirmative – *Yes, it is*, not **it's*, and that we cannot say I **amn't* for the first person negative. Ask students to circle the short answers in exercise 1.

Read Grammar Reference 3.1 on p122 together in class, and/or ask students to read it at home. Encourage them to ask you questions about it.

2 This is a 'Listen and answer' exercise where students reply to your questions. Focus attention on the speech bubbles. Ask the question to a number of students and elicit true short answers *Yes, I am* or *No, I'm not*. Drill the pronunciation of the short answers. Then ask the students further questions to generate a range of true short answers. These can include:

Name: Are you (Yoshi)?
Country: Are you from (Spain)?
City: Are you from (Rio)?
Job: Are you a (teacher)?
Age: Are you (28)?
Married: Are you married?

3 In this exercise students mingle and ask each other *Yes/No* questions. Focus attention on the speech bubbles and get students to ask and answer in open pairs. It's a good idea to give students time to prepare their questions before they mingle, especially with a weaker group. Get students to write five questions using the questions in the book as a model and substituting information where possible.

Get students to stand up and do the activity. Monitor and check for correct intonation and use of short answers.

ADDITIONAL MATERIAL

Workbook Unit 3

Exercise 7 This exercise provides practice of first person short answers.

Exercise 8 A second person question formation exercise.

Exercise 9 This exercise provides practice of first person answers to questions with question words.

PRACTICE (SB p21)

Listening and speaking

1 Focus attention on the photos of Giovanni and Diana. Get students to read through the information in the table so that they know what they have to listen for. Explain that they are going to hear two conversations, one with Giovanni and one with Diana. These are a little longer than in previous units, but reassure students that they only need to complete the information in the table and they don't have to understand every word.

T 3.7 Ask students to listen for the country Giovanni is from. Check the answer (*Italy*). Play the first eight lines of conversation 1 and then pause. Play the recording again from the beginning and get students to complete the information about Giovanni. Pause before moving on to conversation 2.

Play conversation 2 through once and get students to complete the information about Diana. Get students to compare their answers in pairs. Play the conversations again, pausing after conversation 1 and get students to complete/check their answers.

Check the answers with the whole class.

Answers

Name	Giovanni Tomba	Diana Black
Country	Italy	**the United States**
City/Town	**Rome**	**New York**
Phone number	**06 944 8139**	212 463 9145
Age	23	**29**
Job	**Taxi driver**	Shop assistant
Married?	No	**Yes**

T 3.7

1 **I** Good morning.

G Hello.

I What's your name, please?

G My name's Giovanni Tomba.

I Thank you. And where are you from, Giovanni?

G I'm from Rome, in Italy.

I Thank you. And your telephone number, please?

G 06 944 8139.

I How old are you, Giovanni?

G I'm twenty-three.

I And . . . what's your job?

G I'm a taxi driver.
I And . . . are you married?
G No, I'm not.
I Thank you very much.
2 **I** Hello.
D Hello.
I What's your name, please?
D Diana Black.
I And where are you from?
D From New York.
I Ah! So you're from the United States.
D Yes, I am.
I What's your phone number?
D 212 463 9145.
I Thank you. How old are you?
D I'm twenty-nine.
I What's your job, Miss Black?
D I'm a shop assistant.
I And are you married?
D Yes, I am.
I That's fine. Thank you very much.

2 Demonstrate the activity by asking a confident student the first question. Students continue asking and answering in closed pairs. Monitor and check. If students have problems with intonation or with the short answers, drill the questions and answers across the class and get students to repeat.

Check the answers with the whole class.

Answers
No, he isn't.   Yes, she is.
No, he isn't.   No, she isn't.
Yes, it is.   Yes, she is.

> **SUGGESTION**
> If students need further practice, get them to ask and answer more *Yes/No* questions with the information about Giovanni and Diana, e.g.
> Is Giovanni from Italy?
> Is Diana from Chicago?
> Is he a teacher?
> Is he 23?
> Is her phone number 212 463 9145?
> Is she a shop assistant?
> Is he married?
> Is she married?

Talking about you

3 Focus attention on the example. Tell students they need a question word, e.g. *Where*, *What*, in all the questions except number 6. Get students to complete the questions in pairs. Check the answers with the whole class.

Answers
1 **What's your** name?
2 **Where are** you from?
3 **What's your** phone number?
4 How old **are you?**
5 **What's your** job?
6 **Are you** married?

Check the pronunciation of the questions. Make sure students know to use falling intonation on the *Wh-* questions and rising intonation on the *Yes/No* question (number 6). Divide the class into groups of three and get students to interview each other, using the questions. Get students to write down information about one student to use in exercise 4.

4 Get students to use the information they found in exercise 3 to write a short description. This can be done in class time or for homework.

> **SUGGESTION**
> If you want to give students further practice in exchanging personal information, photocopy the role cards on TB p107. There are four cards for female students and four for male students, so photocopy the appropriate number of cards for the gender balance in your class.
> Give out the role cards to the students, telling them this is their new identity. If necessary, review the questions students will need before they start the pairwork. Divide the class into pairs and get them to ask and answer the questions and note down the answers. Pair students with a different partner and get students to describe their first partner in order to review *he/she*, *his/her*.
> If you want students to have more written practice, get them to use the information to write a description as in exercise 4 above.

Check it

5 Focus attention on the first pair of sentences as an example. Remind students of the convention of ticking (✔) to indicate that something is correct. Students continue working individually to choose the correct sentence.

Get students to check their answers in pairs before checking with the whole class.

Answers
1 Her name's Janelle.
2 She's a teacher.
3 Are you from Spain?
4 His phone number is 796542.

5 How old is she?
6 She isn't married.
7 Are you married? Yes, I am.

ADDITIONAL MATERIAL

Workbook Unit 3
Exercise 13 This provides further listening practice.
Exercise 14 This provides further practice of third person short answers.

READING AND SPEAKING (SB p22)

A pop group

1 Check comprehension of the title 'A pop group' by asking students to give names of groups they know. Focus attention on the photo and make sure students understand that it shows a pop group called *4 x 4* (said 'four by four'). Pre-teach/check *on tour*, *great*, and *who?* The text also introduces the subject pronoun *we* and the preposition *at*. Students should understand these from context, but be prepared to explain if necessary.

Ask students to read the text through fairly quickly.

2 Elicit the answer to number 1 (*is 4 x 4*). Students complete the rest of the sentences, working in pairs. Check the answers with the whole class.

> **Answers**
> 1 The name of the group **is 4 x 4**.
> 2 **Melanie Ryan is** from Australia.
> 3 Cath and George Walters **are from** England.
> 4 **Yves Lacoste is from** France.
> 5 'We**'re** on tour in the United States.'

3 **T 3.8** Get students to read the questions through before they listen. If necessary, review numbers 11–30 to help students when picking out the ages of the characters.

Play the first eight lines of the conversation and elicit the answer to question 1 (*Melanie is 22*). Play the rest of the conversation and get students to listen for the answers to 2 and 3. If necessary, refer them back to the text so that they can remember the names of the characters.

Play the recording through again and get students to check/complete their answers.

Check the answers with the whole class.

> **Answers**
> 1 Melanie is 22.
> 2 Cath is 21 and George is 20.
> 3 Yves is 19.
> 4 Melanie is married. Yves, Cath, and George aren't married.

> **T 3.8**
> **I** Hi!
> **All** Hi!
> **I** Now you're Melanie, yes?
> **M** That's right.
> **I** And you're from Australia.
> **M** Uh huh.
> **I** How old are you, Melanie?
> **M** I'm 22.
> **I** And Cath and George. You're from the United States, yeah?
> **G** No, no. We aren't from the United States. We're from England.
> **I** England. Sorry. How old are you both?
> **C** I'm 21 and George is 20.
> **Y** And I'm 19.
> **I** Thanks. Now, who's married in *4 x 4*?
> **Y** Well, I'm not married.
> **C and G** We aren't married!
> **I** Melanie, are you married?
> **M** Yes, I am!
> **I** Well, thank you, *4 x 4*. Welcome to New York!
> **All** It's great here. Thanks!

GRAMMAR SPOT

Check students understand *we* by gesturing to yourself and another student. Focus attention on the affirmative sentence and the contracted form *We're*. Make sure students understand what the contracted form is in full. Ask students to circle the examples of *we're* in the reading text.

Focus attention on the negative sentence and the contracted form *aren't*. Make sure students understand what the contracted form is in full and that the sentence is negative. Ask students to circle the examples of *aren't* in the reading text.

Refer students to Grammar Reference 3.2 on p122.

4 Tell students they are going to invent a pop group. Focus attention on the questions in exercise 4. Check students understand *Where are you now?* by asking the same question about the classroom situation. Divide the class into groups of four. Try to get a mixture of males and females in each group. Give students time to invent their imaginary identities and write down the details. Demonstrate the questions and answers with a confident group. For the answer to *What are your names?* encourage students to use *I'm ...*, and *This is ...* to avoid the need for *our*, which is presented in Unit 4.

Then get the groups to ask and answer about their pop groups. Monitor and check. Get one or two groups to describe themselves to the rest of the class.

ADDITIONAL MATERIAL

Workbook Unit 3
Exercise 15 This provides further reading practice.

EVERYDAY ENGLISH (SB p23)

Social expressions

1 Focus attention on the gapped conversations and the expressions in the box. Focus attention on conversation 1 and elicit the second part of the answer (*Good morning, Mr Brown.*) Students continue completing the conversations in pairs, using the pictures to help.

> **Answers and tapescript**
> 1 **Good morning**.
>   **Good morning**, Mr Brown.
> 2 **Good afternoon**. The Grand Hotel.
>   **Good afternoon**.
> 3 **Good evening**, madam.
>   **Good evening**.
> 4 **Good night**.
>   **Good night**, Peter. Sleep well.
> 5 **Goodbye**.
>   **Goodbye**. Have a good journey!

T 3.9 Play the recording and get students to check their answers. Students then practise the conversations in open and then in closed pairs.

> **NOTE**
> Exercise 2 contains examples of the Present Simple (*I don't know* and *I don't understand*). At this stage, it's best to treat these as useful expressions rather than explain the grammar behind the use of Present Simple. This will be covered in Units 5 and 6.

2 **T 3.10** Focus attention on the first photo and on the gapped conversation. Play the first conversation on tape as an example and elicit the answer (*I don't know*). Play the rest of the recording, pausing at the end of each conversation. Students complete their answers using the words given.
If necessary, play the recording again to allow students to check/complete their answers before checking with the whole class.

> **Answers and tapescript**
> 1 A What's this in English?
>   B I **don't know**.
>   A It's a dictionary.
> 2 C *Hogy hívnak?*
>   M I **don't understand. Sorry**.
>   C What's your name?
>   M My name's Manuel. I'm from Spain.
> 3 A The homework is on page . . . of the Workbook.
>   B **Pardon?**
>   A The homework is on page *thirty* of the Workbook.
>   B **Thank you**.

3 If necessary, play the recording again and get the students to repeat. Students then practise the conversations in open and closed pairs.

ADDITIONAL MATERIAL

Workbook Unit 3
Exercises 16–18 These exercises review and consolidate the social expressions from the *Everyday English* section.

Don't forget!

Workbook Unit 3
Exercise 10 In this exercise students translate sentences containing the main grammar points presented in the unit.
Exercises 11 and 12 Word stress exercises.

Word list
Ask the students to turn to p129 and go through the words with them. Ask them to learn the words for homework, and test them on a few in the following lesson.

Stop and check 1 for Units 1–3 (TB p130).

4

our/their • Possessive *'s*
Family relations • *has/have*
The alphabet • On the phone

Family and friends

Introduction to the unit

The title of this unit is 'Family and friends' and it aims to extend the range of personal information students can give. The unit introduces the possessive *'s* with family vocabulary, *has/have*, and irregular plurals. Students get practice in all four skills with listening and speaking tasks, reading texts on family and friends, and a guided writing task.

The lexical set of family is presented and another important communicative tool – the alphabet – is introduced in *Everyday English*. This section also covers phone language.

Language aims

Grammar – possessive *'s* The possessive *'s* is introduced via the context of family. The way of expressing possession in English is different from many other languages and so students may initially have problems with this. Students are given lots of controlled practice in the Student's Book and Workbook, and the Grammar spot highlights possible confusion with *'s* as a contraction of *is*.

has/have *Has/have* are introduced in the affirmative. We introduce *have* rather than *have got*, as *have* can generate a broader range of uses, e.g. *I have three children* (possession), and *I have lunch at 12* (*have* as main verb). *Have got* operates differently and may cause confusion when students meet the Present Simple and have to deal with *do/does* forms. This is avoided in *New Headway Beginner* as the Present Simple is introduced in Unit 5 after students have practised *has/have* in the affirmative. Apart from in the third person singular affirmative, *have* will operate like all the other verbs presented in the Present Simple and so students won't be overloaded by new language. *Have got* is covered in *New Headway Elementary*.

Irregular plurals These are introduced as part of the presentation on families and are covered in Grammar Reference 4.3.

Possessive adjectives *Our* and *their* are introduced in this unit, and there is a review of all possessive adjectives and subject pronouns.

Vocabulary The lexical set of the family is introduced and practised and there is also a focus on the language of describing a friend. Basic adjective + noun combinations are introduced via the reading texts, e.g. *a good job*.

Everyday English The alphabet is introduced and practised and there is also a focus on phone language.

Workbook The lexical set of the family is recycled.

Possessive *'s* is consolidated. There are exercises to help with potential confusion between both the possessive *'s* and the contracted form of *is*, and plurals.

Possessive adjectives and subject pronouns are consolidated.

Has/have are reviewed and consolidated.

There is a vocabulary categorizing exercise to review vocabulary from Units 1–4.

Students are given extra practice in listening and reading.

There are exercises on word stress.

The alphabet and phone language from *Everyday English* are reviewed.

Notes on the unit

STARTER (SB p24)

1 **T 4.1** This section reviews all the possessive adjectives students have seen in Units 1–3 and also presents *our* and *their*. Focus students' attention on the subject pronoun column and briefly review *I*, *you*, etc. by pointing to yourself and students and eliciting the correct pronoun. Focus attention on the examples in the table. Get students to continue completing the table, working in pairs. Play the recording and let students check their answers. Play it again and get students to repeat chorally and individually. Make sure they can distinguish *you/you*, *they/their*, and that they can pronounce *our* correctly.

> **Answers and tapescript**
>
> | Subject pronoun | I | you | he | she | we | they |
> |---|---|---|---|---|---|---|
> | Possessive adjective | my | **your** | **his** | **her** | our | their |

2 Focus attention on the examples in the speech bubbles. Say the sentences, pointing to relevant objects and getting students to repeat. Elicit more examples by pointing to objects that belong to the students and objects in the classroom.

SALLY'S FAMILY (SB p24)

Possessive 's – family relations

1 Focus attention on the photographs.

T 4.2 Play the recording and ask students to follow the text in their books. Check comprehension of *husband*, *bank manager*, *children*, and *college*.

Point to one member of the family and ask *Who's this?* to elicit the person's name. Take the opportunity to further practise *How old is ... ?* and *(I think) She's ...* by asking *How old is (Sally)?*, etc. to elicit possible ages.

GRAMMAR SPOT

1 Focus attention on the examples. Make sure that students understand that *'s* is the contracted form of *is*.

2 Review the use of *her* and then focus attention on the use of possessive *'s*. Make sure that students understand that we use this form to express possession.

3 Review the use of *his* and then focus attention on the other examples with possessive *'s*. Ask students to circle the examples of possessive *'s* in the text about Sally. Make sure students don't confuse the contracted form of *is* with possessive *'s*.

Read Grammar Reference 4.1 and 4.2 on p123 together in class, and/or ask students to read it at home. Encourage them to ask you questions about it.

Grammar Reference 4.3 on p123 focuses on irregular plurals. Read it together in class, and/or ask students to read it at home. Ask students to find an irregular plural in the text about Sally on p24 (*children*).

2 Elicit the answers to questions 1 and 2 (*Yes, she is.* and *It's in London.*). Get students to continue answering the questions in pairs.

> **Answers and tapescript**
> 1 Is Sally married?
>   **Yes, she is.**
> 2 Where's their house?
>   **It's in London.**
> 3 What is Sally's job?
>   **She's a teacher.**
> 4 Where's her school?
>   **It's in the centre of town.**
> 5 What is Tom's job?
>   **He's a bank manager.**
> 6 Where is his bank?
>   **It's in the centre of town.**
> 7 Are their children doctors?
>   **No, they aren't. They're students.**

T 4.3 Play the recording and get students to check their answers.

3 **T 4.4** Focus attention on the words in the table. Play the recording and get students to repeat as a class.

4 **T 4.5** Focus attention on the family tree. Ask *Who's Sally?* and get students to point to the correct person in the photo. Now focus attention on the example and play sentence 1 on the tape. Continue playing the sentences, pausing at the end of each one and getting students to write the correct words. Play the recording again and get students to check their answers.

> **Answers and tapescript**
> 1 Sally is Tom's **wife**.
> 2 Tom is Sally's **husband**.
> 3 Kirsty is Sally and Tom's **daughter**.
> 4 Nick is their **son**.
> 5 Sally is Nick's **mother**.
> 6 Tom is Kirsty's **father**.
> 7 Kirsty is Nick's **sister**.
> 8 Nick is Kirsty's **brother**.
> 9 Sally and Tom are Kirsty and Nick's **parents**.
> 10 Kirsty and Nick are Tom and Sally's **children**.

Play the recording through again, pausing after each sentence and getting students to repeat chorally and individually. Make sure they reproduce the possessive *'s* accurately.

5 Write the following on the board to reinforce the use of possessive *'s*.

Who('s) Nick? *'s = is*

He's Kirsty('s) brother *'s = possessive, not is*

Drill the question and answers in open pairs. Then drill a plural example, e.g. *Who are Tom and Sally? They're Nick's parents.* Get students to continue asking and answering about Sally's family in open pairs. Make sure that they give all possible answers about the different relationships and that they include plural examples, too. Students continue asking and answering in pairs. Monitor and check for correct use of possessive *'s* and *is/are*.

ADDITIONAL MATERIAL

Workbook Unit 4
Exercises 1 and 2 Further practice of family vocabulary.

The family

1 Focus attention on the photo of Rachel Chang's family and on the names. Ask some general questions about the family: *Where are they from? What are their names?* Focus attention on the table and make sure students understand what information they have to listen for by eliciting *possible* answers for each category, e.g. name – *Bob*, age – *16*, job – *student*.

T 4.6 Play the first part of the recording as far as *He's a student at college.* Elicit the answers about Rachel's brother (*Steve, 15, student*). Play the rest of the recording and get students to complete the table.

Check the answers with the whole class.

Answers

	Name	Age	Job
Rachel's brother	Steve	15	student
Rachel's mother	Grace	42	doctor
Rachel's father	Bob	44	businessman

T 4.6
Hello! My name's Rachel, and I'm from the United States. This is a photo of my family. Our house is in San Diego. This is my brother. His name is Steve, and he's 15. He's a student. This is my mother. Her name's Grace. She's forty-two, and she's a doctor. And this man is my father, Bob. He's forty-four, and he's a businessman.

As a follow-up, point to each of Rachel's relations and get students to give a brief description, e.g. *This is Steve. He's Rachel's brother. He's 15 and he's a student.*

2 Focus attention on the example and then get students to complete the sentences in pairs.

Check the answers with the whole class, making sure students have included possessive *'s* where necessary.

Answers
2 Her **mother's** name is Grace.
3 Grace is Bob's **wife**.
4 'What's **his** job?' 'He's a businessman.'
5 'Where's **their** house?' 'It's in San Diego.'

3 Demonstrate the activity by writing the names of your own family on the board and talking about them. Give the information quite slowly but naturally and then ask a few questions to check understanding, e.g. *Who's this?, What's her job?*, etc.

slowly but naturally and pass them around. Encourage students to ask questions, following the models in exercise 3 on p26.

Get students to draw their own family tree (and have their family photos ready if relevant). Divide the class into pairs and get students to ask about each other's family. Monitor and check for correct use of *he/she*, *his/her*, and *a* + job.

Ask a few students to choose someone in a family tree or in a photo and give a brief description of him/her. The person can be from their own or their partner's family.

ADDITIONAL MATERIAL

Workbook Unit 4
Exercise 3 Further practice of possessive *'s*.
Exercises 4 and 5 Exercises to help with potential confusion between possessive *'s* and the contracted form of *is*, and possessive *'s*, the contracted form of *is*, and plural -*s*.

my/our/your . . .

4   This section consolidates the possessive adjectives covered in the *Starter* section. Focus attention on the example and then get students to complete the sentences. Ask students to check in pairs before checking with the whole class.

> **Answers**
> 2 'What are **your** names?' 'Our names are Kirsty and Nick.'
> 3 Jean-Paul and André are students. **Their** school is in Paris.
> 4 'My sister's married.' 'What's **her** husband's name?'
> 5 'My brother's office is in New York.' 'What's **his** job?'
> 6 We are in **our** English class.
> 7 'Mum and Dad are in Rome.' 'What's **their** phone number?'

ADDITIONAL MATERIAL

Workbook Unit 4
Exercises 6 and 7 Further practice of possessive adjectives.

SALLY'S BROTHER (SB p27)

has/have

1   This section recycles the family vocabulary, possessive *'s*, and possessive adjectives, and also presents *has/have*. Point to the picture of Sally on p24 and ask *Who's this?* Elicit the answer *It's Sally Milton*. Tell students they are going to read about Sally's brother.

T 4.7 Focus attention on the photograph of David and his family and play the first line of the recording as an introduction. Play the rest of the recording through to the end. Check comprehension of *farm* and *dogs* by pointing to the photo, and check students understand that *child* is the singular of *children*.

2   Elicit the answer to sentence 1 with the whole class as an example (true). Then get students to complete the exercise working alone.

Get students to check their answers in pairs before checking with the whole class.

> **Answers**
> 1 ✔ 2 ✔ 3 ✘ 4 ✘ 5 ✘ 6 ✘

GRAMMAR SPOT

Focus attention on the table and the examples. Students complete the table with the other forms of *have*.

> **Answers**
> I **have**
> You have
> He has
> She **has**
> We **have**
> They **have**

Ask students to circle the examples of *has* and *have* in the reading text. Refer students to Grammar Reference 4.4 on p123.

3   **T 4.8** This is a dictation activity. Each sentence is recorded twice, once at normal speed and once more with time for students to write. Demonstrate the activity by playing the first sentence and getting students to listen only, then play it again and get them to write it down. Tell students there are seven sentences in total. Play the rest of the sentences in the same way.

Write the sentences on the board and get students to check their answers.

> **Answers and tapescript**
> 1 I have a small farm in Wales.
> 2 My wife has a job in town.
> 3 We have one son.
> 4 We have two dogs.
> 5 My sister and her husband have a house in London.
> 6 He has a very good job.
> 7 They have a son and a daughter.

Play the recording again, pausing at the end of each sentence and getting the students to repeat as a class. Students then repeat the lines individually.

4   In this exercise students write about themselves. Focus attention on the examples in the speech bubbles. Write a few more examples about yourself on the board and list the categories students can write about: brothers/sisters, children, home, job, animals. Go round helping and checking.

Then ask a few students to tell the rest of the class about themselves and their family.

PRACTICE (SB p28)

has/have

1 Focus attention on the example. Students then complete the exercise working alone.

Get students to check their answers in pairs before checking with the whole class.

> **Answers**
> 2 My parents **have** a house in the country.
> 3 My wife **has** a Japanese car.
> 4 My sister and I **have** a dog.
> 5 You **have** a very nice family.
> 6 Our school **has** fifteen classrooms.
> 7 We **have** English classes in the evening.

2 Focus attention on the examples in the speech bubbles. Drill the sentences chorally and individually. List the categories students can talk about on the board: number of teachers/students/classrooms; size of school; equipment at your school (e.g. TV, video, CD player, computer. You will need to modify the examples to include equipment that students know you have at your school so that they only generate affirmative sentences.)

Divide the class into pairs and get students to talk about their school. Monitor and check for correct use of *has/have*.

ADDITIONAL MATERIAL

Workbook Unit 4
Exercises 12 and 13 Further practice of *has* and *have*.

Questions and answers

3 This exercise reviews the question words students have covered to date and also includes a *Yes/No* question. Focus attention on the example and then get students to match the other questions and answers.

T 4.9 Play the recording and get students to check their answers. Then let them practise the questions and answers in pairs.

> **Answers and tapescript**
> 1 How is your mother?
>   She's very well, thank you.
> 2 What's your sister's job?
>   She's a nurse.
> 3 How old are your brothers?
>   They're ten and thirteen.
> 4 Who is Sally?
>   She's David's sister.
> 5 Where is your office?
>   It's in the centre of town.
> 6 Are you and your husband from Italy?
>   Yes, we are.

Check it

4 Focus attention on the first pair of sentences as an example. Remind students of the convention of ticking (✔) to indicate that something is correct. Students continue working individually to choose the correct sentence.

Get students to check their answers in pairs before checking with the whole class.

> **Answers**
> 1 Mary's children are married.
> 2 What's your daughter's name?
> 3 What's his job?
> 4 They're from Germany.
> 5 Their parents have a house in Bonn.
> 6 My brother has a good job.
> 7 Our house is in the centre of town.

ADDITIONAL MATERIAL

Workbook Unit 4
Exercise 8 This provides further listening practice.
Exercise 9 A vocabulary categorizing exercise that reviews lexis from Units 1–4.
Exercise 10 and 11 Word stress exercises.
Exercise 14 In this exercise students translate sentences containing the main grammar points presented in the unit.

READING AND WRITING (SB p28)

My best friend

> **NOTE**
> Students need access to dictionaries to check new lexis in the reading text. If students don't usually bring dictionaries to class or if there isn't a class set of dictionaries available, ask students to check the new words (in **bold**) in the text for homework before the reading lesson.

1 Working alone or in pairs, students read the text and check the new words (in **bold** in the text). (If students have done the dictionary work for homework before the lesson, ask them to do the reading and matching straightaway.)

2 Demonstrate the activity by eliciting the photo that goes with paragraph a (photo 1). Students continue to match the other photos and paragraphs, and say who they think the people in the photos are. Check the answers with the whole class.

3   Focus attention on the example sentence. Students complete the activity working individually and then check their answers in pairs. Check the answers with the whole class.

4   Focus attention on the speech bubble and then get students to give more information about Andy. Divide the class into pairs and get students to take it in turns to talk about Andy, using the information they underlined in exercise 3. Monitor and check for correct use of *he/she/they, his/her/their, is/are, has/have*, and possessive *'s*.

5   Prepare students for the writing phase by eliciting what sort of information can complete each sentence. If you have time, build up a connected description on the board of an imaginary person to provide the students with a model. Get the students to write their description in class or for homework.

SUGGESTION

It's a good idea to let students look at each other's written work to help correct it. When you correct the work, make a note of the most common mistakes in recent target language and get students to correct them as a class activity before you hand back individual work.

ADDITIONAL MATERIAL

Workbook Unit 4
Exercise 15 A short reading providing further practice of family vocabulary, possessive *'s*, and *have*.

EVERYDAY ENGLISH (SB p30)

The alphabet

This section covers the alphabet and spelling. Once students have learnt the alphabet, take the opportunity whenever possible to spell new words to the students and to get them to spell words in class.

1   **T 4.10** Tell the students they are going to practise the alphabet in English. Play the recording, pausing after each letter and getting the students to repeat as a class.

Review the letters that students find confusing and drill these thoroughly:
a, r
e, i, y
g, j
u, w

2   The letters in this exercise are arranged according to sound. Demonstrate this by reading the first group of letters /eɪ/. Say these letters again and get students to repeat as a class. Repeat for the other groups of letters and then get individual students to read different letter groups aloud.

Write different letters on the board at random and elicit them from the students. Pay special attention to the vowels as these often give problems. Then put some known words on the board and elicit the spelling. (You could feed in *How do you spell … ?* at this point.)

3   **T 4.11** Check comprehension of *first name* and *surname* and tell students they are going to hear five people spelling their names. Play the recording of the first name as an example. Then play the other names, pausing at the end of each surname. Students write the names and then check their answers in pairs. Then check the answers with the whole class by writing the names on the board and getting students to spell them aloud.

4   Focus attention on the examples in the speech bubbles and drill the exchanges chorally and individually. Students practise spelling their own names in open and closed pairs.

5   Focus attention on the examples in the speech bubbles in exercise 5. Drill the exchange chorally and individually. Students practise the exchange with different words from the text, working in open pairs. Students continue working in closed pairs. Monitor and check for accurate pronunciation of the letters.

6 Focus attention on the example. Students continue with the other countries. Get them to check their answers in pairs before checking with the whole class. Get the students to give the spelling of each country, rather than just the name.

SUGGESTIONS

1 You can use anagrams such as the ones in exercise 6 to review vocabulary at any stage. Write the jumbled letters on the board and ask students to work out the word in pairs or teams. Always get the class to give the spelling letter by letter to review the alphabet as often as possible.

2 This is a spelling game called *Hangman*. You can use it at the beginning of lessons as a 'warmer' or as a 'filler' to revise vocabulary. You can divide students into two or three teams for this, or play as a class.

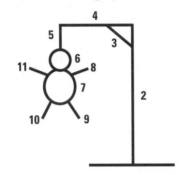

Choose a word and indicate on the board the number of letters it has, using a dash for each letter (i.e. if your word is *doctor*, write _ _ _ _ _ _). One team/The class suggests a letter. If the letter appears in your word, write it in the correct place on the dashes, as many times as it appears (i.e. if the letter suggested is **o**, you should write _ o _ _ o _ for the word *doctor*). If the letter doesn't appear in your word, write the letter in that team's column at the side of the board with a line through it, and draw one line of the gallows. Then the second team suggests a letter, and so on.

If you are playing in teams, the winning team is the one that guesses the final letter to complete the word or that guesses the whole word at an earlier point. If you complete the drawing of the gallows before the teams/the class guess the word, then you win and the teams/class lose.

ADDITIONAL MATERIAL

Workbook Unit 4
Exercises 16 and 17 Further practice of the alphabet and spelling.

On the phone

7 **T 4.12** Focus attention on the first business card and ask *What's his name?*, *Where's his company?*, and *What's his phone number?*. Play the recording through once and get students to follow in their books. Make sure students understand that *And your name is?* is a polite way of asking *What's your name?* over the phone.

Play the recording again, pausing at the end of each line and getting students to repeat chorally and individually. Students practise the conversation in closed pairs. Repeat the above procedure for the second conversation, but use the feminine forms *What's her name?*, *Where's her company?*, and *What's her phone number?* about the second business card.

8 Ask students to write their own information on the blank business card. They should include first name, surname, address, and phone number and they can invent a company name if they like.

Get students to practise conversations 1 and 2 in open pairs, using their own information. Students continue working in closed pairs.

ADDITIONAL MATERIAL

Workbook Unit 4
Exercise 18 Further practice of the phone language in the *Everyday English* section.

Don't forget!

Word list
Ask the students to turn to p129 and go through the words with them. Ask them to learn the words for homework, and test them on a few in the following lesson.

Video
A video accompanies *New Headway Beginner*. It takes the form of six episodes centred around four people sharing a house in Oxford. The first episode can be shown after the end of Unit 4, and subsequent episodes after Units 6, 8, 10, 12, and 14.

Episode 1 *Three plus one*
Helen, David, and Matt are looking for a fourth person to share the house. The interviews go rather badly, with a stream of unsuitable applicants, until Jane turns up, and gets the room.

EXTRA IDEAS UNITS 1–4
On TB p108 there are additional photocopiable activities to review the language from Units 1–4. There is a reading text with tasks, a question formation exercise, and a matching activity on everyday English. You will need to pre-teach/check *divorced* for exercise 1 of the *Language work* section.

5 Sports, food, and drinks • Present Simple – *I/you/they*
a/an • Languages and nationalities • Numbers and prices

It's my life!

Introduction to the unit

This unit introduces the Present Simple with *I*, *you*, and *they* in statement forms. *Wh-* questions, and *Yes/No* questions and short answers are also practised. At this point the Present Simple is used with a limited range of verbs so that students can get used to the new tense. Students get skills practice with reading and listening, and listening and speaking tasks.

Sports, food, and drinks vocabulary is introduced in the context of likes and dislikes. The lexical sets of languages and nationalities are also presented. The *Everyday English* section extends numbers from 31–100 and also focuses on prices.

Language aims

Grammar – Present Simple 1 The Present Simple is the most used tense in the English language and it is therefore important to introduce it to beginners in an accessible way. In *New Headway Beginner*, the tense is presented over two units, starting in this unit with the subjects *I*, *you*, and *they*. The affirmative and negative forms are covered along with *wh-* and *Yes/No* questions. The third person singular forms are covered in Unit 6.

a/an Students have met *a/an* + job in Unit 3 and this focus is extended to cover *a/an* + adjective and noun.

Vocabulary Students practise the lexical sets of sports, food, and drinks in the context of likes and dislikes. Countries are recycled and languages and nationalities are introduced.

Everyday English Numbers 31–100 and prices are introduced and practised.

Workbook The lexical sets of sports, food, and drinks are recycled.

The Present Simple with *I*, *you*, *they* is further practised along with exercises on question formation.

Languages and nationalities are consolidated in a *Vocabulary and pronunciation* section.

Students are given extra practice in reading and listening.

Numbers and prices from the *Everyday English* section are reviewed.

Notes on the unit

STARTER (SB p32)

1 Focus attention on the photos. Demonstrate the activity by matching the first word in each category to the appropriate picture (tennis – 1, Italian food – 13, tea – 4). Students match as many words as possible, working individually or in pairs. Encourage them to guess if they are not sure. Ask them to compare their answers before checking answers with the whole class.

Answers and tapescript		
Sports	**Food**	**Drinks**
1 tennis	13 Italian food	4 tea
8 football	11 Chinese food	10 coffee
14 swimming	2 pizza	12 Coca-Cola
7 skiing	3 hamburgers	9 beer
	15 oranges	6 wine
	5 ice-cream	

T 5.1 Play the recording and get students to repeat chorally and individually. Consolidate the vocabulary by holding up the book and pointing to the pictures. (Alternatively, hold up flash cards if these are available.) Ask *What's this?/What are these?* and elicit replies about three or four examples. Get students to continue asking and answering in pairs.

2 Write on the board three or four things that you like from exercise 1. Tick them and show by your expression that you like them. Get students to tick the things they like in exercise 1.

Repeat the above procedure for the negative, crossing the things you don't like and getting students to do the same.

THINGS I LIKE (SB p33)

Present Simple – *I/you*

1 **T 5.2** Focus attention on the speech bubbles and pictures. Play the recording once or twice before you ask students to repeat. Play the recording again and get students to repeat chorally and individually.

> **GRAMMAR SPOT**
>
> Focus attention on the examples. Make sure students understand that *don't* is the contraction of *do not*.
>
> If students ask what *do* means, you can explain simply (in the students' own language if possible) that it helps to make negatives and questions. However, do not give a detailed grammatical explanation at this stage.

2 **T 5.3** Focus attention on the photo of Bill and ask students to guess what he likes from the lists in *Starter* exercise 1. Play the recording once and get students to check their predictions. Focus on the example and play the first line of the recording again. Play the rest of the recording and get students to write their answers. Students check in pairs. Then check the answers with the whole class.

> **Answers and tapescript**
> Well, I like **swimming** and **football** – American football. I don't like tennis. Mmm yeah, **hamburgers** and **pizza**, I like hamburgers and pizza and **Italian food**, I like Italian food a lot, but not Chinese food – I don't like Chinese food and I don't like tea, but I like **coffee** and **beer**.

3 Drill the example in the speech bubble chorally and individually. Make sure students can reproduce the sentence stress accurately:

● ●   ●   ●
I like tennis, but I don't like football.

Demonstrate the activity by giving examples of what you like and don't like, using the vocabulary from *Starter* exercise 1. Ask students to write down sentences with their likes and dislikes. Then, in pairs, students take it in turns to talk to each other about their likes and dislikes. Ask a few students to read their sentences to the class.

ADDITIONAL MATERIAL

Workbook Unit 5
Exercises 1 and 2 Further practice of food vocabulary and the verb *like*.

Questions

4 **T 5.4** The question form *Do you like … ?* is introduced here. Play the recording a couple of times and let students listen before you ask them to repeat line by line, chorally, and individually. Make sure students can reproduce the pronunciation of *do you* /dju:/ and the rising intonation on the *Yes/No* questions.

> **GRAMMAR SPOT**
>
> Focus attention on the examples. Make sure students understand that we do not use *like* in short answers, i.e. you cannot say **Yes, I like* or **No, I don't like*.
>
> Again, it is probably best not to explain the function of *do* at this stage.
>
> Refer students to Grammar Reference 5.1 on p123. Do not focus on Questions with question words at this stage.

5 Focus attention on the examples in the speech bubbles. Get students to ask you the questions, drilling the pronunciation and intonation again if necessary. Students continue asking about the other things in *Starter* exercise 1.

6 Focus attention on the examples in the speech bubbles. Drill the intonation, making sure students can reproduce the contrastive stress in the second question:

●
Yes, I do. Do you like tennis?

ADDITIONAL MATERIAL

Workbook Unit 5
Exercises 3 and 4 Further practice of Present Simple with *I/you*.

PRACTICE (SB p34)

Reading and listening

1   **T 5.5** Here students are introduced to more Present Simple verbs: *come from, live, work, eat, drink, play, speak,* and *want*. *Have* is also recycled from Unit 4. Other new words are *waiter, drama, restaurant, language,* and *actor*. The languages/nationalities *Italian, English,* and *French* are also introduced in context.

Students read the text and listen to the recording once or twice. Try to get students to understand the new vocabulary in context and get them to refer to the information in the photos for help. Check comprehension of *live* and *work* by making sentences about yourself, e.g. *I live in* (town, country), *I work in* (*this school*), etc. *Eat, drink, play,* and *speak* should be understandable from the context, but if students need further help, mime the actions. (It is probably not worth going into the fact that *drink* is a verb here but a noun on p32.) Students should be able to understand *waiter, drama, restaurant,* and *actor* from the photos. If they query *language* and *Italian, English,* and *French* write the corresponding countries on the board and link them to the languages. You may need to translate *want to* if students query this. If students query the pronoun *it* in *I don't like it,* check they understand what noun *it* refers back to (*beer*). (Object pronouns *it* and *them* are presented in full in Unit 7.)

> #### GRAMMAR SPOT
>
> Focus attention on the examples. Make sure students understand that we use *an* before a vowel – *a, e, i, o,* and *u*. Point out that this can be a noun, e.g. **an actor**, or an adjective, **an Italian restaurant**.
>
> Refer students to Grammar Reference 5.2 and 5.3 on p123.

2   **T 5.6** Play the recording, pausing at the end of each question and getting students to repeat chorally and individually.

T 5.7 Get students to complete Gordon's answers. Then play the recording and check the answers with the whole class.

> #### Answers and tapescript
> 1 Yes, I **do**.
> 2 No, I **don't**. I **live** in London.
> 3 Yes, I **do**. I **live** in a flat near the centre.
> 4 No, I **don't**. I **work** in an Italian restaurant.
> 5 Yes, I **do**. I **like** it a lot.
> 6 No, I **don't**. I want to be **an actor**.
> 7 No, I **don't**. I **don't** like it.
> 8 I **speak** French but I **don't** speak Spanish.

3   Before putting students into pairs, demonstrate by asking individual students the questions from exercise 2. Make sure they answer with information about themselves. Get individual students to ask you the questions and answer with true information. Students continue asking and answering in open pairs. If necessary, drill the pronunciation and intonation of the questions again before getting students to continue in closed pairs. Monitor and check for correct use of the Present Simple.

Talking about you

4   This exercise introduces the Present Simple in *wh-* questions. Briefly review the question words *where, what,* and *how many* by giving short answers and eliciting the appropriate question word, e.g.
a dictionary / an actor – What?
Australia / in a hospital – Where?
three sisters / ten books – How many?

T 5.8 Play the recording, pausing at the end of each line and getting the students to repeat as a class. Students then repeat the questions individually. Make sure students can reproduce the falling intonation on the *wh-* questions.

Demonstrate the activity by giving the answer to the first question yourself. Get students to write their own answers to each question, using the language in *Starter* exercise 1 where appropriate. If students need extra vocabulary, e.g. languages, be prepared to feed these in.

Demonstrate the question and answer phase with a confident student by asking and answering the first two questions. Students continue in open and then in closed pairs. Monitor and check for accurate use of the Present Simple.

Roleplay

5   You will need to photocopy the role cards on TB p109. There is a male and a female role for Student A and for Student B. These are repeated on the page to cut down on photocopying. Make sure you cut out and copy the appropriate number of cards for the gender balance in your class.

Divide the class into pairs and give each student their card, making sure everyone has the correct role in terms of gender. Focus attention on the table on p35 and elicit the questions students will need to ask:
>   *What's your name? How do you spell it?*
>   *Where do you live?*
>   *Do you live in a house or a flat?*
>   *What's your job?*
>   *Where do you work?*
>   *How many languages do you speak?*
>   *What sports do you like?*

Drill the questions, making sure students can reproduce falling intonation.

Ask a confident pair of students to demonstrate the activity in open pairs. Students then continue in closed pairs, completing the table in the Student's Book with information about their partner's character. If possible, get students to stand up to do the roleplay as if they were at a party. Students can then compare role cards to check they have the correct information.

Check it

6 Focus attention on the first pair of sentences as an example. Remind students that the convention of ticking (✔) indicates that something is correct. Students continue working individually to choose the correct sentence.

Get students to check their answers in pairs before checking with the whole class.

Answers
1 Do you live in Berlin?
2 Where do you come from?
3 Do you speak French?
4 I don't speak French.
5 'Do you like football?' 'Yes, I do.'
6 'Are you married?' 'No, I'm not.'
7 He's an actor.

VOCABULARY AND PRONUNCIATION (SB p36)

Languages and nationalities

1 Check comprehension of *Germany*, *China*, and *Portugal* by referring students back to the map on p13. Focus attention on the example. Students continue the matching activity, working individually.

T 5.9 Play the recording through once and let students check their answers.

Answers and tapescript
England	English
Germany	German
Italy	Italian
Mexico	Mexican
Brazil	Brazilian
Japan	Japanese
Portugal	Portuguese
China	Chinese
France	French
The United States	American
Spain	Spanish

Remind students of the system used in *New Headway* to highlight word stress. Play the recording again and get students to repeat the pairs of words as a class. Make sure they can reproduce the change of stress from the country to the nationality/language:

●   ●
Italy   *Italian*

●   ●
Japan   *Japanese*

●   ●
Portugal   *Portuguese*

Play the recording through again and get students to repeat individually.

2 Focus attention on the photos and on the examples in the speech bubbles. Point to the photo of the woman carrying beer and drill the examples chorally and individually. Elicit another pair of examples about different people in the photos. Students continue talking about the people in pairs.

3 This exercise includes the *they* form of the Present Simple with the verb *speak*. Students shouldn't have any difficulty with this form, as it's the same as the *I* form they have already practised.

Check comprehension of *Mexico* and *Switzerland*. Focus attention on the example. Students continue making sentences working individually.

T 5.10 Play the recording and get students to check their answers.

Answers and tapescript
1 In Brazil they speak Portuguese.
2 In Canada they speak English and French.
3 In France they speak French.
4 In Germany they speak German.
5 In Italy they speak Italian.
6 In Japan they speak Japanese.
7 In Mexico they speak Spanish.
8 In Portugal they speak Portuguese.
9 In Spain they speak Spanish.
10 In Switzerland they speak French, German, and Italian.
11 In the United States they speak English.

4 Drill the question form in the speech bubbles. Then get students to practise a few examples in open pairs. Students continue in closed pairs, taking it in turns to ask each other about the countries in exercise 3. Monitor and check for correct use of the question form and for pronunciation of the countries and languages.

5 This exercise consolidates the nationalities and also highlights adjective + noun word order. Focus attention on the photos and the example. Students complete the exercise by writing the correct nationalities.

T 5.11 Play the recording and get students to check their answers.

> **Answers and tapescript**
> 1 an American car
> 2 German beer
> 3 Spanish oranges
> 4 a Japanese camera
> 5 Mexican food
> 6 an English dictionary
> 7 an Italian bag
> 8 Brazilian coffee
> 9 French wine

Refer students to Grammar Reference 5.4 on p123.

6 This exercise gives students the opportunity to practise the Present Simple, nationalities, and noun + adjective word order in a personalized way.

Write the verbs *have*, *eat*, and *drink* on the board and elicit adjectives and nouns that can go with each verb, e.g.

have   a/an Japanese/American/German/French car
an Italian/American bag
a Japanese camera
an English dictionary

eat   Chinese/Italian/Japanese/French food
Spanish oranges
American/Italian ice-cream

drink French/Italian/German/Portuguese/Spanish wine
French/German/English/American beer
Brazilian coffee
Chinese tea

Give examples of your own with *have*, *eat*, and *drink*. Try to highlight the use of *a/an*, e.g. *I have **a** Japanese camera. I don't have **an** Italian car.* Then get students to write their own examples. Monitor and help. Check for accurate use of *a/an* and correct adjective + noun word order.

7 Focus attention on the example questions in the speech bubbles. Give students time to write at least four questions of their own using *have*, *eat*, and *drink*. Monitor and help.

Drill the questions and answers in the speech bubbles. Get students to practise in open pairs across the class and then in closed pairs. Monitor and check for correct use of the Present Simple, *a/an* and adjective + noun word order.

SUGGESTION
You can bring in adverts from magazines to give students further practice with nationality adjectives and nouns. Select pictures of cars, cameras, computers, TVs, food, and drinks. Elicit simple adjective + noun phrases, e.g. *an American computer, Spanish wine,* etc. and then get students to use the pictures to practise *Do you have/eat/drink/like … ?* and short answers *Yes, I do/No, I don't.* If pairs of students interview other pairs, you can also practise the *they* form. (If students try to generate *he/she* forms, tell them these are different and that they will practise them in Unit 6.)

ADDITIONAL MATERIAL

Workbook Unit 5
Exercise 5 A reading text to practise the Present Simple – *they*.
Exercise 6, 7, and 8 Exercises to practise *wh-* questions and answers, and *Yes/No* questions.
Exercises 13 and 14 Further practice of languages and nationalities.
Exercise 15 Further practice of *like* and nationality adjectives + nouns.

LISTENING AND SPEAKING (SB p38)

At a party

1 This is a fairly long, though fairly simple, unseen listening. Set the scene by pointing to Alessandra and Woody in the illustration. Get students to say what nationality they think they are (*I think he's/she's …*).

T 5.12 Play the recording through once and let students check their predictions (Alessandra is Italian and Woody is English.)

Give students time to read the pairs of sentences 1–6. Check pronunciation of *Brighton* in number 2 and comprehension of *love* in number 5 and *very much* in number 6. Play the first part of the recording again, and focus attention on the example. Make sure students understand they have to focus on what *Woody* says. Play the rest of the recording and get students to select the correct sentence from each pair.

Get students to check their answers in pairs before checking with the whole class. Go over the answers by playing the conversation again and pausing the recording after each correct answer.

> **Answers**
> 1 I work in London.
> 2 I live in Brighton.
> 3 I'm an actor.
> 4 You speak English very well.
> 5 I love Italy.
> 6 I like the food and the wine very much.

T 5.12

A Hello. I'm Alessandra.
W Hi, Alessandra. I'm Woody. Woody Bates.
A Do you live here in London, Woody?
W No, I don't. I *work* in London but I *live* in Brighton.
A What's your job?
W I'm an actor. What's your job?
A I work in a hotel.
W You aren't English, but you speak English very well. Where do you come from?
A I'm Italian. I come from Verona.
W Oh, I love Italy.
A Really?
W Oh, yes. I like the food and the wine very much.

2 Turn to the tapescript on p114 and get students to practise the conversation in pairs.

Roleplay

3 Tell students to imagine they are at a party in London. Explain that they have to invent a new identity. Give an example by copying the role card onto the board and writing the information for your new identity. Ask students to complete the role card with their new details. Demonstrate the activity with a confident student, starting with the language in the speech bubbles. Build up a list of possible questions on the board which students could ask each other.

4 Get the class to stand up and complete the roleplay. Monitor but do not expect perfect accuracy or pronunciation. Make notes of major errors to feed back on later but try not to spoil students' enjoyment of the roleplay. If some pairs do well, you could ask them to act it out in front of the class.

ADDITIONAL MATERIAL

Workbook Unit 5
Exercise 10 Students gap-fill another conversation at a party.
Exercise 11 Further listening practice.

Numbers and prices

1 Review numbers 1–30 by getting students to count round the class. Repeat until they can say the numbers accurately without hesitation.

2 **T 5.13** Focus attention on numbers 10–100. Play the recording and get students to repeat chorally and individually. Get students to count to one hundred in tens round the class.

3 This is a pairs number dictation. See Unit 1 *Suggestion* TB p12 for instructions for this task.

4 **T 5.14** This exercise presents prices under and over one pound in English. Play the recording and let students read and listen. Focus attention on the use of *p* /piː/ for prices under a pound. Also point out the plural *pounds*, and that we do not say *pounds* and *p* in the same price, i.e. we do not say * *one pound sixty p* but *one pound sixty*.

Play the recording again and gets students to repeat chorally and individually.

5 Demonstrate the activity by getting students to say the first two prices aloud. Students then continue saying the prices in closed pairs. Monitor and check students can distinguish the stress on:

seventéen pounds and *séventy pounds*

T 5.15 Play the recording and get students to check their answers. If students had problems with pronunciation, play the recording again and get them to repeat. (With a weaker group, you could say the prices as a class activity, drilling the pronunciation as you go along, and then play the recording for reinforcement.)

6 This is a discrimination exercise which gets students to distinguish between prices that sound similar. Focus attention on the objects and prices. (With a weaker group, you could elicit the prices for each object orally first and then get students to listen and tick.)

T 5.16 Play the recording through once and get students to tick the prices they hear. Play it through a second time so that students can check their answers. Get them to check in pairs before checking with the whole class.

Answers and tapescript
1 The cheese sandwich is 90p.
2 The football is £14.
3 The camera is £90.99.
4 The beer is £1.60.
5 The chocolate is 60p.
6 The mobile phone is £24.74.
7 The dictionary is £10.75.
8 The bag is £30.99.

7 Focus attention on the speech bubbles. Drill the question and answer chorally and individually. (If students query the use of *How much … ?*, explain that this is the question we use to ask about prices. Do not go into an explanation of the difference between *How much/How many* at this stage.)

Practise two or three exchanges in open pairs. Then get the students to continue in closed pairs. Monitor and check for correct numbers and prices.

SUGGESTION

You can give students extra practice with numbers and prices by bringing in adverts, leaflets, and menus that show prices and getting students to practise *How much is … ?* Make sure you select the items carefully so that they show objects students know (or ones that you can teach that are in the post-beginner range). If you choose images that show plural objects, you will need to pre-teach/check: *How much are … ?*

ADDITIONAL MATERIAL

Workbook Unit 5
Exercises 16–19 Consolidation of numbers and prices.

Don't forget!

Workbook Unit 5
Exercise 9 A review of *is*, *are*, and *do*.
Exercise 12 In this exercise students translate sentences containing the main grammar points presented in the unit.

Word list
Ask the students to turn to p130 and go through the words with them. Ask them to learn the words for homework, and test them on a few in the following lesson.

Progress test 1 for Units 1–5 (TB p121).

The time • Present Simple – *he/she/it*
usually/sometimes/never • Questions and negatives
Words that go together • Days of the week

Every day

Introduction to the unit

The title of this unit is 'Every day' and it covers the language of daily routines. It presents the third person singular form of the Present Simple and so follows on from the language covered in Unit 5. Basic frequency adverbs, telling the time, and days of the week are also introduced.

The vocabulary syllabus is extended with a focus on an important aspect of English – collocation. The lexical set is of daily routine verbs, allowing students to talk about their own routine and ask about other people's.

Language aims

The time The unit opens with a section on telling the time in English. This is done with digital time so that students can use the numbers they already know to tell the time, e.g. *five fifteen*, and not have to worry about *quarter to/past*, *half past*, etc.

Grammar – Present Simple 2 The *I/you* forms are reviewed and the presentation of the Present Simple is completed with *he/she/it* in the positive, negative, and question forms (both *wh-* and *Yes/No* questions). The third person singular form is the one that causes most problems for students and so it is divided out into a section of its own for the initial presentation. All forms of the Present Simple are reviewed and recycled across the course so that students can deal with the differences in the *I/you/we/they* and *he/she/it* forms.

Frequency adverbs *Usually*, *sometimes*, and *never* are introduced and practised as part of the function of talking about routines.

Vocabulary The vocabulary section focuses on words that go together and so introduces an important aspect of English – collocation. The section includes words that go with common verbs to produce a useful lexical set for talking about routines.

Everyday English Days of the week and prepositions of time are presented and practised.

Workbook The time is reviewed in a range of exercises.

The *he/she/it* forms of the Present Simple positive are reviewed along with the frequency adverbs from the unit. Students are also given the opportunity to personalize the adverbs and review the *I* form.

Students practise third person singular Present Simple negative and questions, and also review the use of the auxiliary verbs *do/does/don't/doesn't* in all forms.

Vocabulary from the units covered to date is consolidated in a crossword.

Students get skills practice with a listening and a guided writing task.

The days of the week and prepositions from *Everyday English* are reviewed and consolidated.

> **POSSIBLE PROBLEMS**
> • The Present Simple has very few inflections when compared with equivalent structures in other languages. The addition of the third person singular *-s* is the only change in the positive and so students often forget to include it. Be prepared to give lots of practice in the *he/she/it* forms!
> • The use of *does/doesn't* is an added complication which students often confuse with *do/don't*. Again, regular review and practice will help students produce the forms accurately.

- The third person singular -*s* can be pronounced in three ways:

works   /wɜːks/
lives   /lɪvz/
watches   /ˈwɒtʃɪz/

Students also need help in distinguishing and producing these endings.

Notes on the unit

STARTER (SB p40)

> **NOTE**
>
> It is useful to have a cardboard clock with movable hands for this lesson and for subsequent revision of telling the time. If you do not have one in your school, then it is quite easy to make one.

The Student's Book presents digital times so that students can tell the time with the numbers they already know, without having to deal with *quarter past/to* and *half past*. The section includes times on the hour, half hour, and quarter hour. The other times, e.g. (9).05, (11).25, etc. are covered in a photocopiable task on TB p110. See the *Suggestion* notes opposite.

1 **T 6.1** Focus attention on the clocks. Play the recording of the first five times, pausing after each one and getting students to repeat chorally and individually. Highlight the use of *o'clock* for times on the hour and make sure students can pronounce it accurately.

Get students to complete the remaining five times, following the examples given in 1–5. Play the recording of numbers 6–10 and get students to check their answers. Play the recording again, getting students to repeat chorally and individually.

> **Answers and tapescript**
>
> | | |
> |---|---|
> | 1 It's nine o'clock. | 6 It's two o'clock. |
> | 2 It's nine thirty. | 7 It's two thirty. |
> | 3 It's nine forty-five. | 8 It's two forty-five. |
> | 4 It's ten o'clock. | 9 It's three o'clock. |
> | 5 It's ten fifteen. | 10 It's three fifteen. |

2 **T 6.2** Focus attention on the conversation. Play the recording once and get students to listen and read. Play the recording again, and get students to repeat chorally and individually. Demonstrate the pairwork with one student. Ask students to give two or three more examples in open pairs before continuing in closed pairs.

> **SUGGESTION**
>
> There is a photocopiable information gap activity on TB p110 which reviews and extends the language of telling the time. Photocopy enough pages for your class (Student A's material and Student B's material are on the same page.) The activity covers times which students haven't met in the Student's Book so you will need to pre-teach/check these first. Write the following times on the board:
>
> 11.05, 1.10, 7.20, 9.25, 8.40, 6.50, 12.55
>
> Remind students of the use of 'oh' /əʊ/, which they met in phone numbers, for 11.05. Get students to say the times aloud, reading them as digital times, e.g. *one ten*.
>
> Explain that each student has six times and six empty clocks and that they have to ask *What time is it, please?* and complete the clocks. Demonstrate the activity with one student before dividing the class into pairs and getting them to complete the task. Monitor and check for the correct use of the times.
>
> Students check their answers by comparing their completed sheets.

WHAT TIME DO YOU . . . ? (SB p41)

Present Simple – *I/you*

1 This section presents daily routine verbs. Focus attention on the pictures. Elicit some basic information about the character: *What's her name?* (Lena). *How old is she, do you think?* (She's about 16.)

Explain that students are going to hear Lena talking about her school day. Review telling the time by getting students to read the pairs of times aloud. (The *Starter* section didn't present (8).40, which appears in number 3, but students should be able to read the time as they already know the numbers.)

T 6.3 Focus on the example and play the first line of the recording. Play the recording to the end and get students to continue circling the correct times. Get students to check their answers in pairs. Play the recording again and get students to check against the tape.

Check the answers with the whole class.

> **Answers**
>
> | | | |
> |---|---|---|
> | 1 7.45 | 4 12.15 | 6 4.30 |
> | 2 8.00 | 5 3.30 | 7 11.00 |
> | 3 8.30 | | |

> **T 6.3**
>
> Well, on schooldays I get up at seven forty-five . I have breakfast at eight and I go to school at eight thirty. I have

lunch in school with my friends, that's at twelve fifteen – it's early in our school. I leave school at three thirty in the afternoon and I walk home with my friends. I get home at four thirty. I go to bed at eleven o'clock on school days, but not at the weekend.

Say the sentences aloud or play the recording again and get students to repeat chorally and individually. Make sure students aren't confused by the spelling of *breakfast* and pronounce it correctly /ˈbrekfəst/. Students practise the sentences in closed pairs.

2 Demonstrate the activity by telling students about your day, giving the same information as in the pictures. Do this in a natural way, but do not add in any new language. Focus attention on the example in the speech bubble and elicit a few single sentences from students about their day with the verbs from exercise 1. Students continue talking about their day working in pairs. Monitor and check for correct use of the Present Simple and the times.

3 **T 6.4** This exercise practises the question *What time ... ?* with the Present Simple. Focus attention on the questions and get students to listen and repeat chorally and individually. Make sure they can reproduce the pronunciation of *do you* /dju:/ and the falling intonation on the *wh-* questions.

Drill the question and answer in the speech bubbles and elicit the other questions students can ask. If students need help, write the verbs on the board:

get up, have breakfast, go to work, have lunch, leave work, get home, go to bed.

Get students to practise the questions in open pairs. Students continue in closed pairs, working with a different partner from exercise 2. Monitor and check for correct use of the Present Simple and the times.

ADDITIONAL MATERIAL

Workbook Unit 6
Exercises 1 and 2 Practice of the time.
Exercise 3 First person singular of the Present Simple and further time practice.

KARL'S DAY (SB p42)

Present Simple – *he/she/it, usually/sometimes/never*

1 This section presents the *he/she/it* positive forms of the Present Simple. Focus attention on the photos of Karl and get students to read the description of him. Check comprehension of *millionaire, director, 24-hour, shopping site,* and *Internet.*

Focus attention on the pictures of Karl's day and check comprehension of *have a shower, work late, buy,* and *go*

out. Focus attention on the example sentence. Get students to continue writing the times, working individually.

Ask students to check their answers in pairs before checking with the whole class.

Answers

1	six o'clock	5	eight o'clock
2	six forty-five	6	nine fifteen
3	seven fifteen	7	nine thirty, eleven thirty
4	one o'clock	8	eleven forty-five

GRAMMAR SPOT

1 Focus attention on the examples of third person singular forms *gets up* and *has.* Students underline the verbs in sentences 2–8. Check the answers with the class.

Answers

2	has	6	buys, eats, gets
3	leaves, goes	7	goes, works
4	has	8	goes
5	works, leaves		

Elicit the key last letter in each of the verbs (*s*).

T 6.5 Play the recording and get students to repeat chorally and individually. Make sure students can distinguish the /s/ endings, e.g. *gets* /gets/ from the /z/ endings, e.g. *has* /hæz/ (The tapescript gives the complete verb forms including nouns and particles.)

Tapescript

1	gets up	6	buys
	has a shower		eats
2	has breakfast		gets home
3	leaves home	7	goes out
	goes to work		works
4	has lunch	8	goes to bed
5	works late		
	leaves work		

2 Focus attention on the adverbs of frequency and their meaning. Make sure that students understand that *usually* and *sometimes* are not fixed references and the actual number of times that they refer to can vary.

Ask students to underline the examples of *usually, sometimes,* and *never* in the sentences about Karl.

T 6.6 Play the recording and get students to repeat chorally and individually. Make sure students reproduce the third person singular ending and encourage them to reproduce the linking in the following sentences:

He sometimes buys a pizza.

He never goes out in the evening.

Read Grammar Reference 6.1 – 6.3 on p124 together in class, and/or ask students to read it at home. Highlight the use of the *-es* ending, e.g. *go – goes*. Encourage them to ask you questions about it. If appropriate, point out that the frequency adverbs can be used with *to be*, but that they usually come after the verb, e.g. *I am **never** at home in the morning.*

ADDITIONAL MATERIAL

Workbook Unit 6
Exercise 4 Present Simple *he/she/it* forms.
Exercises 5 and 6 Present Simple and frequency adverbs *usually/sometimes/never.*

Questions and negatives

2 This section introduces *does/doesn't* in the question and negative forms. Both *wh-* and *Yes/No* questions are presented at the same time, as students are dealing with the third person singular form only at this stage, and they have already had a lot of practice of the individual question types.

T 6.7 Refer students back to the pictures of Karl. Read question 1 aloud and elicit the answer (*gets*). Students continue completing the answers, working individually. Get them to check in pairs before playing the questions and answers on tape. Play the recording through once and let students check their answers.

Play the recording again, pausing after each question and answer exchange, and get the students to repeat chorally and individually. Make sure they can reproduce the falling intonation on the *wh-* questions and the rising intonation on the *Yes/No* questions. Students practise the questions and answers in open and then in closed pairs.

Answers and tapescript
1 What time does he get up?
   He **gets** up at six o'clock.
2 When does he go to bed?
   He **goes** to bed at eleven forty-five.
3 Does he go to work by taxi?
   Yes, he does.
4 Does he have lunch in a restaurant?
   No, he doesn't.
5 Does he go out in the evening?
   No, he **doesn't**.

Focus attention on the example sentences. Make sure students understand that the *-s* is on the verb in the positive form and on *does* in the question and negative. Highlight *doesn't* as the contracted form of *does not*. Ask students to circle the *-s* ending and the use of *does/doesn't* in the questions and answers in exercise 2.

3 Focus attention on the language in the speech bubbles. Drill the question and answer. Elicit two or three more examples with students working in open pairs. Students continue asking and answering in closed pairs. Monitor and check for correct use of third person *-s* and of *does/doesn't* in the questions and negatives.

T 6.8 Play the recording and get students to check their answers. If students had difficulties with questions and answers 1–7, drill the questions and answers and get students to practise them in pairs again.

Answers and tapescript
1 What time does he have breakfast?
   He has breakfast at six forty-five.
2 When does he leave home?
   He leaves home at seven fifteen.
3 Does he go to work by bus?
   No, he doesn't. He goes to work by taxi.
4 Where does he have lunch?
   He has lunch in his office.
5 Does he usually work late?
   Yes, he does.
6 Does he eat in a restaurant?
   No, he doesn't. He sometimes buys a pizza and eats it at home.
7 What does he do in the evening?
   He works at his computer.

1 Focus attention on the table. Elicit the forms for *you* (*work* and *don't work*) and then get students to complete the rest of the table. Check the answers with the whole class.

Answers

	Positive	Negative
I	work	don't work
You	**work**	**don't work**
He	**works**	**doesn't work**
She	works	doesn't work
We	**work**	**don't work**
They	**work**	**don't work**

Highlight again that the *he/she* form is the only one that is different.

2 Get students to complete the *wh-* questions. Then check the answers with the class.

> **Answers**
> 1 When **do** you get up?
> 2 When **does** he get up?

Highlight the use of *does* in the second question. Refer students to Grammar Reference 6.4 on p124. Make sure students understand that we repeat *do/does* or *don't/doesn't* in the short answers rather than the main verb, i.e. we cannot say: *Do you get up at 7.30?* * *Yes, I get up.*

PRACTICE (SB p44)

Katya's day

1 Remind students of Karl from the previous section. Point to the photos of Katya and ask *Who is she?* (She's Karl's sister.) Pre-teach/check *artist, country, early, toast, go for a walk, paint, studio, cook,* and *play the piano.*

Read the heading of the text aloud. Ask *How old is Katya?* and *What's her job?* (She's 25. She's an artist.) Focus attention on the example. Elicit the second verb (*gets up*) and then get students to complete the text, working individually.

T 6.9 Get students to check their answers in pairs before playing the recording and letting them check against the tape.

> **Answers and tapescript**
> Katya is twenty-five. She's an artist. She **lives** in a small house in the country. She usually **gets up** at ten o'clock in the morning. She never **gets up** early. She **has** coffee and toast for breakfast and then she **goes** for a walk with her dog. She **gets** home at eleven o'clock and she **paints** in her studio until seven o'clock in the evening. Then she **cooks** dinner and **drinks** a glass of wine. After dinner, she sometimes **listens to** music and she sometimes **plays** the piano. She usually **goes** to bed very late, at one or two o'clock in the morning.

2 Focus attention on the two examples. Make sure students realize that *he* refers to Karl and *she* to Katya. Get students to complete the answers and then check in pairs. Check the answers with the whole class.

> **Answers**
> 1 He 2 She 3 She 4 He 5 He 6 She 7 She
> 8 He 9 She 10 He

Ask a few students to read the sentences aloud. Then get students to practise the sentences in pairs. If they have

serious problems with pronunciation, drill the sentences with the whole class and get them to repeat.

Negatives and pronunciation

3 This exercise practises the negative form and also highlights the importance of contrastive stress when correcting or disagreeing with a statement. Focus attention on the example and ask *positive or negative?* about each sentence in the answer (first sentence – negative, second sentence – positive). Explain that the circles indicate where the main stress falls in each sentence.

Pre-teach *stay at home* for sentence 8. Elicit the answer to sentence 2 (*He doesn't get up at ten o'clock. He gets up at six o'clock.*) Tell students to continue correcting the sentences, referring back to the information about Karl and Katya on pp42 and 44. (With a weaker group, you could do this as a class activity on the board and then play the tape for reinforcement.) Tell them not to worry about the stress in the sentences at this stage.

T 6.10 Play the recording through once, getting students to check their sentences for grammatical accuracy. Then write the pairs of sentences for numbers 2 and 3 and elicit where the main stress falls with the whole class. Remind students that the stress helps to indicate the main difference in the information in the pairs of sentences, and so falls on the key words.

Get students to work in pairs and mark where they think the main stress falls in the rest of the pairs of sentences. Play the recording again and get students to check their answers. Also, check the answers orally with the whole class in case students have problems hearing the main stress.

Play the recording again and get students to repeat chorally and individually.

> **Answers and tapescript**
> 1 She doesn't live in the town. She lives in the country.
> 2 He doesn't get up at ten o'clock. He gets up at six o'clock.
> 3 She doesn't have a big breakfast. She has coffee and toast.
> 4 He doesn't have a dog. She has a dog.
> 5 She doesn't work in an office. She works at home.
> 6 He doesn't cook dinner in the evening. He buys a pizza.
> 7 She doesn't go to bed early. She goes to bed late.
> 8 They don't go out in the evening. They stay at home.

Talking about you

4 Demonstrate the activity by writing the names of two people (one male, one female) from your family on the board. Get students to ask you questions about them, using the language in the speech bubbles and the cues in the Student's Book. If students have problems switching from questions with *be* to the Present Simple questions, drill the language as a class.

Get students to write the name of two family members on a piece of paper. Remind them to choose one male and one female. Students work in pairs and ask and answer about the family members. Monitor and check for correct use of *he/she*, *his/her* and the third person singular Present Simple forms.

> **SUGGESTION**
> You could ask students to bring in family photos for the above activity.

Check it

5 This exercise consolidates the auxiliary forms *do/don't* and *does/doesn't* in Present Simple questions and short answers. Focus attention on number 1 and elicit the answers (*Do, do*). Students continue completing the questions and answers, working individually.

Ask students to check their answers in pairs before checking with the whole class.

> **Answers**
> 1 '**Do** you like ice-cream?' 'Yes, I **do**.'
> 2 '**Does** she work in London?' 'Yes, she **does**.'
> 3 'Where **does** he work?' 'In a bank.'
> 4 '**Do** you go to work by bus?' 'No, I **don't**.'
> 5 '**Does** she go to bed early?' 'No, she **doesn't**.'
> 6 '**Do** they have a dog?' 'Yes, they **do**.'
> 7 '**Does** he speak German?' 'No, he **doesn't**.'
> 8 '**Do** they live in the US?' 'No, they **don't**.'

ADDITIONAL MATERIAL

Workbook Unit 6
Exercise 7 Word order in *he/she/it* forms of Present Simple *wh-* questions.
Exercise 8 A reading task to consolidate Present Simple *he/she/it* forms.
Exercises 9 and 10 Present Simple *he/she/it* forms in the negative.
Exercise 11 *he/she/it* forms of Present Simple *Yes/No* questions.
Exercise 12 A review of *do/does/don't/doesn't*.

Words that go together

1 Check comprehension of *shopping*. Focus attention on the examples. Students continue working in pairs to match the verbs and nouns/phrases.

T 6.11 Play the recording and get students to check their answers.

> **Answers and tapescript**
>
> | | |
> |---|---|
> | get up early | go shopping |
> | go to bed late | have a shower |
> | listen to music | eat in restaurants |
> | watch TV | drink beer |
> | cook dinner | play the piano |
> | work in an office | stay at home |

2 This is a questionnaire activity to practise *Yes/No* questions. As a variation, students use *Yes, usually.*, *Yes, sometimes.*, and *No, never.* in their answers, rather than *Yes, I do./No, I don't.* This allows them to practise the frequency adverbs in a simple but meaningful way.

T 6.12 Focus attention on the questionnaire. Play the recording and get students to repeat chorally and individually.

3 Focus attention on the language in the speech bubbles. Drill the question and three possible answers. Get students to ask you a few of the questions and give true answers. Demonstrate how to record the answers by putting the three adverbs on the board and ticking under the appropriate one.

Students then work in closed pairs, asking and answering, and filling in their partner's answers.

4 This follow-up phase allows students to talk about themselves and their partner and so get practice in switching from first to third person. Focus attention on the example and then elicit more information from individual students about themselves and their partner.

ADDITIONAL MATERIAL

Workbook Unit 6
Exercises 14 A crossword to review vocabulary covered in Units 1–6.

Days of the week

1   **T 6.13** Explain that students are going to learn the days of the week in English. Play the recording and get students to write the days in the correct order. Play the recording again and get students to repeat chorally and individually. Make sure they can distinguish *Tuesday* and *Thursday* and that they only produce two syllables in *Wednesday* /ˈwenzdeɪ/.

> **Answers and tapescript**
> Monday   **Tuesday   Wednesday   Thursday   Friday**
> **Saturday**   Sunday

Students practise the days again with each student saying one day of the week in the correct order.

2   Elicit the answer to question 1 as an example. Students do the exercise in pairs. Have a brief feedback session by getting students to give their answers to individual questions.

3   Here students learn which prepositions are used with the days, parts of the day, and times. Elicit the answer for times and *the weekend* (*at*) and then get students to write the correct preposition for the other phrases.

   T 6.14 Play the recording and get students to check their answers. Highlight the difference between *in the evening* but *on Saturday evening*, *in the afternoon* but *on Friday afternoon*, etc.

> **Answers and tapescript**
> on Sunday
> on Monday
> on Tuesday
> on Saturday evening
> on Thursday morning
> on Friday afternoon
>
> at nine o'clock
> at ten thirty
> at twelve fifteen
> at the weekend
>
> in the morning
> in the afternoon
> in the evening

4   Elicit the answer to number 1 (*at*) and then get students to complete the other sentences with either *in*, *on*, or *at*. Check the answers.

> **Answers**
> 1 at   2 on   3 in   4 on   5 at

Focus attention on the example answers in the speech bubbles. Get students to practise asking and answering questions 1–5 in closed pairs. This allows them to practise the *we* form of the Present Simple. Get them to complete the sentences in writing about when they do have English lessons. Encourage them to include the day, part of the day, and time: *We have English lessons on (Monday evening) at (seven thirty).*

5   Students complete the questions with the correct preposition, then ask and answer the questions in closed pairs. Monitor and check for correct question formation, use of short answers and prepositions of time. If you have time, conduct a brief feedback session to allow students to talk about their partner and so practise the third person singular.

ADDITIONAL MATERIAL

Workbook Unit 6
Exercises 17 and 18 Days of the week.
Exercise 19 Prepositions of time *in/on/at*.

Don't forget!

Workbook Unit 6
Exercise 13 In this exercise students translate sentences containing the main grammar points presented in the unit.
Exercise 15 Further listening practice.
Exercise 16 A guided writing task to consolidate the language of routines.

Word list
Ask the students to turn to p131 and go through the words with them. Ask them to learn the words for homework, and test them on a few in the following lesson.

Video
Episode 2 *Home movie*
Jane has a video camera and is making a film about the new house (and the people in it) for her sister, Alison. David's a reluctant interviewee, Helen rather enjoys it, and Matt has an unpleasant surprise.

Stop and check 2 for Units 4–6 (TB p133).

7

Question words • *it/them*
this/that • Adjectives
Can I . . . ?

Places I like

Introduction to the unit

The title of this unit is 'Places I like' and it gives practice in describing places. The grammar input includes revision and extension of question words, the introduction of object pronouns, and the demonstratives *this* and *that*. Students get skills practice with a reading and writing section linked to the focus on places.

Useful adjectives and their opposites are introduced and practised. Making requests with *Can I ... ?* is the focus of the *Everyday English* section.

Language aims

Question words The question words introduced in previous units are reviewed and *how* to refer to manner and *why* are introduced. *Who* in subject questions is also included for recognition.

Object pronouns Subject pronouns (*I*, *you*, *he*, etc.) are reviewed and object pronouns (*me*, *you*, *him*, etc.) are introduced. Grammar Reference 7.2 also lists possessive adjectives so that students can see potential areas of confusion.

this/that *This* and *that* are introduced in the context of asking about objects: *What's this/that?*

Vocabulary A set of key everyday adjectives and their opposites is introduced. This gives an opportunity to review objects introduced in earlier units. Students also review the use of *a/an* + adjective + noun.

Everyday English Requests with *Can I ... ?* are introduced and practised in a range of situations.

Workbook There are exercises to practise object pronouns and help students with potential confusion with subject pronouns and possessive adjectives.

This, *that*, and objects are consolidated.

Students practise question words in matching and word order exercises. Students are given an opportunity to give their own answers to questions. There is an exercise to practise the newly-introduced question word *why* and answers with *because*.

The adjectives from the unit are consolidated in a range of exercises.

Students get skills practice with a listening and a reading task.

Requests with *Can I ... ?* from *Everyday English* are reviewed and consolidated.

> **POSSIBLE PROBLEMS**
> The similarity between subject and object pronouns, and possessive adjectives often present problems for students. The Student's Book and Workbook give practice to help students with these areas, but be prepared to monitor these areas during pairwork and review as necessary.

Notes on the unit

STARTER (SB p48)

> **NOTE**
> *How much?* and *How many?* are reviewed together in this exercise. Students have used *How much?* to talk about prices and *How many?* to talk about numbers, so they should not have any problem with the matching exercise.

It is not advisable at this stage to present the use of *much/many* with countable and uncountable nouns. This is covered in *New Headway Elementary*. Similarly, at this stage, don't explain the use of *Who lives … ?* in the subject question in number 7 or contrast it with the object question form *Who does … ?* Just let students recognize which answer goes with *Who?*

1 Focus attention on the example to demonstrate the activity. Students continue to match the questions and answers, working in pairs.

T 7.1 Play the recording and get students to check their answers.

Answers and tapescript
1 What is the capital of Australia?
   Canberra.
2 How old are the Pyramids?
   4,500 years old.
3 What time do Spanish people have dinner?
   Late. At 10.00 in the evening.
4 Where does the American President live?
   In the White House.
5 How many floors does the Empire State Building have?
   86.
6 How much is a hamburger in the US?
   $3.50.
7 Who lives in Buckingham Palace?
   The Queen of England.

If you feel students need practise with the intonation of *wh-* questions, play the recording and get them to repeat the questions and answers chorally and individually.

SUGGESTION
To give more practice with question words, you can have a quiz in which the students generate the questions. You can give different groups sets of answers and get them to write the questions. You will need to choose answers that can only generate one question and only focus on the present tense at this stage. Check the questions with each group and then divide the students into pairs so that each student has a different set of questions. Students ask and answer in pairs, scoring a point for each correct answer.

2 Give an example by talking about your favourite town or city. Include known adjectives, e.g. *big, small, beautiful*, etc., and information about what the place has, e.g. *restaurants, hotels*, etc. Take the opportunity to pre-teach *why* and *because*, which will be used in the next section. Check the pronunciation of *because* /bɪˈkɒz/.

Elicit another example from a confident student. Students then continue in pairs. Monitor and check, but only feedback on major errors. Let students have the opportunity to say what they can in a relatively free way.

I LOVE IT HERE! (SB p48)

it/them, this/that

1 This exercise reviews questions and answers, including *why* and *because*. Review these words but don't pre-teach all the new vocabulary unless you feel students will have difficulty understanding from context. If this is the case or if you have a weak group, you can pre-teach/check the following by referring to a film star students will know: *famous, film star, journalist, fantastic, nice, first, movie* (American usage), *visit* (verb), *vacation* (American usage), *wedding, happy, together*.

Focus attention on the photo of Céline. Ask questions to get students to predict information about her: (*What's her job? Where is she from? Where is she now? Is she married? Does she have children?*)

T 7.2 Play the recording through once and get students to check the predictions above: (*She's a film star. She's from the United States. She's in her house in London now. Yes, she is. Yes, she does.*)

Play the recording again and get students to complete the conversation.

Get the students to check in pairs before checking with the whole class.

Answers and tapescript
G This is a very beautiful house.
C Thank you. I like it very much, too.
G Céline, you're American. Why do you live here in London?
C Because I just love **it** here! The people are fantastic! I love **them**! And of course, my husband, Charles, is English, and I love **him**, too!
G That's a very nice photo. Who are they?
C My sons. That's Matt, and that's Jack. They go to school here. My daughter's at school in the US. Her name's Lisa-Marie.
G **Why** does Lisa-Marie go to school in the US?
C **Because** she lives with her father. My first husband, you know, the actor Dan Brat. I hate **him** and all his movies. I never watch **them**.
G I see. And does Lisa-Marie visit you?
C Oh, yes. She visits me every vacation. She's here with **me** now.
G And is this a photo of **you** and Charles?
C Oh yes. It's us in Hawaii. It's our wedding. We're so happy together!

2 Get students to practise the conversation in closed pairs while you monitor. If students have problems with pronunciation and intonation, drill key sentences and then get students to continue practising the conversation in closed pairs.

3 This exercise reviews Present Simple questions and answers, and also practises object pronouns and *why* and *because*. Focus on the example and remind students of the use of *does* in the third person question. Students complete the sentences, working individually.

Get students to check their answers in pairs before checking with the whole class.

Answers
1 Why **does** Céline live in London?
  Because she **loves** it in England.
2 Does she like English people?
  Yes, she loves **them**.
3 How **many** children does she have?
  Three.
4 Where **do** her sons go to school?
  In England.
5 **Why** does Lisa-Marie go to school in the US?
  Because she lives with her father.

GRAMMAR SPOT

Check comprehension of the terms *subject* and *object pronouns* by writing this simple table on the board.

Subject	Verb	Object
I	like	you.
You	like	it.
She	likes	them.
We	like	him.

1 Focus attention on the examples *What* and *How old* from sentences 1 and 2 in *Starter* exercise 1. Elicit the question words in sentences 3 and 4 (*What time* and *Where*). Students continue underlining the question word(s) in *Starter* exercises 1 and 2. Check the answers with the whole class.

2 Focus attention on the table in the Student's Book and on the examples. Get students to complete the object pronouns, working in pairs. Check the answers with the whole class.

Answers
Subject pronoun	I	you	he	she	it	we	they
Object pronoun	**me**	**you**	**him**	her	**it**	us	**them**

Ask students to underline the object pronouns in the conversation in exercise 1.

3 Elicit the first examples of *this* and *that* in the conversation in exercise 1 (*This is a very beautiful house. That's a very nice photo.*) Students continue to find examples of *this* and *that*.

Read Grammar Reference 7.1–7.3 on p124 together in class, and/or ask students to read it at home. Encourage them to ask you questions about it.

What's that?

1 Pre-teach/check the use of *What's this?* by holding an object/picture of an object close to you and eliciting the answer *It's a (book).* Repeat the procedure for *What's that?* by pointing to an object/picture of an object at a distance from you. Drill the questions and answer *It's a/an …* chorally and individually. Make sure you include an object/picture of an object beginning with a vowel so that students review *It's an (ice-cream).*

Focus attention on the picture. Review the names of all the objects, without asking *What's this/that?* at this stage, and check the pronunciation. Focus attention on the examples in the speech bubbles. Drill the examples in open pairs and then get students to ask and answer about the objects in the pictures in closed pairs. Monitor and check for correct use of *What's this/that?* Check the answers by getting students to ask and answer across the class.

Answers
What's that? It's a dog / camera / bag / photograph / glass / computer.
What's this? It's a/an phone / television / orange / sandwich / dictionary / cat.

2 Focus attention on the examples in the speech bubbles. Drill the language across the class and then get students to continue asking about objects in the classroom in closed pairs. Encourage them to use the possessive *'s* where appropriate, e.g. *It's Juan's book.* Monitor and check for correct use of *What's this/that?* and the possessive *'s*.

ADDITIONAL MATERIAL

Workbook Unit 7
Exercises 4 and 5 *this* and *that*.

I like them!

3 This section practises object pronouns and allows students to personalize the language by talking about people and things. Pre-teach/check *hate* and *of course*. Focus attention on the example and make sure students understand what the answer *it* refers back to (*ice-cream*). Students complete the other sentences, working individually.

T 7.3 Get students to check their answers in pairs before letting them check against the tape. Ask students what the pronoun refers back to each time (given in brackets in the key below). Sentence 5 assumes the teacher is a woman. Check what pronoun would be used if the teacher were a man (*him*).

Answers and tapescript
1 Do you like ice-cream?
   Yes, I love **it**. (ice-cream)
2 Do you like dogs?
   No, I hate **them**. (dogs)
3 Do you like me?
   Of course I like **you**! (me)
4 Does your teacher teach you French?
   No, she teaches **us** English. (you)
5 Do you like your teacher?
   We like **her** very much. (your teacher)

[handwritten: No Answers + Answers]

What do you like?

4 Check comprehension of the items in the list. Focus attention on the speech bubbles and check comprehension of *love*, *hate*, and *all right*. This can be done with simple board drawings of faces – a smiling face ☺ for *love*, a neutral face ☺ for *all right*, and a frowning face ☹ for *hate*.

Drill the language in the speech bubbles chorally and individually. Check for correct sentence stress in the answers:

Yes, I do. I love it.

No, I don't. I hate it.

It's all right.

Get students to give two or three more examples in open pairs across the class. Then get students to continue in closed pairs. Monitor and check for the correct use of object pronouns.

ADDITIONAL MATERIAL

Workbook Unit 7
Exercises 1–3 Consolidation of object pronouns.

Questions and answers

5 Pre-teach/check *champagne*, *marry*, *maths*, *homework*, *present* (noun). Focus attention on the question in the example and review the formation of the third person Present Simple question. Focus attention on the answer and review the use of third person -*s* and the object pronoun *it*. Check students know what the pronoun refers back to (*champagne*).

▪ **T 7.4** Give students time to write the questions and answers individually and then ask and answer in pairs. Monitor and check for grammatical accuracy. Play the recording and get students to check their answers.

Answers and tapescript
1 Why does Céline drink champagne?
   Because she likes it.
2 Why do you eat oranges?
   Because I like them.
3 Why does Annie want to marry Peter?
   Because she loves him.
4 Why do you eat Chinese food?
   Because I like it.
5 Why don't you like your maths teacher?
   Because he gives us a lot of homework.
6 Why does Miguel buy presents for Maria?
   Because he loves her.

[handwritten: no answer]

If students had a lot of problems with the question formation or the object pronouns, go over the key grammar in each question and answer and then get students to listen and repeat each exchange.

6 Pre-teach/check *learn*, *start* (verb), *a lot* (of groups). Check comprehension of *How?* to refer to manner by focusing on the answer to question 1 (*By bus.*). Then get students to continue matching the questions and answers, working individually.

▪ **T 7.5** Play the recording and get students to check their answers.

Answers and tapescript
1 How do you come to school?
   By bus.
2 What do you have for breakfast?
   Toast and coffee.
3 Who is your favourite pop group?
   I don't have a favourite. I like a lot.
4 Where does your father work?
   In an office in the centre of town.
5 Why do you want to learn English?
   Because it's an international language.
6 How much money do you have in your bag?
   Not a lot. About two pounds.
7 When do lessons start at your school?
   They start at nine o'clock.
8 How many languages does your teacher speak?
   Three.

[handwritten: Answers]

Get students to practise the questions and answers in closed pairs. Monitor and check for correct pronunciation and intonation. If students have problems, drill the questions and answers chorally.

Demonstrate the personalization phase by getting the students to ask you the questions. Students then continue in closed pairs, talking about themselves.

Check it

7 Focus attention on the first pair of sentences as an example. Students continue working individually to choose the correct sentence.

Get students to check their answers in pairs before checking with the whole class.

> **Answers**
> 1 What do you do at the weekend?
> 2 Who is your boyfriend?
> 3 How much money do you have?
> 4 I don't drink beer. I don't like it.
> 5 Our teacher gives us a lot of homework.
> 6 She loves me and I love her.

ADDITIONAL MATERIAL

Workbook Unit 7
Exercises 6–8 Further practice of question words.
Exercise 9 *why* and *because*.

VOCABULARY (SB p52)

Adjectives

1 This exercise introduces some key adjectives and their opposites and also reviews *it's* and *they're*. Focus attention on the pictures and the example. Get students to tell you any other of the adjectives they recognize or let them guess. Pre-teach the remaining adjectives, using mime. Elicit a plural example to remind students of the use of *They're*. Make sure students understand they only have to write *It's/They're* and the appropriate adjective, not the name of the objects.

> **T 7.6** Play the recording and get students to check their answers in pairs.

> **Answers and tapescript**
> | 1 It's lovely. | 6 It's small. |
> | 2 It's horrible. | 7 He's hot. |
> | 3 They're old. | 8 She's cold. |
> | 4 They're new. | 9 They're expensive. |
> | 5 It's big. | 10 They're cheap. |

Drill the pronunciation of the sentences chorally and individually.

2 Focus attention on the adjectives and opposites. Elicit the opposite of *new* as an example (*old*). Get students to write the other opposites in the table and then to check their answers in pairs.

> **Answers**
> | Adjective | Opposite |
> | --- | --- |
> | new | old |
> | expensive | cheap |
> | lovely | horrible |
> | small | big |
> | cold | hot |

> **SUGGESTION**
> You can practise adjective and noun combinations in the 'pictionary'-type activity on TB p111.
> Ask students to work in pairs. You will need one copy of the worksheet cut up into cards for each pair. Each student takes an adjective card and a noun card. If their noun card cannot be matched with their adjective card then they replace it at the bottom of the pile and take another, until they find a combination which they are able to depict in a drawing. Each student then draws a picture of their combination. When they have finished drawing, they show their pictures to their partner, asking *What this?* Partners have to guess which adjective/noun combinations have been depicted, and reply using *It's a(n) … .* Continue until all the adjective cards have been used.

ADDITIONAL MATERIAL

Workbook Unit 7
Exercises 11–13 Consolidation of adjectives from the unit.

READING AND WRITING (SB p53)

A postcard from Dublin

1 This section extends the focus on adjectives in the context of a description of a place. Focus attention on the photos and elicit information about the places shown, e.g. *Is it a hot place? Is it in the United States? Where do you think it is?* Tell students they are going to read and listen to the postcard. Encourage them to guess the meaning of new words.

> **T 7.7** Play the recording and get students to follow in their books. Check comprehension of the following, using the context to help where possible: *on holiday, comfortable, friendly, delicious, building, weather, wet, see you soon.*

2 Elicit the answer to question 1 as an example (*It's from Dona and Sergio.*) Get students to answer the other questions, working individually. Check the answers with the whole class.

3 Focus attention on the adjectives Dona and Sergio use to describe their hotel. Get students to continue finding the appropriate adjectives. Point out that for Dublin they will need to use a negative formed with *not*.

Get students to check their answers in pairs before checking with the whole class.

4 Focus attention on the skeleton of the postcard. Check comprehension of *beach*. You can get students to write their postcard in full in class, feeding in vocabulary where relevant, or give it for homework. With a weaker class, you could draft the postcard as a class activity on the board, and then get students to write a different postcard for homework, based very closely on the draft.

ADDITIONAL MATERIAL

Workbook Unit 7
Exercise 15 Further reading practice.

EVERYDAY ENGLISH (SB p54)

Can I . . . ?

1 This section focuses on requests in everyday situations. Students are introduced to *Can I . . . ?*, but do not give a detailed explanation of the grammar of *can* at this stage. Check comprehension of the vocabulary in the activities list by reading out each activity and getting students to point to the correct picture. Check comprehension of any other individual words, e.g. *ham, return ticket*. Repeat this procedure for the places vocabulary. Students then write the correct numbers and letters for each picture. Check the answers.

2 **T 7.8** Explain that students are going to hear Keiko, a Japanese girl, in different places in town. Focus on the example and play the first conversation. Play the other four conversations, pausing after each one. Get students to complete their answers, choosing from the options in exercise 1. Play the conversations through again if necessary. Check the answers with the whole class. Highlight the use of *at* with railway station, rather than *in*.

3 Focus attention on the gapped conversations. Pre-teach/check *changing room, PC* (personal computer), *pay, at the end, Can I help you?, change* (noun in money context). Elicit as many answers for conversation 1 as the students can remember. Play the recording and get students to check. Students continue to complete the other conversations, working in pairs.

Play the recording again and get students to check/complete their answers.

Get students to practise the conversations in closed pairs. Monitor and check for correct pronunciation and intonation. If students have problems, drill key sections chorally and then get students to repeat the closed pairwork.

4 Check comprehension of *jacket*, *T-shirt*, and *single ticket*. Put students in pairs and assign a role, A or B, to each student. Make sure they understand that they have to ask about the things in their list. Check students know which item can go with which conversation:
conversation 1 – a coffee, an ice-cream
conversation 2 – this jacket, this T-shirt
conversation 5 – a return ticket to Edinburgh, a single ticket to Manchester

Elicit likely prices for a coffee and an ice-cream. Choose a pair of students to demonstrate the conversation with Student A asking for a coffee. Then choose another pair, with Student B asking for an ice-cream. Get students to continue practising the conversations, working in closed pairs and taking it in turns to be the assistant and the customer. Monitor and check for correct pronunciation and intonation. If students have problems, drill key sections of the conversations and get them to practise again in pairs.

ADDITIONAL MATERIAL

Workbook Unit 7
Exercises 16 and 17 Further practice in making requests with *Can I … ?*

Don't forget!

Workbook Unit 7
Exercise 10 Further listening practice.
Exercise 14 In this exercise students translate sentences containing the main grammar points presented in the unit.

Word list
Ask the students to turn to p132 and go through the words with them. Ask them to learn the words for homework, and test them on a few in the following lesson.

8

Rooms and furniture
There is/are • *any*
Prepositions • Directions

Where I live

Introduction to the unit

The title of this unit is 'Where I live' and the theme is homes. *There is/are* and *any* are introduced in the context of talking and asking about rooms and furniture. Prepositions of place are reviewed and extended. There is a range of skills practice, including a reading and speaking section on the city of Sydney, and a listening and writing section on the students' own home town.

The lexical set is of rooms and furniture. The language of asking about local amenities and giving directions is introduced and practised in the *Everyday English* section.

Language aims

There is/are *There is/are* are introduced in the positive, question, and negative forms.

any *Any* is introduced for negatives and plural questions with the structure *there is/are*. It is not used with any other structures at this stage so that students have the opportunity to get used to using it. *Some* is included for recognition, but is not given a full presentation or contrasted with *any*, as this is covered in *New Headway Elementary*.

> **POSSIBLE PROBLEMS**
>
> • *There is/are*
> Students will be familiar with the forms *is/are* from their knowledge of the verb *to be*. However, students may find it confusing to have a singular and plural form to talk about what exists, especially if the equivalent structure has a single form in their own language.
>
> Students can also confuse *there* and *their*, so they may need help in this area in written work. In terms of pronunciation, students need practice in the /ð/ sound in *there* and also need help with linking *There's a* and *There are*. The intonation of the question form may need careful drilling. Students should be encouraged to use a broad voice range, starting high with a fall in the voice and then ending the question with a rise.
>
> • *any*
> Students often ask what *any* means, as there is usually no direct translation in their own language. There is of course no real answer to this, so simply tell students that they need to use *any* in negatives and plural questions with *there is/are*. Students also sometimes have a tendency to use *any* in the positive, so be prepared to monitor and check for this.

Prepositions of place *In, on, under*, and *next to* are introduced and practised in the context of talking about furniture in rooms.

Vocabulary The lexical set is of rooms and furniture. Students are given the opportunity to personalize the language by talking about their own home.

Everyday English This covers the language of asking about local amenities and giving simple directions.

Workbook The lexical set of rooms and furniture is consolidated.

There is/are and *any* are practised in a range of exercises.

There is a word stress exercise, reviewing key language from this and earlier units.

The prepositions of place from the unit are practised.

There is further practice in reading and writing.

The language of local amenities and directions from *Everyday English* is consolidated in a range of exercises.

Notes on the unit

STARTER (SB p56)

1 Focus attention on the questions in exercise 1. Pre-teach/ check *garden* and the difference between *house* and *flat*. You can draw these on the board to highlight the difference. Demonstrate the activity by talking briefly about your own home. Only include language that students have already met, e.g. adjectives *big*, *small*, etc. As a class, students talk briefly about where they live.

2 **T 8.1** Focus attention on the picture of the house. Play the recording and get students to point to the correct room and repeat the words chorally and individually. Check for accurate pronunciation of:

kitchen /ˈkɪtʃn/
toilet /ˈtɔɪlət/

> **Tapescript**
> living room
> dining room
> kitchen
> bedroom
> bathroom
> toilet

3 Focus attention on the example. Then get students to find the rest of the things in the house and write the correct number, working in pairs. Check the answers with the class.

> **Answers**
> 1 a bed   4 a TV
> 6 a CD player   11 a picture
> 12 a cooker   3 a shower
> 7 an armchair   8 a magazine
> 9 a sofa   10 a table
> 2 a lamp   5 a video recorder

T 8.2 Students listen and repeat the words chorally and individually. Check for accurate pronunciation and word stress on:

shower /ˈʃaʊə/
picture /ˈpɪktʃə/
sofa /ˈsəʊfə/
magazine /mægəˈziːn/

NICOLE'S LIVING ROOM (SB p57)

There is/are, any

1 Focus attention on the photograph and the rubric for exercise 1. Ask *What's her name?* (*Nicole*) and *Where is she?* (*In her living room.*).

T 8.3 Play the recording through once and get students to read and listen to the text, not writing anything at this stage. Write the sentence *There's a sofa and there are a lot of books* on the board. Underline *There's* and *there are*. Focus attention on the first gap and elicit the answer (*There*). Play the recording again and get students to complete the text. Check the answers with the whole class.

> **Answers and tapescript**
> My living room isn't very big, but I love it. **There**'s a sofa, and there are two armchairs. **There**'s a small table with a TV on it, and there **are** a lot of books. **There's** a CD player, and **there are** some CDs. **There are** pictures on the wall, and **there are** two lamps. It's a very comfortable room.

If students query the use of *some*, ask *How many CDs?* and elicit *We don't know* to get over the idea of indefinite quantity.

2 Focus attention on the speech bubbles. Write the sentences on the board and ask *Singular or plural?* (*There's a sofa* – singular and *There are two armchairs* – plural). If you know the students' mother tongue, you can translate *There is/are*. If you don't, they should be able to pick up the meaning from the context.

Drill the language in the speech bubbles chorally and individually. Check students can accurately reproduce the linking in both forms:
There's a sofa.
There are two armchairs.

Elicit more singular and plural examples from the class, using the other nouns in the exercise. Students then repeat the sentences working in closed pairs. Monitor and check for correct use of *there is* and *there are*.

Get students to practise *there is* and *there are* with the objects in the classroom. Write lists on the board of the things you have in your classroom, e.g.
Singular *a picture, a table, a TV, a photo*
Plural *lots of books, chairs, desks, bags*

Students work in pairs and take it in turns to make sentences about objects in the classroom. Monitor and check for correct use of *there is* and *there are*.

3 **T 8.4** In this exercise, students practise the question form and short answers. Focus attention on the questions and answers. Play the recording and get students to listen to the questions and repeat chorally

and individually. Check students can accurately reproduce the intonation in the question, and the linking in the short answers:

Are there any photographs?
Yes, there is.
No, there isn't.
Yes, there are.
No, there aren't.

Highlight the singular and plural forms and point out that we use *any* in questions in the plural. Get students to practise the questions and answers in closed pairs. Monitor and check for correct formation of the questions and short answers, and the correct use of *any*.

GRAMMAR SPOT

Focus attention on the completed examples. Check students know that *there's* is singular and is the contracted form of *there is*, and that *Are there* is plural.

Focus attention on the gapped sentences. Check students notice that the first and third gaps require plural forms and the second gap singular by focusing on the nouns. Students then complete the sentences.

Give students the opportunity to practise the negative statements by referring to the classroom, e.g. *There isn't a CD player. There aren't any magazines.* Write a list of nouns on the board and get students to make negative sentences.

Read Grammar Reference 8.1 and 8.2 on p125 together in class, and/or ask students to read it at home. Encourage them to ask you questions about it.

4 Tell students they are going to talk about Nicole's living room. Check comprehension of the items in the list. Focus attention on the speech bubbles and get students to ask and answer the questions in open pairs. Elicit one or two more exchanges using different nouns and then get students to continue in closed pairs. Monitor and check for correct formation of the questions and short answers, and the correct use of *any*.

Check the answers with the whole class by getting students to ask and answer across the class.

Answers	
Is there a TV?	Yes, there is.
Are there any pictures?	Yes, there are.
Is there a radio?	No, there isn't.
Is there a CD player?	Yes, there is.
Is there a telephone?	No, there isn't.
Is there a video recorder?	Yes, there is.
Are there any lamps?	Yes, there are.
Are there any photographs?	No, there aren't.

5 Demonstrate the activity by describing your own living room. Include positive and negative sentences. Get students to work in closed pairs. Encourage students to ask questions if their partner runs out of things to say. Monitor and check for correct use of *there is/are* in all forms, *any*, and pronunciation and intonation. Feed back on any common errors with the whole class.

ADDITIONAL MATERIAL

Workbook Unit 8
Exercises 1–3 Further practice of rooms and furniture vocabulary.
Exercises 4–8 Further practice of *there is/are* and *any* in a range of exercises.

NICOLE'S BEDROOM (SB p58)

Prepositions

1 Focus attention on the prepositions. Check students understand the difference between *in* and *on* by putting something in your book and then on your book and eliciting the correct preposition.

2 Focus attention on the photograph. Ask *What room is this?* (*Nicole's bedroom.*) Briefly review the vocabulary in the picture by pointing to the objects/furniture and eliciting the correct word. Pre-teach/check the new vocabulary in the gap-fill: *car keys*, *drawer*, and *floor*.

Focus attention on the example. Students then complete the sentences, working individually.

T 8.5 Get students to check in pairs before checking with the whole class.

Answers and tapescript
1 Nicole's mobile phone is **on** the bed.
2 The magazine is **next to** the phone.
3 Her CD player is **on** the floor **next to** the bed.
4 Her car keys are **in** the drawer.
5 Her bag is **on** the floor **under** the chair.
6 The books are **under** her bed.

Students practise the sentences. Monitor and check for accurate pronunciation. If students have problems, drill the sentences and get students to practise them again.

3 This exercise practises questions with *Where?* and the prepositions. Focus attention on the speech bubbles. Remind students of the singular form *is* and the plural form *are*. Highlight the use of *It's* in the singular answer and *They're* in the plural. Drill the questions and answers chorally and individually. Make sure students can reproduce the falling intonation on the questions. Check comprehension of the items in the lists. Elicit two or three more exchanges using the nouns in the list.

Students then continue in closed pairs. Monitor and check for correct use of *is/are*, *It's/They're* and the prepositions.

Check the answers with the whole class by getting students to ask and answer across the class.

4 Give students time to write about six questions each. Demonstrate the activity by closing your eyes and getting students to ask you one or two questions. Then get them to continue in closed pairs. Monitor and check for correct use of *is/are*, *It's/They're* and the prepositions.

> **SUGGESTION**
> You can use the picture of Nicole's bedroom on p58 to review *there is/are* in the positive, negative, and in questions. This can be done as a warm-up activity at the beginning of a lesson or as a 'filler'. For further practice, bring in pictures of rooms from magazines. These can be used for vocabulary consolidation, question and answer practice, and describe and draw activities.

ADDITIONAL MATERIAL

Workbook Unit 8
Exercises 10–12 Further practice of the prepositions of place from the unit.

PRACTICE (SB p59)

Questions and answers

1 Focus attention on the example. Then get students to write the words in the correct order to form questions.

T 8.6 Play the recording and get students to check their answers.

Answers and tapescript
1 Do you live in a house or a flat?
2 How many bedrooms are there?
3 Is there a telephone in the kitchen?
4 Is there a television in the living room?
5 Is there a video recorder under the television?
6 Are there a lot of books in your bedroom?
7 Are there any pictures on the wall?

2 Demonstrate the activity by asking a few students the questions in exercise 1. Students continue asking and answering in closed pairs. Encourage them to ask different questions from those in exercise 1. Monitor and check.

Different rooms

3 This is an information gap using different pictures. Tell students that they are going to work with a partner and ask questions to find the difference between two similar pictures of a room. Pre-teach/check *window*. Divide the class into pairs. Refer the Student As to p59 and Student Bs to p139. Tell them they shouldn't look at each other's picture. Focus attention on the examples in the speech bubbles and drill the language. Tell students to circle the differences they find in their pictures. Students work in pairs to find all six differences. Monitor and check.

Students compare their pictures to check they have found the differences.

4 **T 8.7** Tell students they are going to hear a description of one of the rooms and that they have to decide which one it is. Play the recording through once and get students to vote for either picture A or B. If there is disagreement, play the recording again. Check the answer with the whole class.

Answer
Student A's picture, p59
T 8.7
The living room

There's a cat on the sofa and there's a telephone on a small table next to the sofa. There's a CD player with some CDs under it. Not a lot of CDs. There isn't a television and there aren't any pictures or photographs on the walls. There's one lamp, it's next to the table with the telephone. There are two tables and two armchairs. There are some books under one of the tables.

Check it

5 Focus attention on the first pair of sentences as an example. Students continue working individually to choose the correct sentence.

Answers
1 Is there a sofa in the living room?
2 There's a CD player.
3 Are there any lamps?
4 Your keys are in the drawer.
5 The lamp is next to the bed.

Sydney

1 Ask students *What do you know about Australia?* and let students give any information that they know. Focus attention on the photos. Ask students to find the Opera House as an example and then get students to find the other things in the lists, working in pairs. Monitor and help as necessary.

2 This text is slightly longer than in previous units and there are some new words. Tell students not to worry if they don't understand every word and just to focus on the matching task. Check comprehension of the headings. Get students to read the text as far as *it is very hot*. Elicit what heading goes in the first space (*When to go*). Students continue reading and putting in the headings.

T 8.8 Play the recording and get students to check their answers.

> **Answers and tapescript**
> **How to have a good time in . . .**
> **Sydney**
> Sydney has everything you want in a city. It's beautiful, it has old and new buildings, there are fantastic beaches, and the food is delicious.
> **When to go**
> The best times to visit are spring and autumn. In summer it is very hot.
> **Where to stay**
> There are cheap hotels in King's Cross. A room is about $50 a night. There are international hotels in the centre. Here a room is about $150 a night.
> **What to do**
> Sydney has theatres and cinemas, and of course, the Opera House. The best shops are in Pitt Street.
> Go to the harbour. There are beaches, walks, parks, and cafés and, of course, the wonderful bridge.
> Sydney has the famous Bondi Beach. People go swimming, surfing, windsurfing, and sailing.
> For night-life, there are clubs and bars in Oxford Street.
> **What to eat**
> There are restaurants from every country – Italian, Turkish, Lebanese, Japanese, Thai, Chinese, and Vietnamese. Australians eat a lot of seafood – it's very fresh!
> **How to travel**
> There are fast trains and slow buses. The best way to see Sydney is by ferry.

Check comprehension of the following vocabulary: *everything, spring, autumn, summer, theatre, walk, park, surfing, night-life, club, Turkish, Lebanese, Thai, Vietnamese, seafood, fresh, fast, train, slow.*

3 Focus attention on the examples in the chart. Students continue finding the nouns and adjectives, working in pairs. Check the answers with the whole class.

> **Answers**
>
> | Adjective | Noun |
> |---|---|
> | old/new | buildings |
> | fantastic | beaches |
> | delicious | **food** |
> | **cheap** | hotels in King's Cross |
> | **international** | hotels in the centre |
> | **best** | shops |
> | **wonderful** | bridge |
> | **famous** | Bondi Beach |
> | fresh | **seafood** |
> | fast | **trains** |
> | **slow** | buses |

4 Elicit the answer to the first question as an example (*The best times to go are spring and autumn*.) Students ask and answer in closed pairs. Monitor and help where necessary. Check the answers.

> **Answers**
> 1 The best times to go are spring and autumn.
> 2 No. There are cheap hotels in King's Cross.
> 3 People go shopping in Pitt Street.
> They go swimming, surfing, windsurfing, and sailing at the beach.
> They go to clubs and bars in Oxford Street.
> 4 There are Italian, Turkish, Lebanese, Japanese, Thai, Chinese, and Vietnamese restaurants in Sydney.
> 5 The best way to see Sydney is by ferry.

My home town

1 **T 8.9** Focus attention on the photograph. Ask *What's his name?* (*Darren*) and *Where does he live?* (*Bondi, Sydney*). Focus attention on the example. Play the tape as far as *We live in Bondi and we all love surfing*. Tell students they are going to listen to the rest of the recording. Tell them to focus just on the list of things at this stage and not to worry about the details of what Darren says. Make sure students understand they have to write ✔ for the things Darren talks about and ✘ for the things he doesn't. Play the recording through once and get students to complete the task. Let them check in pairs and play the recording through again if necessary. Check the answers with the whole class.

> **Answers**
> Darren talks about: his brother, surfing, train, the Harbour, the Opera House, his girlfriend, Oxford Street, ferry, Manly Beach

Focus attention on the information Darren gives about his brother. Tell students to listen to the recording again and to focus on the details of what Darren says about each thing. Play the recording through again if necessary. Check the answers with the whole class.

Answers
Darren says:
his brother: Darren lives in a house with his brother and a friend.
surfing: They (Darren, his brother, and a friend) all love surfing. They often go surfing in the morning before work.
train: He goes to work by train.
the Harbour: His office is in Macarthur Street, very near the Harbour.
the Opera House: They go running near the Opera House.
his girlfriend: His girlfriend likes to go shopping on Saturday.
Oxford Street: There are some great clothes shops in Oxford Street.
Manly Beach: They go to Manly Beach on Sunday if the weather is good.
ferry: They go to the beach by ferry.

T 8.9

G'day! My name is Darren, and I live in a house with my brother and a friend. We live in Bondi and we all love surfing. We often go surfing in the morning before work.
I'm an engineer. I work in the centre of Sydney for a big international company. I go to work by train. My office is in Macarthur Street, very near the Harbour. On Monday, Wednesday, and Friday I go running at lunchtime. It's very hot in summer, but it's beautiful. I sometimes go with friends from work. We run near the Opera House.
My girlfriend likes to go shopping on Saturday. There is a great market in Paddington, and there are some great clothes shops in Oxford Street. On Saturday night, we often go to Chinatown. The food is fantastic, and really cheap. Or we stay in Bondi because there are a lot of really good little Thai and Italian restaurants here.
I usually relax on Sunday. When the weather is good, we go to the beach, Manly Beach. We go by ferry. When it's wet, we go to the pub.

2 Get students to ask you the questions in the Student's Book and give true answers. Write up relevant vocabulary on the board in the categories given below and get students to add to each list, e.g.
Where/live? *house with a garden, flat, in the centre, near the beach*
Where/work/go to school? *in a hospital/office/school/shop/restaurant/café, from home, in the centre of town, near my house*

What do/with your friends? *go to restaurants/the cinema/theatre/Internet café, watch TV/videos, play football/tennis, go shopping/swimming/sailing/surfing/windsurfing*
Where/go shopping? *in the town centre, at the supermarket/department store/clothes shop/market*
What do/when go out? *see friends, go to clubs and bars* (also see above examples of pastimes with friends.)

Put the students into groups and get them to talk about their home town or a town they like. Get them to refer to the ideas on the board to help them, but also encourage them to say as much as they can for themselves. Monitor and check, but only help if asked, as it's important for students to have the opportunity for free practice and to rely on each other for help. Feed back on any common errors but only focus on things which are potential blocks to communication. Correcting every small mistake will only discourage the class.

3 This writing task can be done in class or for homework. Tell students they are going to write about a town they know. Focus attention on the paragraph headings and the ideas. If you have time, you might like to build up a full writing model on the board, based on the town where students are studying. If the writing is done in class, get students to exchange their descriptions with a partner for checking/editing. If you check the writing, feed back on any general errors, but again do not pick up on every small mistake.

ADDITIONAL MATERIAL

Workbook Unit 8
Exercises 13 and 14 Further reading and writing practice.

EVERYDAY ENGLISH (SB p63)

Directions

1 Pre-teach/check the items in the box. Drill the pronunciation chorally. Demonstrate the activity by getting students to find and point to the bank and the chemist. Students continue locating the places on the map.

2 Focus attention on the signs. Copy them onto the board and drill the pronunciation of *turn left*, *turn right*, and *go straight on*.

Answers
a turn left
b turn right
c go straight on

3 **T 8.10** Tell students they are going to listen to some directions which they have to follow on the map. Tell students to find the start point YOU ARE HERE on the map. Play the first conversation as an example and get students to follow on the map.

Play the rest of the conversations, pausing after each one and getting students to write in their final location. Get students to check in pairs. Play the recording again and get students to check/complete their answers.

Check the answers with the whole class. If students had problems, go over the exercise again, holding up your book and following the route as you read the tapescript aloud.

Answers
1 At the chemist.
2 At the park.
3 At the railway station.
4 At the Chinese restaurant.
5 At the Internet café.

T 8.10
1 Go down King's Road. Turn right at the Grand Hotel into Charles Street. It's next to the cinema.
2 Go straight on, past Charles Street and past Park Lane. It's on the left, next to the supermarket.
3 Go down King's Road. Turn right at the church. Go down Station Road. It's a big building on the right.
4 Go down King's Road. Turn left at the bank into Charles Street. It's on the right, next to the theatre.
5 Go straight on. It's on King's Road, on the left, next to the post office.

Refer students to the tapescript on p116. Get students to practise in pairs. Monitor and check. If they have problems with pronunciation, drill key phrases and then get them to repeat the pairwork.

4 Focus attention on the language in the speech bubbles. Drill the language chorally and individually. Check students can reproduce the falling intonation on *Excuse me!* and the rise on *Is there a … near here?*

Excuse me!

Is there a … near here?

Elicit the directions to the cinema and the post office as examples. Students continue in closed pairs. Monitor and check.

5 Focus attention on the speech bubbles. Check comprehension of *get to, bus station, go out,* and *far*. Drill the language chorally and individually. Briefly review the numbers 1–50 by getting students to count round the class in fives. This will help students with the numbers of minutes. Get one pair of students to practise the

conversation in front of the class. Students then continue in closed pairs. Monitor and check.

ADDITIONAL MATERIAL

Workbook Unit 8
Exercises 16–18 Further practice of giving directions.

Don't forget!

Workbook Unit 8
Exercise 9 Word stress.
Exercise 15 In this exercise students translate sentences containing the main grammar points presented in the unit.

Word list
Ask the students to turn to p133 and go through the words with them. Ask them to learn the words for homework, and test them on a few in the following lesson.

Video
Episode 3 *Do it yourself*
Helen is tired of her bedroom but isn't the decorating kind. Jane, David, and Matt offer to decorate it for her. So while Helen goes out for the day, the other three choose the colour, paint her room, and wait for Helen to return. When Helen does get back, her reaction isn't quite what they had bargained for.

EXTRA IDEAS UNITS 5–8
On TB p112 there are additional photocopiable activities to review the language from Units 5–8. There is a reading text with tasks, a question formation exercise, and a matching activity on everyday English. You will need to pre-teach/check *fridge, message,* and *light* (adjective) for the reading text.

9

Saying years • *was/were born*
Past Simple – irregular verbs
When's your birthday?

Happy Birthday!

Introduction to the unit

The title of this unit is 'Happy Birthday!' and it focuses on the birth dates and lives of famous people. This is the vehicle for the presentation of *was/were born*, which is extended to general uses of the past of *to be*. The positive forms of Past Simple irregular verbs are also presented in a story context. Students learn how to say dates in English with focuses on months, ordinal numbers, and years. Skills practice is provided in the *Vocabulary and reading* section.

Language aims

Saying years The *Starter* section teaches students how to read dates in English. This highlights dates before 2000, e.g. *1961 – nineteen sixty-one*, and the use of *and* in dates after 2001, e.g. *2008 – two thousand and eight*.

> **POSSIBLE PROBLEMS**
> How students say dates in their own language can often create problems with dates in English. Some languages divide the date differently, e.g. *1999 – *one thousand nine hundred and ninety-nine*, so students need help with dividing the century and years correctly. The use of *and* in dates after 2001 also needs highlighting.

was/were The past of *to be* is introduced in all forms. Students' first contact with the past forms is with *was/were born*, and then students move on to general uses of *was/were*.

> **POSSIBLE PROBLEMS**
> *was/were*
> Students usually make the switch from present of *be* to past relatively smoothly, although they need a lot of practice in which subjects take *was* and which take *were*. Pronunciation can present a problem in that the vowels in *was* and *were* both have weak and strong forms: *was* /ə/ and /ɒ/; and *were* /ə/ and /ɜ:/. The weak form /ə/ is in the positive and question forms, and strong forms /ɒ/ and /ɜ:/ are in negatives and short answers:
>
> | | |
> |---|---|
> | She was at school. | /ʃi: wəz ət sku:l/ |
> | She wasn't at school. | /ʃi: wɒznt ət sku:l/ |
> | Was she at school? | /wəz ʃi: ət sku:l/ |
> | Yes, she was./ No, she wasn't. | /jes ʃi: wɑz/ /nəʊ ʃi: wɒznt/ |
> | They were at school. | /ðeɪ wə(r) ət sku:l/ |
> | They weren't at school. | /ðeɪ w ɜ:nt ət sku:l/ |
> | Were they at school? | /wɜ: ðeɪ (j)ət sku:l/ |
> | Yes, they were./No, they weren't. | /jes ðeɪ wɜ:/ /nəʊ ðeɪ wɜ:nt/ |
>
> The pronunciation of the negative forms is highlighted and practised in the *Negatives and pronunciation* section on p67.

was/were born The equivalent structure in students' own language is often different, leading students to say **I am born* or **I born*. The unit provides a whole section on this structure to help students become familiar with the correct forms.

Past Simple – irregular verbs The unit introduces the Past Simple in the positive. The focus is on a limited number of irregular verbs which are presented as a lexical set in a story context. This allows students to get initial familiarization with some of the highest frequency irregular past forms before they move on to the use of *did* in negatives and questions in Unit 10.

POSSIBLE PROBLEMS

There are a lot of irregular verbs for students to learn in the course of their studies. The initial presentation is limited to a small number of verbs and students access them by matching to their present forms. Students are referred to the irregular verb list on p142 to help them do this and they should be encouraged to refer to the list as they work through the remaining units in the book.

Vocabulary This is the small number of irregular past forms which students use to complete a story.

Everyday English This covers months of the year, ordinal numbers in dates, and personalizes the language by talking about students' birthdays.

Workbook Saying years is consolidated in writing and listening exercises.

A listening exercise reviews family vocabulary and further consolidates years.

was/were born is further practised.

was/were is consolidated through a range of exercises, including guided writing, question formation tasks, cued sentences, and gap-fill. Some of these exercises are based on profiles of famous people from the past.

Irregular pasts are further practised.

Vocabulary from earlier units is reviewed and consolidated in a categorizing activity.

The *Everyday English* section focuses on months, ordinal numbers, and dates.

Notes on the unit

STARTER (SB p64)

1 **T 9.1** Briefly review numbers 1–20 round the class. Write numbers in the 30s, 40s, 50s, etc. on the board to review numbers up to 100. Pre-teach/Check *a thousand*. Play the recording for the first date and focus attention on the answer. Play the rest of the recording and get students to underline the correct date.

Get students to check their answers in pairs before checking with the whole class.

Answers and tapescript
1 fourteen twenty-six
2 seventeen ninety-nine
3 eighteen eighty
4 nineteen thirty-nine
5 nineteen sixty-one
6 two thousand and seven

! Focus attention on the Caution Box. Read the first two dates aloud and write them on the board. Highlight that we divide the dates like this in English:

18 – 41   19 – 16

T 9.2 Focus attention on the last three dates. Read them aloud and highlight the use of *and* in dates after 2000. Play the recording and get students to repeat chorally and individually. Elicit how we read each of the dates in exercise 1. Then get students to practise saying the dates in closed pairs. Monitor and check.

2 Elicit the answers to the questions. The second question includes *was* for recognition. If students query it, just tell them it's the past of *be*, but do not go into a full presentation of *was/were* at this point.

WHEN WERE THEY BORN? (SB p64)

was/were born

1 **T 9.3** Focus attention on the photos. Ask *Who was he/she?* about each of them to check the names. Check comprehension of *When were they born?* Focus attention on the information about the people. Check comprehension of *painter*, *scientist*, and *Poland*. Tell students that they will hear a short description of each person and that they have to write the year they were born. Play the recording and get students to write the years. Check the answers with the class.

Answers and tapescript
Leonardo da Vinci was a painter and scientist. He was born in **1452** in Tuscany, Italy.
Marie Curie was a scientist. She was born in **1867** in Warsaw, Poland.

---

2 **T 9.4** Focus attention on the sentences. They present the *I/he/she* forms with *was*. Play the recording and get students to repeat chorally and individually. Encourage students to reproduce the weak form /ə/ in *was*.

3 Focus attention on the speech bubbles. Get students to ask you the questions and give the answers. Drill the language chorally and elicit a few exchanges in open pairs. Students continue in closed pairs. Monitor and check for correct use of *am* and *was* and correct pronunciation.

4 **T 9.5** This exercise presents the *you* and *they* forms with *were*, the *wh-* question form, and also reviews dates. Play the recording and get students just to listen. Play the recording again and get students to repeat chorally and individually. Encourage students to reproduce the weak form /ə/ in *was* and *were*, and the correct intonation and sentence stress:

When were you born? I was born in 1986.

Get students to practise the questions and answers in open pairs and then in closed pairs. Monitor and check for correct reading of dates, pronunciation, and intonation.

GRAMMAR SPOT

Focus attention on the table. Read out the present forms of *to be* and focus on the past examples *was* and *were*. Elicit the *you* form in the past (*were*). Then get students to complete the rest of the table.

Answers		
	Present	**Past**
I	am	was
You	are	**were**
He/She/It	is	**was**
We	are	were
They	are	**were**

Read Grammar Reference 9.1 on p125 together in class, and/or ask students to read it at home. Encourage them to ask you questions about it.

5　**T 9.6** Focus attention on the photo. Ask *What's her name?* (*Calico Jones.*) *How old do you think she is?* (Students guess age – about 15.) Draw a family tree on the board and review the following vocabulary: *brother, sister, mum, dad, grandmother*. Focus attention on the names of Calico's family. Read the names aloud so that students can recognize the pronunciation. Tell the students they are going to hear Calico describing her family. Ask *When was Calico born?* Play the recording as far as *I was born in 1987* and elicit the answer. Play the next part of the recording as far as *one year later in 1993*. Elicit the answers about Henry and William (Henry – *1992*, William – *1993*). Play the rest of the recording and get students to complete their answers.

Get students to check their answers in pairs. Play the recording again if necessary to allow students to check/complete their answers. Check the answers with the whole class.

Answers	
Calico Jones	
Calico's family	
Henry and William	1992, 1993
Cleo	1999
Linda and Alan	1961
Violet	1932

T 9.6

My name's Calico. I know, it's a funny name! I was born in 1987. My two brothers are Henry and William, they were born . . . er . . . Henry in 1992 and William just one year later in 1993. Ugh – they're horrible! My little sister is Cleo, she's OK. She was born in 1999. Mum and dad are Linda and Alan. My mum was born in 1961 and my dad . . . er . . . I think he was born in 1961, too. And my grandmother . . . er, she was born in 1930 something . . . yes, 1932. Her name's Violet. I think it's a beautiful name.

Focus attention on the speech bubbles. Highlight the uses of present and past forms. Ask the questions and get students to give complete answers (*She was born in 1999. They're her parents. Linda was born in 1961. Alan was born in 1961, too.*)

Drill the questions and answers chorally. Elicit some questions and answers about the other people in Calico's family with students working in open pairs. Students continue in closed pairs. Monitor and check for correct use of *is/are*, *was/were born*, dates, pronunciation, and intonation.

6　Demonstrate the activity by writing the names of some of your family on the board. Focus attention on the speech bubbles. Elicit similar questions about your family from the class. Briefly review *he/she* if students have problems with this and make sure they use *is* and *was* correctly. Students work in closed pairs and ask and answer about their respective families. Encourage them to make brief notes of the dates when people were born in preparation for the next exercise. Monitor and check for correct use of *is/are*, *was/were born*, dates, pronunciation, and intonation.

7　This is a transfer activity to consolidate the third person singular form. Elicit information from several students about their partner's family.

ADDITIONAL MATERIAL

Workbook Unit 9

Exercises 1 and 2 Further practice of writing and understanding years.

Exercise 3 A listening exercise to review family vocabulary and years.

Exercises 4 and 5 Further practice of *was/were born* in positive and question forms.

Who were they?

1 Pre-teach/check the words in the box, and *India*. Drill the pronunciation chorally and individually. Focus attention on the example. Get students to continue matching the people to the jobs in the box.

> **Answers**
> 1 writer
> 8 politician
> 3 musician
> 2 painter
> 7 racing driver
> 4 actor
> 6 princess

2 **T 9.7** Tell the students they are going to hear when each of the people in exercise 1 was born. Play the first sentence and elicit the answer (*1564*). Play the rest of the recording and get students to write the other years. Get students to check their answers in pairs. Play the recording again if necessary to allow students to check/complete their answers. Check the answers with the whole class.

> **Answers and tapescript**
> 1 Shakespeare was born in England in **1564**.
> 2 Van Gogh was born in Holland in **1853**.
> 3 Beethoven was born in Germany in **1770**.
> 4 Marilyn Monroe was born in the US in **1926**.
> 5 Elvis Presley was born in the US in **1935**.
> 6 Diana Spencer was born in England in **1961**.
> 7 Ayrton Senna was born in Brazil in **1960**.
> 8 Indira Gandhi was born in India in **1917**.

3 **T 9.8** This exercise extends *wh-* question forms with *was*. Play the recording and get students just to listen. Play the recording and get students to repeat chorally and individually. Encourage students to reproduce the weak form /ə/ in *was* and the correct intonation and sentence stress.

Get students to practise the questions and answers in open pairs and then in closed pairs. Monitor and check for correct pronunciation and intonation.

Focus attention on the speech bubbles. Ask the question about Van Gogh and elicit the answer (*He was a painter.*) Elicit the other questions with *Where* and *When* and get students to practise in open pairs. Students continue asking and answering in closed pairs. Monitor and check for correct question formation and intonation, and for correct reading of the dates.

SUGGESTION

You can give students further practice in *was born* and dates with the photocopiable information gap activity on TB p113. Student A and Student B have six pictures of famous people from the past, but only information for three of those people. They have to ask questions to complete the information. Photocopy enough pages for your class. Pre-teach *politician*, *dancer*, and *Jamaica*. Divide the class into pairs and hand out the copies, one for Student A and one for Student B. Elicit the questions students will need to ask: *Who was number (1)? What was his/her job? When was he/she born? Where was he born?* Remind students to ask *How do you spell that?* when they don't know the spelling of the proper nouns. Demonstrate the activity by getting one pair of students to ask about picture 1 (*Einstein*). Students then complete the task, working in closed pairs. Monitor and check for correct use of *was*, reading of the dates, and use of the alphabet. Get students to compare their sheets to check they have exchanged the information correctly.

Negatives and pronunciation

4 This exercise introduces the negative forms and highlights the change in pronunciation of the vowel from positive to negative. It also highlights the need for contrastive stress when students correct information.

T 9.9 Focus attention on the examples. Remind students that the circles indicate the main stress of each sentence. Play the recording and get students to repeat chorally and individually. Encourage them to reproduce the correct sentence stress and strong vowel forms in *wasn't* and *weren't*.

> ! Focus attention on the Caution Box.
> 1 Make sure students understand that *wasn't* and *weren't* are contracted forms and what the corresponding full forms are.
> 2 Focus attention on the examples and read the full sentences aloud. Then read the positive and negative verb forms in isolation, emphasizing the change from the weak form /ə/ in *was* and *were* to the strong forms /ɒ/ in *wasn't* and /ɜː/ in *weren't*. Drill the sentences and individual verb forms chorally and individually.

5 Elicit the answer to number 1 as an example (*No, he wasn't. He was a racing driver.*) Remind students they will need a plural verb form in numbers 3 and 5. Students continue correcting the information working individually.

T 9.10 Play the recording and get students to check their answers.

Answers and tapescript
1 Ayrton Senna was an actor.
   No, he wasn't. He was a racing driver.
2 Marie Curie was a princess.
   No, she wasn't. She was a scientist.
3 Marilyn Monroe and Elvis Presley were Italian.
   No, they weren't. They were American.
4 Beethoven was a scientist.
   No, he wasn't. He was a musician.
5 Leonardo da Vinci and Van Gogh were musicians.
   No, they weren't. They were painters.
6 Indira Gandhi was a singer.
   No, she wasn't. She was Prime Minister of India.

Play the recording again and get students to repeat. If students have problems, highlight the weak and strong verb forms in the Caution Box again and elicit where the main stress goes on each sentence. Then get students to repeat again. Get students to practise the sentences in pairs, Student A reading the first sentence and Student B the correction. Monitor and check for correct sentence stress and correct pronunciation of the past verb forms.

ADDITIONAL MATERIAL

Workbook Unit 9
Exercises 6 and 7 A gap-fill and guided writing task to consolidate *was/were* and *was/were born*.
Exercise 8 Further practice of *was/were* in questions, short answers, and positive forms.
Exercise 9 Further practice of *was/were* in positive and negative forms.
Exercise 10 Consolidation of *was/were* in all forms.

Today and yesterday

6 Pre-teach/check *yesterday* and briefly review the days of the week round the class. Briefly elicit other items that can fit in the table, e.g.
   Today/Yesterday . . .
      I'm/I was *in town/at the shops/at the cinema/in the country/in the park*
      the weather is/was *good/all right/bad*
      my parents are/were (see above examples)
   Demonstrate the activity by saying where you and your parents are today and were yesterday. Elicit an example of the days of the week and the weather and then get students to continue in closed pairs. This exercise can be extended also to practise the negative. Monitor and check for correct present and past verbs forms, and for correct pronunciation.

Check it

7 Elicit the answer to number 1 as an example (*was*). Students complete the other sentences, working individually.

   Get students to check their answers in pairs before checking with the whole class. Get students to read the complete sentences out in order to get more pronunciation practice.

Answers
1 Where **was** your mother born?
2 When **were** your parents born?
3 No, my parents **weren't** *both* born in 1951. My *father* **was** born in 1951, and my mother in 1953.
4 Yes, I **was** in New York in 1999.
5 **Was** he at home yesterday? No, he **wasn't**.
6 **Were** you at work yesterday? Yes, we **were**.
7 **Were** they at school yesterday morning? No, they **weren't**.

VOCABULARY AND READING (SB p68)

Past Simple – irregular verbs

1 This section introduces a small set of irregular past forms in a story context. Students access the verbs through their knowledge of the verbs in the Present Simple and the main focus is a lexical rather than grammatical one. It is therefore not advisable to go into a detailed presentation of the Past Simple at this stage. This is covered in Unit 10.

   Check the meaning of *present* and *past* and review the meaning of the verbs in their present form. Demonstrate the activity by eliciting the past of *is* and *are* (*was* and *were*). Refer students to the irregular verb list on p142. Get students to match the verbs forms, working in pairs.

T 9.11 Play the recording through once and get students to check their answers.

Answers and tapescript

are	were
is	was
buy	bought
go	went
say	said
see	saw
take	took

Play the recording and get students to repeat chorally and individually. Make sure students aren't confused by the spelling of *bought* – /bɔːt/. Say the present forms and get students to say the past equivalent round the class.

Refer students to Grammar Reference 9.2 on p125.

2 Pre-teach the new vocabulary in the sentences: *market, painting, expert* (noun), *be worth, million, franc, upset, dirty, for sale*, using the pictures where appropriate.

Focus on the example to demonstrate the activity. Students continue matching the pictures and sentences, working in pairs. Check the answers with the whole class.

> **Answers**
> 1d   2f   3a   4c   5e   6b

3 Tell students they are going to read a report of the story about the painting. Focus attention on the example to demonstrate the activity. Tell students to complete the rest of the story, working individually. Encourage them not to worry if they come across new words and to try to understand them from the context.

T 9.12 Get students to check in pairs before checking with the whole class.

> **Answers and tapescript**
> In August 1999 three friends, Jacques Proust, Guy Fadat, and François Leclerc, **were** on holiday in the town of Laraque in France. On Sunday they **went** shopping in the market and they **saw** a dirty, old painting of the Virgin Mary. They **bought** it for 1,400 francs and they **took** it to Paris. In Paris, an expert said that the painting was by Leonardo da Vinci and it **was** worth 500,000,000 francs. The man in Laraque market **said**: 'I was happy to sell the painting but now I'm very upset. I don't want to think about it!'

Check any vocabulary students had problems with. Students then read the story to a partner. Monitor and check for pronunciation. If students have problems, drill key sections and get students to repeat the task.

4 Get students to cover the text in exercise 3. Focus attention back on the pictures. You can either re-tell the story as a class activity first and then get students to repeat in pairs. Alternatively, set up the pairwork first and then re-tell as a class in a checking phase. Either way, when you monitor, don't expect students to reproduce the story with complete accuracy. Do not over-correct in the feedback stage – just pick up on common errors in the irregular past forms.

ADDITIONAL MATERIAL

Workbook Unit 9
Exercises 11 and 12 Further practice of irregular past simple forms.

EVERYDAY ENGLISH (SB p70)

When's your birthday?

1 Focus attention on the months. Pre-teach *calendar* and elicit the second month of the year (*February*). Get students to continue writing the months in order on the calendar.

T 9.13 Play the recording and get students to check their answers.

> **Answers and tapescript**
> January, February, March, April, May, June, July, August, September, October, November, December.

Focus attention on the stress marks on each word. Play the recording again and get students to repeat chorally and individually. Get students to say the months in order round the class. Check for accurate pronunciation and drill the months again if necessary.

2 Focus attention on the speech bubbles. Check comprehension of *So is my birthday!* Drill the language chorally and then get students to stand up and practise the language in a mingle activity. Get them to note down the months of other students' birthdays as they ask. Elicit the answers to the follow-up questions and establish which is the most common month for birthdays in your class.

3 This exercise presents ordinal numbers. Check students understand the difference between cardinal numbers and ordinal numbers with the following examples: *There are seven days in a week and there are twelve months in a year. The first day is Monday and the seventh day is Sunday. The first month is January and the twelfth month is December.* Get students to tell you the ordinal numbers (*first, seventh*, and *twelfth*).

T 9.14 Focus attention on the numbers and on how we form the abbreviations with the numeral and the last two letters of the ordinal number. Play the recording and get students to repeat chorally and individually. Write the abbreviated numbers on the board in random order and elicit the ordinal from individual students.

4 Elicit the first ordinal as an example (*sixteenth*). Get students to say the other ordinal numbers, working in pairs. Monitor and check and note any common errors.

T 9.15 Play the recording and let students check their answers. If necessary, drill any ordinals students had problems with.

5 **T 9.16** This exercise presents how we read dates in English. Tell students they are going to hear eight dates and that they should write down the correct ordinal. Play the first date and focus on the example answer (*the first of January*). Play the rest of the dates and get students to complete the task.

Get students to check their answers in pairs before checking with the whole class.

> **Answers and tapescript**
> the **first** of January
> the **third** of March
> the **seventh** of April
> the **twentieth** of May
> the **second** of June
>
> the **twelfth** of August
> the **fifteenth** of November
> the **thirty-first** of December

> **!** Focus attention on the Caution Box and highlight the use of *the* and the ordinal in spoken dates and the use of the abbreviation, but not *the* in writing. If appropriate, point out that students may also see dates written as *3rd January*, *10th March*, etc.

Elicit the dates in exercise 5 orally and then get students to continue practising in closed pairs. Monitor and check for correct use of *the*, correct ordinals, and pronunciation of the months.

6 Focus attention on the speech bubbles. Get students to ask you the questions and give answers. Drill the language chorally and then get students to practise in open pairs. Students continue in groups. Monitor and check for correct falling intonation in the questions and for the correct use of prepositions – *on* + date and *at* + time. Tell the class again the date and time of your birth, following the example in the last speech bubble. Elicit more examples from the class.

> **SUGGESTION**
> You can give students regular practice in dates by asking *What's today's date?* at the beginning of every class. Encourage students to write the dates in full at the top of any written work, i.e. *January 3rd 2002*, rather than *3/1/02*.

ADDITIONAL MATERIAL

Workbook Unit 9
Exercises 15 and 16 Consolidation of the months of the year.
Exercise 17 Consolidation of ordinal numbers.
Exercise 18 Consolidation of dates.
Exercise 19 Further practice of ordinal numbers.

Don't forget!

Workbook Unit 9
Exercise 13 In this exercise students translate sentences containing the main grammar points presented in the unit.
Exercise 14 A review of the key lexical sets from previous units.

Word list
Ask the students to turn to p134 and go through the words with them. Ask them to learn the words for homework, and test them on a few in the following lesson.

10

Past Simple – regular and irregular
Questions and negatives
Sports and leisure • Filling in forms

We had a good time!

Introduction to the unit

The title of this unit is 'We had a good time!' and the overall theme is leisure and holidays. The unit follows on from Unit 9 with the introduction of all forms of the Past Simple with both regular and irregular verbs. Skills practice is provided with speaking, listening, and writing tasks.

The lexical set of sports and leisure is reviewed and extended. The *Everyday English* section focuses on filling in an application form.

Language aims

Grammar – Past Simple regular and irregular; questions and negatives The set of irregular past forms from Unit 9 is extended and the regular forms are also introduced. The unit covers positive, negative, and question forms. Students' knowledge of the Present Simple usually helps them with the Past Simple, in that students are already familiar with the uses of the auxiliary *do*, and so will grasp how *did* functions. The past auxiliary is easier in that it is the same in all persons. It is important for students to see the contrast in the use of Present Simple and Past Simple and practice in using the two tenses in parallel is provided in the unit.

POSSIBLE PROBLEMS

- Although knowledge of the Present Simple helps students to access the Past Simple, students often make mistakes in the new tense. Common errors are:
  * *Did they watched TV?*
  * *They no played tennis.*
  * *When you lived in the US?*

- Irregular verbs need constant use and reviewing. Students often try to apply the regular *-ed* ending to irregular verbs, e.g.
  *I goed to the cinema.

  Encourage students to refer to the irregular verb list on p142 and get students to review the verbs regularly for homework.

- There are different ways of pronouncing the *-ed* regular ending and students need help with this. There is a pronunciation focus on p72 highlighting the /t/ and /d/ *-ed* endings, e.g.
  worked /wɜːkt/
  played /pleɪd/

  Students often try to divide out the *-ed* ending in the pronunciation inappropriately, e.g.
  watched /wɒtʃed/ rather than /wɒtʃt/

  Monitor and check for this mistake, and also help students to perceive the different *-ed* endings, but do not insist that they produce the endings each time.

Vocabulary The lexical set of sports and leisure activities is reviewed and extended. Students focus on sports/activities collocations with *go/play*, e.g. *go swimming, play hockey*, etc.

Everyday English This section focuses on filling in an application form. The theme of leisure and sports is maintained with a form to join a sports centre.

Workbook Regular and irregular Past Simple verbs in the positive are reviewed and consolidated in a range of exercises.

There is a *Listening and writing* section focusing on a day in the life of a character.

A *Writing* section gets students to talk about what they did last Saturday.

Past Simple questions and negatives are reviewed in a range of exercises.

There is further practice on the lexical set of sports and leisure.

A short *Reading* section gives further consolidation of negative and positive Past Simple forms.

There is further practice in filling in forms in the *Everyday English* section.

Notes on the unit

STARTER (SB p72)

1 This section reviews days and dates, Present and Past Simple forms, and key time expressions. Focus attention on the questions and elicit the answers. Make sure students use *is/was* correctly, pronounce the days correctly, and use ordinal numbers and *the* in the dates.

2 **T 10.1** Focus attention on the sentences. Go through and ask *Past or present?* about each one, and also elicit which verb is used in each sentence. Demonstrate the activity by eliciting the time expression for line 1 (*now*). Elicit from students the fact that the other time expressions are not possible and establish that this is because they refer to the past. Students then match the remaining lines and time expressions. Play the recording and get students to check their answers.

> **Answers and tapescript**
> 1 We're at school now.
> 2 You were at home yesterday.
> 3 I went to Australia in 1997.
> 4 She lives in London now.
> 5 They bought their house in 1997.
> 6 It was cold and wet yesterday.

Play the recording again and get students to repeat chorally and individually.

YESTERDAY (SB p72)

Past Simple – regular and irregular

1 This section reviews and extends the irregular verbs students met in Unit 9 and also presents regular *-ed* forms. Focus attention on the photo and ask *What's her name?* (*Betsy.*) *Where is she?* (*At home.*) Tell students they are going to hear Betsy talking about what she did yesterday. Focus attention on the list of verbs and ask *Past or present?* Check comprehension of each verb and

get students to tell you the infinitive of the irregular past forms. (If students query the regular *-ed* endings, tell them this is the ending for most verbs in the Past Simple, but do not go into a long explanation at this stage.)

T 10.2 Play the first line of the recording as far as *half past eleven* and focus attention on the example. Play the recording through to the end and get students to tick the remaining verbs. Get students to check their answers in pairs before checking with the whole class.

> **Answers**
> 1 ✔ got up late
> 2 ✔ had a big breakfast
> 3 ✔ went shopping
> 4 ✔ stayed at home
> 5 ✔ bought a newspaper
> 6 ✔ listened to music
> 7 ✔ watched TV
> 8 ✔ cooked a meal
> 9 ✔ went to bed early

> **T 10.2**
> Yesterday was Sunday, so I got up late, eleven thirty. I had a big breakfast, orange juice, toast, eggs, and coffee. Then I went shopping, to the supermarket, and I bought some chocolate and a Sunday newspaper, the *Sunday Times*. In the afternoon I listened to music for a bit and then I watched a film on TV. In the evening cooked a meal just for me, not a big meal, just soup and a salad. I went to bed early. It was a lovely, lazy day.

2 Focus on the speech bubble and highlight the use of *Then* to link a series of actions. Elicit from the class what Betsy did yesterday. Students then take it in turns to say what Betsy did, working in closed pairs. Monitor and check for pronunciation of the *-ed* regular endings but do not overcorrect if students have problems during this initial production stage.

GRAMMAR SPOT

1 Focus attention on the list of verbs and on the examples *worked* and *played*. Ask students to write the other past forms. Check the answers with the whole class.

> **Answers and tapescript**
>
> | /t/ | work | watch | cook |
> | --- | --- | --- | --- |
> | | worked | **watched** | **cooked** |
> | /d/ | play | stay | listen |
> | | played | **stayed** | **listened** |

Explain that these are regular verbs and so are different from those students met in Unit 9. Elicit the last two letters in each of the verb forms: *-ed*.

Establish that adding *-ed* is the rule for the formation of the Past Simple in the majority of verbs.

T 10.3 Pronounce the sounds /t/ and /d/ and then play the recording. Get students to repeat chorally and individually. Make sure students don't divide out the *-ed* ending into a syllable of its own, e.g. */kʊked/. Encourage them to reproduce the /t/ and /d/ endings accurately, but do not overdo this if students find it difficult. It is enough at this stage for them to perceive the difference.

2 Ask students to write the past tense of the verbs ending in /t/. Check the answers.

T 10.4 Pronounce the sound /ɪd/ and then play the recording. Get students to repeat chorally and individually. Elicit the difference between these verbs and the ones in exercise 1: the *-ed* ending is pronounced /ɪd/.

Answers and tapescript		
/ɪd/ visit	want	hate
visited	**wanted**	**hated**

3 Read the sentence aloud. Check students understand there is no difference in the verb forms for different persons in the Past Simple. Contrast this with the third person *-s* in the Present Simple.

Read Grammar Reference 10.1 on p125 together in class, and/or ask students to read it at home. Encourage them to ask you questions about it.

3 Refer students back to the list in exercise 1. Get students to underline the things that they did yesterday. Demonstrate the activity by telling the class things that you did yesterday. If appropriate, write the sentences on the board and underline the verbs, e.g. *I had a big breakfast*. Elicit a few more short examples from the class and then get students to continue in closed pairs. Monitor and check for correct use of regular and irregular past forms.

ADDITIONAL MATERIAL

Workbook Unit 10
Exercises 1–3 Further practice of Past Simple regular verbs.
Exercises 4 and 5 Further practice of Past Simple irregular verbs.
Exercises 6 and 7 Listening practice to review the Past Simple.
Exercise 8 Personalized writing practice.

Questions and negatives

4 **T 10.5** This section presents the Past Simple question and negative forms. Focus attention on the photo. Ask *What's her name?* (*Betsy*.) and *What's his name?* (*Dan*.) Tell students they are going to hear Betsy and Dan talking about their weekend. Play the recording as far as *tennis with some friends* and elicit the verb for the first gap (*played*). Play the recording to the end and get students to complete the conversation. Get students to check their answers in pairs. Play the recording again if necessary. Check the answers with the whole class.

Answers and tapescript
B Hi, Dan. Did you have a good weekend?
D Yes, I did, thanks.
B What did you do yesterday?
D Well, yesterday morning I got up early and I **played** tennis with some friends.
B You **got up** early on Sunday!
D I know, I know. I don't usually get up early on Sunday.
B Did you go out yesterday afternoon?
D No, I didn't. I just **stayed** at home. I **watched** the football on TV.
B Ugh, football! What did you do yesterday evening?
D Oh, I didn't do much. I **worked** a bit at my computer. I didn't go to bed late. About 11.00.

5 **T 10.6** Focus attention on the first question in the conversation and elicit the answer (*Did you have a good weekend?*). Ask students to complete the rest of the conversation. Play the recording and get them to check their answers. Play the recording again and get students to repeat chorally and individually. Encourage falling intonation on the *wh-* questions.

Answers and tapescript
1 B **Did** you **have** a good weekend?
  D Yes, I did.
2 B What **did** you **do** yesterday?
  D I played tennis.
3 B **Did** you **go** out yesterday afternoon?
  D No, I didn't.
4 B What **did** you **do** yesterday evening?
  D I **didn't** do much. I **didn't** go to bed late.

6 Focus attention on the speech bubbles. Drill the questions and answers chorally and individually. Elicit other questions and answers in open pairs.

7 **T 10.7** Focus attention on the examples, and then get students to continue in closed pairs. Encourage accurate pronunciation of *didn't*. Monitor and check for correct formation of the negatives. A common error is the repetition of the positive past form after the auxiliary *didn't* – * *He didn't cooked a meal*. If students have this problem, highlight the errors in a general feedback session, then refer students to the *Grammar Spot*.

1 Read the notes on the formation of questions and negatives. Highlight the use of *did* and *didn't* and make sure students understand that *didn't* is the contracted form of *did not*.

T 10.7 Play the recording. Get students to repeat the sentences chorally and individually.

2 Read the notes on the difference between Present Simple and Past Simple. Highlight the use of *do/did* in the questions. Remind students that *did* is used for all persons in Past Simple questions. Highlight the use of *doesn't/didn't* in the negatives and remind students that the other present forms require *don't*.

Ask students to underline the time expressions that are used with the different tenses (Present Simple: *every morning, every Sunday*; Past Simple: *yesterday morning, last Sunday*). Elicit other time expressions that can be used with the tenses, e.g. :

Present Simple: *every day/week/month, on Sunday, at the weekend, on Saturday afternoon*

Past Simple: *last week/month/year/weekend, yesterday*

Refer students to Grammar Reference 10.2 on p125.

SUGGESTION

You can give students further practice in Past Simple *wh-* and *Yes/No* questions by using the photocopiable memory game on TB p114. This shows two flats, one for Student A and one for Student B, which show what the occupants did yesterday.

Photocopy enough sheets for your class. Pre-teach/check *write a letter* and irregular past *wrote, read a book/newspaper* and irregular past *read* /red/, *have a bath, have a shower,* and *play the guitar* /gɪˈtɑː/.

Demonstrate the activity with two confident students. Get Student A to look carefully at the picture of Jane's flat for 30 seconds and then put it out of sight. Student B then uses the question cues to ask about what Jane did yesterday. Pre-teach *I can't remember.* Get students to complete the task in closed pairs for Student A's picture. Students then change roles with Student B looking at Paul's flat for 30 seconds and Student A using the question cues to ask about what Paul did yesterday.

Monitor and check for correct question formation and use of regular and irregular pasts. (With a weaker class, you could put all the A and B students together in separate groups to give them time to write out the cues as full questions. Then divide the class into A and B pairs and continue as above.)

Workbook Unit 10
Exercise 9 Past Simple *Yes/No* questions and short answers.
Exercises 10 and 11 Past Simple *wh-* questions and answers.
Exercise 12 Past Simple negatives.

PRACTICE (SB p74)

Did you have a good weekend?

1 Exercises 1, 2, and 3 focus on *Yes/No* questions in the Past Simple. Tell students they are going to talk about what *they* did last weekend. Focus attention on the list of activities in the chart and check comprehension of each one. Double-check comprehension of the difference between *do homework* and *do housework*. Students then continue to form the questions, working individually. Explain that there are three columns in the chart – one for each student, one for the teacher, and one for the student's partner. Get students to tick the activities they did last weekend in the *You* column.

2 Focus attention on the speech bubbles. Drill the question chorally and individually and then give your answer. Get students to ask you the rest of the questions and record the answers in the *Teacher* column.

3 Demonstrate the activity in open pairs and then get students to continue in closed pairs. Monitor and check for correct question formation and short answers.

Focus attention on the examples and then get students to tell the class about what they and their partner did last weekend.

4 This exercise focuses on *wh-* questions in the Past Simple. Briefly review the question words *what, who, where, what time,* and *how much.* Focus attention on the example.

T 10.8 Tell students they are going to hear the questions on tape, each preceded by a statement. Play the recording through once and get students to listen to the statements and check that they have formed the questions correctly. Play the recording again and elicit what the man says before each question.

5 **T 10.9** Pre-teach/check *meal*, and *steak and chips*. Play the recording and get students to listen. Get students to practise the conversations in closed pairs. Monitor and check for pronunciation. If students have problems, drill key sections, and then get them to practise again in closed pairs.

Refer students back to exercises 1 and 4. Explain that they are going to ask each other about the activities in question 1 again. If their partner answers 'Yes' about an activity, they should ask the appropriate follow-up question from exercise 4. If you think they need it, demonstrate by building a model dialogue on the board.

Model conversation
A Did you go shopping last weekend?
B Yes, I did.
A What did you buy?
B A new jumper.
A Was it expensive?
B Yes, it was.

Get students to continue working in closed pairs. Monitor and check for the correct form of Past Simple questions, short answers, and positive forms, and for the use of *was/were*.

6 This exercise reviews short answers in the Present and Past Simple. Pre-teach/check *party* and *newspaper*. Focus attention on the examples and then get students to complete the answers, working individually.

T 10.10 Get students to check their answers in pairs before checking with the whole class.

Get students to practise the questions and answers in open and then in closed pairs. Monitor and check for pronunciation. If students have problems, drill key sentences and then get students to practise again in closed pairs.

Check it

7 Focus attention on the first pair of sentences as an example. Students continue working individually to choose the correct sentence.

Get students to check their answers in pairs before checking with the whole class.

SUGGESTION
Take the opportunity to review the Past Simple by getting students to ask and answer about the weekend in the first lesson that you have each week. This provides a useful review and also highlights the value of what students are learning in a realistic situation.

VOCABULARY AND SPEAKING (SB p76)

Sports and leisure

1 Focus attention on the photographs. Elicit the activity that goes with photo 1 (*swimming*). Students continue to match the photos and activities. Check the answers with the whole class.

Answers

1 swimming
2 windsurfing
3 skiing
4 dancing
5 sailing
6 walking
7 baseball
8 tennis
9 ice-skating
10 football
11 cards
12 ice hockey
13 golf

Check the pronunciation of the activities and drill if necessary.

2 This exercise focuses on collocations with *play* and *go* + *-ing*. Focus attention on the examples and then get students to complete the categorizing, working in pairs. Check the answers with the whole class. As a general rule, you could tell students that sports with a ball and games like cards, chess, etc. take *play*, and physical activities ending in *-ing* take *go*.

Answers

play	go + *-ing*
tennis	skiing
football	sailing
golf	windsurfing
baseball	ice-skating
cards	dancing
ice hockey	walking
	swimming

3 This exercise practises *Yes/No* and *wh*- questions with the collocations from exercise 2. Focus attention on the speech bubbles. Highlight the use of the tenses – Present Simple to talk about general habits in the present and Past Simple to ask *When?* in the past. Drill the language chorally and individually. Elicit two or three more examples from students working in open pairs. Students continue in closed pairs. Monitor and check for correct use of tenses, correct use of *play* and *go*, and pronunciation.

4 This exercise practises the third person forms. Focus attention on the examples. Elicit more examples from students about their partner. Check for accurate use of the third person forms in the Present Simple. Highlight common errors and get students to correct them.

ADDITIONAL MATERIAL

Workbook Unit 10
Exercise 14 Consolidation of sports and leisure vocabulary.

LISTENING AND SPEAKING (SB p77)

Holidays

1 This section gives further practice of the Present Simple and Past Simple in the context of holidays. It also reviews the sports and leisure activities from the *Vocabulary and speaking* section. Revise the months of the year by getting students to say them round the class. Check for accurate pronunciation. Check comprehension of *season*. Elicit the seasons students have already met – *spring*, *summer*, and *autumn*, and pre-teach *winter*. Get students to say the months that correspond to each season in their country, e.g. *In England, Spring is March, April and May.*

Focus attention on the speech bubble and give an example about yourself. Elicit more examples from the class, and then get students to continue in pairs.

2 **T 10.11** Focus attention on the photos. Ask *Who are they?* (*Colin and Fran.*) Focus attention on the list of information, A and B. Check students recognize that A is Present Simple and B is Past Simple. Focus attention on the examples. Tell students to listen and underline the correct information about Colin and Fran's holidays. Make sure they understand that the information will come in slightly different order from the order on the page. Play the recording through once and get students to complete the task.

Get students to check their answers in pairs. Play the recording through again and get students to check/complete their answers. Check the answers with the whole class.

Answers

A	B
They usually ...	**Last year they ...**
go in summer	went in winter
go to Spain	went to Switzerland
stay in a hotel	stayed in a chalet
eat in restaurants	cooked their own meals
go swimming	went skiing / ice-skating
play golf	played cards
have a good time	had a good time

T 10.11

C Well, usually we go on holiday in summer.

F Yes, and usually we go to Spain ... but last year we ...

C ... last year we went to Switzerland, and we went in winter.

F We stayed in a chalet and we cooked all our own meals there. It was lovely.

C Yes, in Spain we usually stay in a hotel and eat in restaurants.

F It was good to do different things too. Usually we just go swimming and sit in the sun ...

C And I sometimes play golf. I love that!

F Ah yes, you do. But of course in Switzerland we went skiing every day, and sometimes we went ice-skating in the afternoons – it was great fun.

C And in the evenings we cooked a meal and then played cards. We had a very good time.

F We love holidays – we always have a good time in Spain too.

3 This exercise practises questions in the Present Simple and Past Simple. Focus attention on the speech bubbles. Drill the questions and answers encouraging students to reproduce the correct sentence stress:

●　　　●　　　●　　　●

When do they usually go on holiday?

●　　　●　　　●

When did they go last year?

Elicit the questions and answers for the second prompt in open pairs. (*Where do they usually go on holiday? To Spain. Where did they go last year? They went to Switzerland.*) Remind students that the questions for the last prompt are a different type (*Yes/No* questions). Get students to ask and answer in closed pairs. Monitor and check for correct question formation in both tenses, for correct sentence stress, and for correct use of prepositions *to* and *in*. Check the answers by getting students to ask and answer in open pairs across the class. Feed back on any common errors if necessary.

Answers

- Where do they usually go on holiday? To Spain.
  Where did they go last year? They went to Switzerland.
- Where do they usually stay? In a hotel.
  Where did they stay last year? They stayed in a chalet.

- Where do they usually eat? In restaurants.
  Where did they eat last year? They cooked their own meals.
- What do they usually do? Go swimming and play golf.
  What did they do last year? They went skiing and ice-skating.
- Do they usually have a good time? Yes, they do.
  Did they have a good time last year? Yes, they did.

WRITING (SB p78)

My last holiday

1 This section reviews Past Simple negative and positive forms. Establish that this exercise is about Colin and Fran's holiday last year and so students will need to use the Past Simple tense. Focus attention on the example and highlight the need for a negative form, then a positive form. (With a weaker group, you might like to elicit the verbs students will need to use before they start: 2 – *go*, 3 – *stay*, 4 – *eat/cook*, 5 – *go*.) Get students to complete the sentences working individually.

T 10.12 Let students check their answers in pairs before checking against the tape.

Answers and tapescript

1 Last year Colin and Fran **didn't go** on holiday in summer.
   They **went** in winter.

2 They **didn't go** to Spain.
   They **went** to Switzerland.

3 They **didn't stay** in a hotel.
   They **stayed** in a chalet.

4 They **didn't eat** in restaurants.
   They **cooked** their own meals.

5 They **didn't go** swimming.
   They **went** skiing.

2 This exercise allows students to personalize the language of holidays and the Past Simple in a guided writing task. Tell students they are going to write to a friend about their last holiday. Ask *Present or past?* and establish that students need to use the past tense. Focus attention on the model sentences and elicit what language can complete the skeleton. Highlight the use of *was* in *Was the weather good?* and check students recognize this as the past of *be*.

Tell the class about your own last holiday and then get students to write their description, using the skeleton in the Student's Book. Go round and help, correcting as necessary.

Get students to read their description to the class. If time is short, or if you have a very large class, get students to read their descriptions in groups of four.

Filling in forms

> **NOTE**
> Students may need help with understanding the titles used with surnames in English:
> *Mr/Mrs/Ms/Miss.* Be prepared to give a brief explanation of the titles.
> *Mr* – used for men
> *Mrs* – used for married women
> *Ms* /mz/ – used before a woman's surname when you do not know whether she is married or not, or when she prefers for this not to be known
> *Miss* – used for unmarried women

1 This section focuses on the language of forms and extends the overall unit theme of leisure. Focus attention on the form and ask *What does Jennifer Cottrell want to do?* (*Join a sports centre.*) *What's the name of the Sports Centre?* (*Olympic.*) Focus attention on the categories that applicants have to fill in. Check comprehension of the titles *Mr/Mrs/Miss/Ms, full name, postcode, date of birth, squash, athletics, fitness training, signature, type of card* (= card that applicant will be allocated), *data input date* (= date when applicant's details were processed).

2 Get students to complete the form with their own details. Go round and help as necessary.

3 Focus attention on the speech bubbles. Highlight the use of *both* to say students share interests, and the way of contradicting information with *but I'm not.* Also highlight the preposition *in.* Drill the language chorally and individually, encouraging students to reproduce the sentence stress correctly:

  ●   ●   ●   ●   ●
Georges and I are both interested in athletics.

        ●   ●   ●
Maria is interested in fitness training, but I'm not.

Divide the class into groups and give students time to compare their forms and decide who is interested in what. Elicit examples from the class of similarities and differences in interests.

ADDITIONAL MATERIAL

Workbook Unit 10
Exercise 16 Further practice of filling in forms as part of a listening task.

Don't forget!

Workbook Unit 10
Exercise 13 In this exercise students translate sentences containing the main grammar points presented in the unit.
Exercise 15 Reading practice.

Word list

Ask the students to turn to p134 and go through the words with them. Ask them to learn the words for homework, and test them on a few in the following lesson.

Video

Episode 4 *Surprise, surprise!*
During a dull evening at home, Matt reveals that Jane's birthday is on Saturday – in two days' time. Helen, Matt, and David decide to give her a surprise party. They buy all they need, and are getting everything ready in the kitchen, when Jane gets back to the house early. Matt tries to stall her in the hall. When she finally gets past him, we discover that Matt has yet again got the wrong idea – and misunderstood the date.

Stop and check 3 for Units 7–10 (TB p136).

Progress test 2 for Units 6–10 (TB p124).

11

can/can't • Requests and offers
Verbs and nouns that go together
What's the problem?

We can do it!

Introduction to the unit

The title of this unit is 'We can do it!' and it introduces *can* for ability. The positive, negative, and question forms are introduced and practised. The focus on *can* is extended to cover requests and offers. There is a *Reading and vocabulary* section with a text on the Internet, and a focus on verb and noun collocations. The *Everyday English* section focuses on basic problems.

Language aims

Grammar – *can/can't* *Can* for ability is introduced in all forms. It is presented and practised with key verbs and the adverbs *well* and *fast*. There is also a pronunciation focus highlighting the different sounds in *can/can't*. Students are given both receptive and productive practice in the different forms.

POSSIBLE PROBLEMS

* After having practised the Present Simple, students can sometimes want to use the auxiliaries *do/does* and *don't/doesn't* to form negatives and questions with *can*:
  * We don't can run fast.
  * Do you can swim?
* The pronunciation of *can/can't* needs careful presentation and practice. Students often have problems with the different vowel sounds (weak form /ə/ and strong form /æ/ in *can*, and /ɑː/ in *can't*). Students can also have problems distinguishing positive from negative forms, as the final *t* in *can't* is often not fully pronounced.
  I can swim.   /aɪ kən swɪm/
  Can you swim?   /kən juː swɪm/
  Yes, I can.   /jes aɪ kæn/
  I can't swim.   /aɪ kɑːnt swɪm/
  The pronunciation is highlighted as part of the Grammar Spot and students are given both receptive and productive practice.

Requests and offers Requests and offers with *can* are presented and practised.

Vocabulary There is a focus on key noun–verb collocations as an introduction to a text about what you can do on the Internet.

Everyday English The language associated with describing and solving basic problems is introduced and practised.

Workbook The vocabulary and collocations syllabus is extended with a focus on activities. Vocabulary from previous units is also reviewed in an 'odd one out' exercise.

can/can't is consolidated in a range of exercises.

A listening exercise gives further practice of *have* and *can*.

There is a pronunciation exercise on *can*.

Requests and offers with *can* are further practised.

The *Everyday English* focus on problems is consolidated.

Notes on the unit

STARTER (SB p80)

> **NOTE**
> In *New Headway*, we have chosen to spell *email* without a hyphen. Students may have seen the hyphenated form *e-mail* and both are acceptable in current usage.

1 This *Starter* section focuses on possible uses of a computer and provides a useful introduction to the overall topic of computing and the Internet. Pre-teach/check the language in the list of questions. Drill the pronunciation as necessary.

2 Focus attention on the examples in the speech bubbles. Highlight the contrastive stress in the first speech bubble (*don't, home, use, work*). Check that students understand what *it* refers back to in the second sentence of the second speech bubble (a computer). Give an example of how you use a computer.

Elicit one or two more examples from the students and then get them to continue in closed pairs. Monitor and check.

Elicit a few more examples in a short class feedback session.

WHAT CAN THEY DO? (SB p80)

can/can't

1 This section presents different people and their skills and so highlights the use of the positive form *can*. It also reviews the use of *a/an* with jobs/roles.

Focus attention on the photos and on the example. Students continue matching the words and photos, working in pairs. Check the answers with the whole class.

> **Answers**
> | | | | |
> |---|---|---|---|
> | 2 | athlete | 5 | farmer |
> | 3 | architect | 6 | grandmother |
> | 4 | interpreter | | |

2 Pre-teach/check *run fast*, *draw well*, *drive a tractor*, and *make cakes*, using the information in the photos. Focus attention on the example, highlighting the use of *a*. Students complete the rest of the sentences with *a* or *an*.

T 11.1 Play the recording and let students check their answers.

> **Answers and tapescript**
> 1 Josh is **a schoolboy**. He can use a computer.
> 2 Sharon is **an athlete**. She can run fast.
> 3 Lucy is **an architect**. She can draw well.
> 4 Ted is **an interpreter**. He can speak French and German.
> 5 Archie is **a farmer**. He can drive a tractor.
> 6 Mabel is **a grandmother**. She can make cakes.

Play the recording again line by line and get students to repeat. Encourage them to reproduce the weak form in the positive form of *can* /kən/. If students find this hard, get them to highlight the main stresses in each sentence and then practise the sentences again. Students practise in closed pairs. Monitor and check for correct pronunciation of *can*.

3 Focus attention on the language in the speech bubble. Drill the example chorally and individually. Give another example about yourself and elicit one or two more examples from the class. Students then continue in closed pairs. Monitor and check for correct use and pronunciation of *can*. Do not overdo the practise of the weak form /kən/, as students will have the opportunity to review this in contrast with the other forms at various points in the unit.

Questions and negatives

4 **T 11.2** This section presents the question and negative forms. Play the recording through once and get students to just listen. Play the recording again and get students to repeat the questions and answers. Encourage them to reproduce the weak form /kən/ in the question, the strong form /kæn/ in the positive short answer, and the negative form /kɑːnt/. Get students to ask and answer in open pairs across the class. Students then continue in closed pairs. Monitor and check for correct pronunciation of the different forms of *can*. If students have severe problems with the pronunciation, drill the sentences again, but do not make students self-conscious about using the new language.

5 Focus attention on the examples in the speech bubbles. Highlight the use of *can* for both the *she* and the *I* forms. Drill the examples in open pairs. Elicit some more examples about the people in exercise 1, and also some student–student examples. Students then continue in closed pairs. Monitor and check for correct use and pronunciation of *can* and *can't*.

GRAMMAR SPOT

1 Read the notes with the whole class. Highlight that *can/can't* is used with all persons, and that *can't* is the contraction of *can not*.

2 Read the notes with the whole class. Highlight the use of *can* in the positive and question forms.

3 **T 11.3** Tell students they are going to hear the three ways of pronouncing *can*. Play the recording and get

students to just listen. Play the recording again and get students to repeat chorally and individually.

Read Grammar Reference 11.1 on p126 together in class, and/or ask students to read it at home. Encourage them to ask you questions about it.

6 **T 11.4** Focus attention on the photo. Ask *What's his name? Does he have a job?* (*Josh. No, he's a schoolboy.*) Ask *What's her name?* (*Tessa.*) Pre-teach/check *a bit*, *planes*, *cook* (verb) and *grandma*. Play the recording through once and get students to fill in the gaps. Ask them to check their answers in pairs. Play the recording again and get students to check/complete their answers. Check the answers with the whole class.

Answers and tapescript
T Can you use a computer, Josh?
J Yes, of course I **can**. All my friends **can**. I use a computer at school and at **home**.
T That's very good. What other things can you do?
J Well, I can **run** fast, very fast, and I can draw a bit. I can draw planes and **cars** very well but I can't drive a car of course. When I'm big I want to be a farmer and **drive** a tractor.
T And I know you can speak French.
J Yes, I can. I **can** speak French very well because my dad's French. We sometimes **speak** French at home.
T Can you speak any other languages?
J No, I **can't**. I can't speak German or Spanish, just French – and English of course! And I can cook! I can **make** cakes. My grandma makes lovely cakes and I sometimes help her. Yesterday we made a big chocolate cake.

Get students to practise the conversation in closed pairs. Monitor and check. If students have problems with pronunciation, drill key sections of the conversation and get students to practise again in closed pairs.

7 Elicit the answer to question 1 as an example (*He can use a computer, run fast, draw planes and cars, speak French and English, cook, and make cakes.*) Students continue asking and answering in closed pairs.

Check the answers by getting students to read the questions and answers across the class.

Answers
1 He can use a computer, run fast, draw planes and cars, speak French and English, cook, and make cakes.
2 He can't drive, or speak German or Spanish.
3 Yes, he does.
4 He wants to be a farmer.
5 He can speak French well because his dad is French.
6 He made a chocolate cake with his grandma.

SUGGESTION
You could ask students to practise similar conversations to the one in exercise 6 by getting them to role play the other people in the photos in exercise 1. Students can imagine the skills for their character and then ask and answer, using the conversation in exercise 6 as a model.

ADDITIONAL MATERIAL

Workbook Unit 11
Exercise 1 A vocabulary exercise on activities including some verb–noun collocations.
Exercises 2 and 3 Further practice of *can/can't*.
Exercises 4 and 5 Questions and answers with *can*.

PRACTICE (SB p82)

Pronunciation

1 **T 11.5** This is a discrimination exercise to practise recognizing and producing *can* and *can't*. Play sentence 1 as an example and elicit the answer (*can*). Play the rest of the sentences, pausing at the end of each one and get students to underline the correct word.

Get students to check their answers in pairs before checking with the whole class.

Answers and tapescript
1 I can use a computer.
2 She can't speak German.
3 He can speak English very well.
4 Why can't you come to my party?
5 We can't understand our teacher.
6 They can read music.
7 Can we have an ice-cream?
8 Can't cats swim?

Play the recording again line by line and get students to repeat chorally and individually. Students then practise the sentences in closed pairs. Monitor and check for correct pronunciation of *can/can't*, but don't insist on perfect pronunciation from all students.

Can you or can't you?

2 Focus attention on the chart. Check comprehension of the verbs in the list. Tell students that they will get the answers for Tito on tape, they will complete the *You* column, the teacher will give answers for the *T* column, and another student for the *S* column.

T 11.6 Focus attention on the photo. Ask *What's his name?* (*Tito*). Tell students they are going to hear Tito in the recording and that they should tick the things he can do in his column of the table. Play the recording as far as *French, German, and English*. Focus attention on the example, and elicit the next verb that requires a tick (*speak French*). Play the rest of the recording and get students to complete their answers.

Play the recording and get students to check their answers before checking with the whole class.

3 Students complete the *You* column in the chart. Drill the pronunciation of the verbs in the list if necessary and then elicit the questions from the class. Give true answers for yourself and get students to complete the *T* column.

Then focus attention on the language in the speech bubbles. Drill the language chorally and individually. Elicit two or three more examples in open pairs. Then get students to continue asking and answering in closed pairs, noting their partner's answer to each question in the *S* column.

4 Focus attention on the example in the speech bubble. Drill the language and highlight the different pronunciation of *can* and *can't* and the contrastive stress in the second sentence:

　　　　　/ə/
Isabel and I can speak French.

● /ə/　　　●　　　　●/ɑ:/
She can speak Spanish too, but I can't.

Elicit two or three more examples from the class and then get students to continue in closed pairs. Monitor and check for the correct use and pronunciation of *can/can't*. Feed back on any major common errors, but do not expect students to produce perfect pronunciation of *can/can't* as this may prove demoralizing.

ADDITIONAL MATERIAL

Workbook Unit 11
Exercise 6 A listening exercise to consolidate *have* and *can/can't*.
Exercises 7 and 8 Exercises to consolidate the pronunciation of *can/can't*.

Requests and offers

5 Focus attention on the example. Then get students to write the other questions, working individually. Get students to check their answers in pairs but don't check with the whole class until after exercise 6.

6 Elicit the answer to question 1 (c *It's about three thirty.*) Students continue matching, working individually.

T 11.7 Play the recording and let students check their answers to the question formation and the matching phase.

Focus attention on the examples in the speech bubbles. Highlight how the conversation can be continued. Get students to practise the conversation in open pairs. Get students to continue with the other conversations in closed pairs. Remind them to continue the conversations in an appropriate way. With a weaker class, you could get students to repeat after the tape, and also elicit ways of continuing the conversations before students start the pairwork. Possible ways of continuing the conversations:
2 Yes, I can. Thanks.
3 Say 'Happy Birthday' from me.
　OK. Thanks.
4 That's 90p please.
　Thank you.
5 Orange juice, please.
　Here you are.
　Thanks.

Check it

7 Focus attention on the first pair of sentences as an example. Students continue working individually to choose the correct sentence.

Get students to check their answers in pairs before checking with the whole class.

ADDITIONAL MATERIAL

Workbook Unit 11
Exercises 9 and 10 Further practice of requests and offers.

READING AND LISTENING (SB p84)

The things you can do on the Internet!

> **NOTE**
> The reading text in this section contains a number of new lexical items and some topic-specific lexis, e.g. *computer network, the Net, go worldwide*. In order to save time in class, you might like to ask students to look up the following words in their dictionary for homework before the reading lesson: *history, start* (verb), *Department of Defense* (US spelling), *computer network, military* (noun), *telephone company, communicate, the Net, go worldwide, north, south, partner* (in a game), *list, endless*.

1 This section gives practice in vocabulary, reading, and listening based on a subject of interest to many students – the Internet. The first exercise reviews and extends useful verb–noun collocations and also pre-teaches some of the vocabulary used in the reading text.

    Pre-teach/check *chat to, book* (verb), and *chess*. Focus attention on the example. Students continue matching, working individually. Get students to check in pairs before checking with the whole class.

> **Answers**
> listen to a CD   read a magazine
> watch a video   chat to a friend
> play chess   book a hotel

2 Focus attention on the website addresses and elicit where you can find them (on the Internet). Elicit what 'www' means – *world wide web*.

3 Read the questions through as a class and elicit possible answers. Focus attention on the example in the speech bubble. Divide the class into pairs or groups of three and get students to discuss the questions. Allow them to use whatever language they can to express their ideas, but be prepared to feed in language if students request it. Do not feed back on the questions at this stage as students will find answers to the questions in the reading text.

4 **T 11.8** If you haven't set the vocabulary checking as homework pre-teach/check the items listed in the Note opposite. Ask students to read and listen to the text and to find the answers to the questions in exercise 3. Get students to compare their predictions in exercise 3 with the information in the text. Check the answers with the whole class.

> **Answers**
> 1 The Internet started in the 1960s.
> 2 It started because the US Department of Defense wanted a computer network to help the American military.
> 3 You can buy a car or house; you can book a holiday; you can watch a video; you can read an Australian newspaper or a Japanese magazine; you can buy books and CDs from North and South America, you can play chess with a partner in Moscow; you can chat to people from all over the world.

Elicit any other uses of the Internet that the students thought of in exercise 3 and that don't appear in the text.

5 Get students to read the text again and find and correct the false sentences. Ask students to check their answers in pairs before checking with the whole class.

> **Answers**
> 1 The Internet started in the 1960s.
> 2 The US Department of Defense started it.
> 3 ✔
> 4 ✔

6 Give the names of a few good websites that you know and describe what you can do at these sites. Feed in useful language for talking about websites:
    (Name of site) is good for (shopping).
    I visit (name of site) for (information on travel).
    You can (read the news) at (name of site).
    A good site for (games) is (name of site).

    Divide the class into groups and get them to talk about good websites that they know. Monitor and check. Get students to tell the whole class of any interesting sites in a brief feedback session. Highlight any common errors to the class, but do not over-correct as this may prove demoralizing.

7 **T 11.9** Tell students they are going to hear different people talking about when and why they use the Internet. Play the first extract and focus attention on the example. Play the rest of the recording and get students to note down their answers in the chart.

    Get students to check their answers in pairs. Play the recording again and get students to check/complete their answers. Check the answers with the whole class.

Answers

	When?	Why?
Fleur	every day	help with homework
Anya	in the evening	talk to her brother
Tito	at weekends	find songs
Henry	every day	get information about his family name
Tommy	after school	play games
Iris	every Friday	shopping

T 11.9

1 Fleur

I use the Internet a lot. Every day, I think. It helps me with my homework. It helps me with everything. Yesterday I did an English test. It was quite difficult.

2 Anya

My brother's in Japan. I can't phone Japan, it's very expensive – so Paul (that's my brother) and me – we 'talk' in chat rooms on the Internet. We talk late, at about 11 o'clock in the evening – well, it's evening here, but it's eight o'clock in the morning in Japan.

3 Tito

I play the guitar and I can find lots of songs on the Internet. Yesterday I got the words and music for *Can't buy me love,* you know, by the Beatles. I can play it now. I use the Internet at weekends because it's cheap then.

4 Henry

Well, my family's name is Krum and I want to write about my family, so every day I chat to people from all over the world, Canada, Germany, Argentina – people who have the name Krum. They send me information about their families. It's really interesting.

5 Tommy

I play games. And I go to chat rooms. And I go on websites for my favourite pop groups and football players. I want to be on the web all the time, but my mum says I can't. She says I can only use it after school for an hour, and then I stop.

6 Iris

I go shopping on the Internet. Every Friday I go to my son's house and I use his computer. It's fantastic – the supermarket brings all my shopping to my home.

SUGGESTION

You can review and extend the verb–noun collocations from the *Reading and listening* section with the photocopiable activity on TB p115. Photocopy enough pages for your students to work in pairs. The page is divided into two sections – a matching activity and a gap-fill to practise the collocations. Divide the page along the cut lines, cutting out the verbs in the heading strip and each square which contains a noun. Divide the bottom half of the page so that you have two separate gap-fills. Keep each set of verbs and nouns and the gap-fills separate. Divide the class into pairs.

Give each pair a set of verbs and nouns. Explain that they have to match the nouns and verbs. Elicit an example, e.g. *listen to music.* If appropriate, you could do the activity as a competition with the fastest students to match the nouns and verbs as the winners. When students have finished matching, check the answers with the whole class.

Answers

(Note: these answers are based on the collocations that are presented in the Student's Book. Other combinations may be possible, e.g. *read the news,* and accept these at the checking phase.)

listen to: music, a CD, a cassette, the news
play: the piano, chess, basketball, cards, computer games, the guitar, tennis
book: a hotel, a room, a table, a holiday, a ticket
watch: TV, a video, the news, a film
read: a newspaper, a magazine, a book, music, a letter

Hand out a copy of the gap-fill to each student. Pre-teach/check *show* (verb). Focus attention on the example and then get students to complete the conversation, working individually. Check the answers with the whole class.

Answers

1	watched	4	listen to
2	booked	5	read
3	play	6	book

Get students to practise the conversation in closed pairs.

EVERYDAY ENGLISH (SB p86)

What's the problem?

1 Focus attention on the problems and check students understand them. Pre-teach/check the following words from the conversations as you elicit from the class which problem goes with which photo: *airport, push a button, borrow, What's the matter, perhaps, it doesn't matter, flowers.*

2 Elicit the sentence to complete conversation 1 (*I can't find my passport.*) Students complete the other conversations, working individually. Get students to check their answers in pairs.

T 11.10 Play the recording and get students to check against the tape.

Answers and tapescript

1 **A** Come on! It's time to go to the airport.
   B But **I can't find my passport**.
   A You put it in your bag.
   B Did I? Oh, yes. Here it is! Phew!

2 **A** Excuse me!
   B Yes?
   A **This ticket machine doesn't work**. I put in two pounds, but I didn't get a ticket.
   B Did you push this button?
   A Oh! No, I didn't.
   B Ah, well. Here you are.
   A Thank you very much.

3 **A** Excuse me.
   B Yes?
   A Can you help me? **I'm lost**.
   B Where do you want to go?
   A To the railway station.
   B Go straight on. About two hundred metres. It's on your left.

4 **A** **I don't understand this word**.
   B Check it in your dictionary.
   A My dictionary's at home. Can I borrow yours?
   B OK. No problem. Here you are.

5 **A** Oh no!
   B What's the matter?
   A **The TV's broken**.
   B Good! Perhaps we can talk this evening.
   A But I want to watch a film.
   B Go to the cinema, then.

6 **A** I'm really sorry. **I forgot your birthday**.
   B It doesn't matter.
   A It was on the tenth, wasn't it?
   B Yes, it was.
   A Well, here are some flowers.
   B Oh, thank you very much. They're beautiful.

3 Get students to practise the conversations in closed pairs. Monitor and check for pronunciation. If students have problems, drill key sections from the tape and get students to repeat the pairwork.

Get students to choose two conversations to learn and act out for the rest of the class. Encourage them to stand up and role play the situation, rather than just say the conversations face to face. This helps students with the acting out and with the overall delivery. Encourage the other students to listen carefully to the students who are acting and give feedback on pronunciation.

SUGGESTION

If class time is short, you could get students to learn their lines for homework and then give them a short time to rehearse in pairs. With a weaker group, you could put simple cues on the board to help if students forget their lines.

ADDITIONAL MATERIAL

Workbook Unit 11
Exercise 13 Further practice of talking about and solving problems.

Don't forget!

Workbook Unit 11
Exercise 11 In this exercise students translate sentences containing the main grammar points presented in the unit.
Exercise 12 An 'odd one out' exercise to review word groups from previous units.

Word list
Ask the students to turn to p135 and go through the words with them. Ask them to learn the words for homework, and test them on a few in the following lesson.

12

want and would like
Food and drink
In a restaurant • Going shopping

Thank you very much!

Introduction to the unit

This unit is called 'Thank you very much!' and it focuses on the function of asking for things in a range of contexts. The structures *want* and *would like* are practised and the difference in register is highlighted. *Like* is also reviewed and contrasted with *would like*. The lexical set of shops and amenities is reviewed and extended, and there is a vocabulary and speaking section on food and drink, and ordering in a restaurant. The *Reading* section also focuses on food with a text on junk food. There is further functional practice in the *Everyday English* section with the language used when going shopping.

Language aims

Grammar – *want* and *would like* Students have already met *want* as part of their practice of the Present Simple. In this unit, *want* + noun and *want* + *to*-infinitive are reviewed and practised. *Would like* + noun and *would like* + *to*-infinitive are also introduced as more polite ways of asking for things, or saying that you want to do something. The question form *Would you like … ?* is also introduced for offering things.

> **POSSIBLE PROBLEMS**
> Students have already seen *like* as a main verb in the presentation of the Present Simple in Unit 5. This is the first time students have seen *would like* and it is easy for students to confuse the two. Common mistakes are:
> * *Do you like a cup of tea?*
> * *I like to buy a dictionary.*
> * *You like a coffee?*
> Students can usually understand the difference between liking in general (expressed with *like*) and a specific request (expressed with *would like*) but the similarity in form can lead to confusion. Students are given both receptive and productive practice in both forms, but be prepared to monitor and check for mistakes and review as necessary. (There is no need to highlight at this stage that *would* is a modal verb, as students will meet *would* and its various uses in later levels of *New Headway*.)

Vocabulary Shops and amenities are reviewed and extended. The lexical set of food and drink is practised in the context of ordering things in a restaurant. The food and drink theme is carried through in the *Reading* section with a text on an elderly lady who only eats junk food!

Everyday English This highlights and practises the language used when shopping in a range of situational conversations.

Workbook *Would like* is reviewed and consolidated in a range of exercises.

There is a pronunciation exercise to practise discrimination in vowel sounds.

The lexical set of food and drink and the function of ordering things in a restaurant are consolidated in a range of exercises.

Further reading practice is given with a series of short texts on eating habits.

The language of shopping from the *Everyday English* section is further practised.

Notes on the unit

STARTER (SB p88)

This *Starter* section reviews and extends the lexical set of shops and amenities and also reviews *can*.

1. Focus attention on the example and then get students to continue matching in pairs.

2. Get students to make sentences with the phrases in exercise 1 using *You can ... .*

   T 12.1 Play the recording and get students to check their answers. Explain any individual words that students query. (If you think students need further practice in the pronunciation of *can*, you could get students to listen and repeat the sentences.)

   > **Answers and tapescript**
   > You can buy stamps in a post office.
   > You can buy a dictionary in a book shop.
   > You can buy a computer magazine in a newsagent.
   > You can change money in a bank.
   > You can buy a CD in a music shop.
   > You can get a cup of coffee in a café.
   > You can send an email in an Internet café.

A TRIP INTO TOWN (SB p88)

want and *would like*

1. Focus attention on the shopping list and check comprehension of the items. Highlight the use of *want +* noun and *want + to*-infinitive in the examples and drill the sentences. Check students' pronunciation of *wants* /wɒnts/. Check the pronunciation of the other items in the list. Students make sentences with the other items in the list, working in pairs. Monitor and check for correct use of third person *-s* on *wants*.

   Check the answers with the whole class by getting students to say the sentences aloud.

   > **Answers**
   > He wants Gary Alright's new CD.
   > He wants to send an email to Rosa in the US.
   > He wants a Spanish/English dictionary.
   > He wants a PC Worldwide computer magazine.

2. This exercise introduces *would like* in different situations. Pre-teach/check *change* (noun) in conversation 1. Make sure students understand that this is a noun form and contrast it with the verb form in *change my money*. Also pre-teach/check *black or white coffee* in conversation 2, and *minidictionary* in conversation 3. Highlight the use of *I'd like* and *Would you like* in the example answers in conversations 1 and 2,

but do not go into a full grammatical explanation, as this is covered in the *Grammar Spot*.

T 12.2 Ask students to read and listen to Enrique and complete the conversations from the tape. Play the recording through once. With a weaker group, you may need to play the recording through again. Check the answers with the whole class. (If students query the use of *one* in conversation 3, check they understand it stands for *dictionary*, but do not go into a full explanation of the use of *one/ones* at this stage.)

> **Answers and tapescript**
> 1 **E** Good morning. **I'd like** a stamp for this letter to Venezuela, please.
>   **A** That's 75p.
>   **E** Thank you.
>   **A** Here you are, and 25p change.
>   **E** Thanks a lot. Bye.
> 2 **E** **I'd like** a cup of coffee, please.
>   **B** **Would you like** black or white?
>   **E** Black, please.
>   **B** All right. Here you are. One pound twenty, please.
> 3 **E** Hello. **I'd like** to buy a Spanish/English dictionary.
>   **C** OK. **Would you like** a big dictionary or a minidictionary?
>   **E** Just a minidictionary, please.
>   **C** This one is £4.99.
>   **E** That's fine. Thank you very much.

3. **T 12.3** Focus attention on the examples in the speech bubbles. Play the recording, pausing at the end of each sentence, and get students to repeat chorally and individually. Encourage them to reproduce *I'd like* correctly and make sure students don't say *I like*. Also encourage accurate intonation:

Would you like black or white?

Would you like a big dictionary or a minidictionary?

Get students to practise the conversations in exercise 2 in closed pairs. If students have problems with pronunciation, drill key sections of the conversations and get students to practise again in closed pairs.

GRAMMAR SPOT

1. Read the notes as a class. Make sure students understand the difference in register between *want* and *would like*, and that *'d like* is the contracted form. Focus attention on the examples and highlight the use of the noun and *to*-infinitive with *would like*.

2. Read the notes as a class. Make sure students understand that *Would you like ... ?* is used when we

offer things. Focus attention on the examples and highlight the use of the noun and *to*-infinitive in questions with *would like*.

Read Grammar Reference 12.1 on p126 together in class, and/or ask students to read it at home. Encourage them to ask you questions about it.

4 **T 12.4** This exercise gives further practice of *would like* in different situations. Explain that students are going to hear Enrique from exercise 2 in different places in town. Check comprehension of the places in the list by asking *What can you do/buy in a (newsagent)?* Play the first conversation and elicit the correct place from the list (*a music shop*). Get students to write number 1 in the correct box. Play the rest of the recording and get students to number the other boxes.

Ask students to check their answers in pairs. If there is disagreement, play the recording again and get students to check/amend their answers. Check the answers with the whole class.

Answers
3 a newsagent
2 an Internet café
1 a music shop
5 a bank
4 a cinema

T 12.4
1 A Can I help you?
  E Yes. I'd like the new CD by Gary Alright, please.
  A There you are.
  E How much is that?
  A £11.99.
  E Thank you very much.
2 E I'd like to send an email, please.
  B Take PC number ten.
  E Thanks a lot.
3 E Hello. I'd like this month's PC Worldwide magazine, please.
  C Here you are. That's £2.20, please.
  E Thank you very much. Bye.
4 E Two tickets for James Bond, please.
  D Eight pounds forty, please.
  E Thanks. What time does the film start?
  D Seven thirty.
  E Thanks very much.
5 F Good afternoon. Can I help you?
  E Yes, please. I'd like to change some traveller's cheques, please.
  F Certainly. Are they in American dollars?
  E Yes, they are.
  F Fine. That's £115 and 25p.
  E Thank you very much.

SUGGESTION
If appropriate, you could ask students what were the key words which gave them the correct answer, e.g. conversation 1 – *CD*, conversation 2 – *send an email*, conversation 3 – *this month's PC Worldwide magazine*, conversation 4 – *James Bond, film*, conversation 5 – *traveller's cheques, American dollars*.)

Refer students to the tapescript on p119. Get students to practise conversation 1 in open pairs. Students continue practising in closed pairs. If students have problems with pronunciation, drill key sections of the conversations and get students to practise again in closed pairs.

PRACTICE (SB p90)

What would you like?

1 This exercise practises question forms with *would like*. Focus attention on the picture and get students to imagine they are at home with a friend. Check comprehension of *feel at home*. Focus attention on the examples in the speech bubbles. Remind students of the use of *would like* + noun and *would like* + *to*-infinitive. Drill the examples chorally and individually. Encourage students to reproduce correct intonation – rising intonation on the *Yes/No* questions and falling on the *wh-* question, and a wide voice range on the answers, starting 'high'.

Check comprehension of the food, drinks, and activities on offer. (If students query the use of *some* in *some cake*, explain that we use it when we don't know exactly how much of something is being referred to. Do not go into a full explanation of *some* versus *any* at this stage.) Elicit two or three different exchanges from the students in open pairs. Then get them to continue in closed pairs. Monitor and check for correct use of *would you like* + noun and *to*-infinitive, and pronunciation.

It's my birthday!

2 Tell students they are going to hear three people talking about their birthday. Focus attention on the table and elicit possible answers to the two questions, e.g.
What would she/he like? a book, a CD, a picture, a jumper, a camera, etc.
What would she/he like to do in the evening? go to the theatre, have a party, go to a restaurant, go shopping, etc.

T 12.5 Play the recording of Suzanne and elicit the answers (*breakfast in bed* and *to go to the theatre*). Play the rest of the recording and get students to complete the chart.

Get students to check their answers in pairs before checking with the whole class.

Answers

	What would she/he like?	What would she/he like to do in the evening?
Suzanne	breakfast in bed	to go to the theatre
Tom	a new computer	to go to a good restaurant
Alice	a mobile phone	to go out with her friends

T 12.5

Suzanne

What would I like for my birthday? That's easy. I'd like to have breakfast in bed. With the newspapers. And in the evening I'd like to go to the theatre.

Tom

Well, I'd like a new computer, because my computer is so old that the new programs don't work on it. And then in the evening, I'd like to go to a good restaurant. I don't mind if it's Italian, French, Chinese, or Indian. Just good food.

Alice

I don't have a mobile phone, and all my friends have one, so what I'd really like is my own mobile. They aren't expensive these days. And in the evening, I'd like to go out with all my friends and have a great time!

3 Ask students to imagine it's *their* birthday soon. Focus attention on the examples in the speech bubbles. Drill the language and check students say *I'd like* rather than *I like*. Get students to give one or two more examples, working in open pairs. Students continue in closed pairs. Monitor and check for correct use of *would like* + noun and *would like* + *to*-infinitive.

Talking about you

4 Focus attention on the examples in the speech bubbles. Review the difference between *like* and *would like* by asking *General or specific?* about each sentence (*like* = general meaning; *would like* = a specific wish). Also highlight the use of *like* + *-ing* and *would like* + *to*-infinitive. Drill the examples in the speech bubbles. Elicit open question and answer exchanges to the questions about travelling and living in another country. Then get students to continue working in closed pairs, asking and answering all the questions in the list. Monitor and check for correct use of *like* + *-ing* and *would like* + *to*-infinitive. Feed back on any common errors which might interfere with comprehension, e.g. * *I like to learning French.*

GRAMMAR SPOT

1 Read the notes as a class. Make sure students understand that *like* is used to talk about something which is always true. Focus attention on the example sentences and elicit other examples from the class.

2 Read the notes as a class. Make sure students understand that *'d like* is used to talk about

something we wish to have or do now or in the future. Focus attention on the example sentences and elicit other examples from the class.

Read Grammar Reference 12.2 on p126 together in class and/or ask students to read it at home. Encourage them to ask you questions about it. Draw students' attention to the difference between *would like* and *want* in Grammar Reference 12.3 on p126.

Listening and pronunciation

5 **T 12.6** This is a discrimination exercise to help students distinguish *like* and *would like*. Play the first sentence as an example and elicit the sentence that is recorded (*Would you like a Coke?*) Play the rest of the recording and get students to choose the correct sentence. Get students to check in pairs. If there is disagreement on the answers, play the recording again and then check the answers with the class.

Answers and tapescript
1 Would you like a Coke?
2 I like orange juice.
3 We'd like to go for a walk.
4 What do you like doing at the weekend?
5 We like our new car.

If students need more practice in pronunciation of *like* and *would like*, drill the sentences chorally and individually. Then get students to repeat the task sitting back to back – Student A should say a sentence and Student B should say if it is sentence 1 or 2.

Check it

6 Focus attention on the first pair of sentences as an example. Students continue working individually to choose the correct sentence.

Get students to check their answers in pairs before checking with the whole class.

Answers
1 I'd like to go home now, please.
2 What would you like to do?
3 I like swimming.
4 Would you like a coffee?
5 Do you like listening to music?

ADDITIONAL MATERIAL

Workbook Unit 12
Exercises 1–3 Further practice of *would like* in a range of exercises.

In a restaurant

1 This section reviews and extends the lexical set of food and drink, and recycles *would like* and *can* in the context of ordering in a restaurant. Focus attention on the words and photos. Elicit the answer for number 1 (*cheese*). Students continue matching, working in pairs. Check the answers with the whole class.

T 12.7 Play the recording and get students to repeat chorally and individually. Check students can reproduce the word stress on the following words:

• •
mineral water

•
vegetables

•
tomato

> **Answers and tapescript**
> 1 cheese
> 2 fish
> 3 fruit
> 4 salad
> 5 vegetables
> 6 chicken
> 7 soup
> 8 tomato
> 9 fries
> 10 mineral water

2 Pre-teach/check the main headings in the menu – *Joe's diner, To start, Burgers, Meat, Side orders,* and *Desserts.* There are two ways to approach the rest of this exercise – you can either put the students into groups and get them to complete as much of the menu as they can. Alternatively, you can pre-teach the words in the list and then get students to complete the menu. Whichever way you choose, check the pronunciation of the food and drink items when students give the answers.

> **Answers**
> **To start**   seafood cocktail, **tomato soup**
> **Burgers**   hamburger, salad and fries, **cheeseburger**, salad and fries
> **Sandwiches** ham, chicken, **cheese**
> **Meat**   steak and fries, **roast chicken** and salad
> **Side orders** fries, **mixed salad**
> **Desserts**   ice-cream, chocolate cake, **apple pie and cream**
> **To drink**   wine, orange juice, **beer, mineral water**

3 **T 12.8** Tell students they are going to hear Renate and Paul ordering a meal. Check they understand that Renate is a woman's name and Paul a man's name. Also check what the letters *W, R,* and *P* stand for. Give students time

to read through the sentences. Check comprehension of *How would you like it cooked?* Focus attention on the example and play the first line of the recording. Play the rest of the recording and get students to complete the task.

Ask students to check their answers in pairs. If there is disagreement on the answers, play the recording again and get students to check/amend their answers. Check the answers with the whole class.

> **Answers**
> **P** Renate, what would you like to start?
> **R** Can I have the tomato soup, please?
> **P** And I'd like the seafood cocktail.
> **P** Can I have the steak, please?
> **W** How would you like it cooked?
> **W** What would you like to drink?
> **R** And we'd like a bottle of mineral water, too.
> **R** Delicious, thank you.
>
> **T 12.8**
> **W** Are you ready to order?
> **P** Yes, we are. Renate, what would you like to start?
> **R** Can I have the tomato soup, please?
> **P** And I'd like the seafood cocktail.
> **W** And for your main course?
> **R** I would like the er . . . roast chicken, please.
> **W** Certainly. And for you?
> **P** Can I have the steak, please?
> **W** How would you like it cooked?
> **P** Medium.
> **W** What would you like to drink?
> **P** Can we have a bottle of red wine, please?
> **W** Very good.
> **R** And we'd like a bottle of mineral water, too.
> **W** Thank you very much.
> (*Pause*)
> **W** Is everything all right?
> **R** Delicious, thank you.

4 Refer students to the tapescript on p119. Check comprehension of *ready to order, main course,* and *medium* (for a steak). Divide the class into groups of three. Get students to practise the conversation in groups. If students have problems with pronunciation, drill key sections of the conversations and get students to practise again.

5 Give students time to prepare their roles and what they want to order. Encourage them to rehearse the conversation a few times. Once they are more confident with the language, encourage them not to refer to the text in the Student's Book, but to work from their own memory. (With a weaker group, you could write simple sentence cues on the board to help with the roleplay.) Monitor and help as necessary. Get students to act out their conversations for the rest of the class.

ADDITIONAL MATERIAL

Workbook Unit 12
Exercises 4–8 A range of exercises to practise the lexical set of food and drink and the language of ordering in a restaurant.

READING (SB p94)

She only eats junk food

1 Focus attention on the title of the text and check comprehension of *junk food*. Elicit an example of food from the list that is good for you, e.g. *fruit*. Students decide which other food they think is good for you and then compare answers in pairs. Check students' ideas with the whole class.

2 Tell the students your favourite food and then elicit examples from the class. Be prepared to feed in relevant vocabulary if students request it.

3 Pre-teach/check *oldest* (as a lexical item only – don't do a full presentation of superlatives at this stage), *generations, popcorn, die, granddaughter, grandma*, and *hairdresser*. Ask students to read the article. Elicit students' reactions to the text and what they find unusual about Mary Alston. Ask them *Who is the oldest person you know? What does he/she eat?*

4 This exercise focuses on the details in the text and also provides question and answer practice. Focus attention on the example and then get students to continue matching and completing the sentences, working individually.

T 12.9 Get students to check their answers in pairs and then play the recording so that they can check against the tape.

Answers
1c 2e 3h 4g 5a 6i 7j 8b 9f 10d

T 12.9
1 When was Mary Alston's birthday?
  It was yesterday.
2 **Did** she have a party?
  Yes, she did.
3 Does she eat fresh food?
  No, she **doesn't**.

4 What **does** she eat?
  Popcorn, pizza, and burgers.
5 What was her job?
  She was **a** teacher.
6 **Where** was she born?
  On a farm in Pennsylvania.
7 When did she marry?
  She married **in** 1915.
8 What time does she **get** up?
  She gets up at six o'clock.
9 Where does she go every Friday?
  She **goes** to the hairdresser.
10 What did she say to her granddaughter?
  'I**'d like** a cheeseburger and fries!'

Divide the class into pairs and get them to practise the questions and answers. If students have problems with the intonation, drill key questions and answers and get students to repeat in pairs.

ADDITIONAL MATERIAL

Workbook Unit 12
Exercise 11 Further reading practice on food and eating habits.

EVERYDAY ENGLISH (SB p95)

Going shopping

1 **T 12.10** Focus attention on the photos. Use them to help you pre-teach/check *film* (for a camera), *metre, shirt, medium* (size), *try on, pair of jeans, size, potatoes, anything else?* Focus attention on the first conversation in the Student's Book and on the example. Play the corresponding conversation on tape and elicit the missing sentences (*Is there a chemist near here?* and *next to the bank*). Play the rest of the recording, pausing at the end of each one, and get students to complete the conversations, using the words given.

If necessary, play the recording again to allow students to check/complete their answers. Check the answers with the whole class.

Answers and tapescript

1 **A** Excuse me! **Where can I buy a film** for my camera?
  B In a chemist.
  A **Is there a chemist near here?**
  B Yes, two hundred metres from here, **next to the bank.**
2 **C** Can I help you?
  A **No, thanks.** I'm just looking.
3 **A** Excuse me! **Do you have this shirt** in a medium?
  C No, I'm sorry. **That's all we have.**
4 **A** **I'd like to try on** a pair of jeans, please.
  C Sure. **What size are you?**
  A I think I'm a forty.
  C Fine. The changing rooms are over there.
5 **D** Yes, madam. **What would you like?**
  A **I'd like a kilo of** potatoes, please.
  D Anything else?
  A **No, that's all,** thanks. How much is that?
6 **A** Excuse me! **Do you sell Spanish** newspapers?
  E **No, I'm sorry,** we don't.
  A Where **can I buy them?**
  E Try the railway station.

2 **A** Excuse me! Do you sell *Le Monde*?
  B No, I'm sorry. We don't.
  A Where can I buy French newspapers?
  B Try the railway station.
3 **A** I'd like to try on this shirt, please.
  B Sure. What size are you?
  A Medium, I think.
  B OK. The changing rooms are over there.

Elicit where the speakers are in each conversation (1 – in the street, 2 – in a newsagent, 3 – in a clothes shop). Then get students to practise the conversations in closed pairs.

2 Pre-teach/check *birthday card, phone card, T-shirt, small/medium/large.* Put students in pairs and assign a role, A or B, to each student. Make sure they understand they have to ask for the things in their list. Check where you can buy a birthday card and a phone card (in a newsagent). Choose a pair of students to demonstrate the conversation with Student A asking for a birthday card. Then choose another pair with Student B asking for a phone card. Get students to continue practising the other conversations, working in closed pairs. Monitor and check for correct pronunciation and intonation. If students have problems, drill key sections of the conversations and get students to practise again in closed pairs.

SUGGESTION
You can give students further practice in the language used when shopping with the photocopiable activity on TB p116. Photocopy enough pages for students to work in pairs. Cut up the lines of conversation and keep each set of lines together in an envelope. Hand out a set of lines to each pair of students and explain that they have to put the lines in order to make three shopping conversations. Give students time to do this and then check the answers.

Answers
1 **A** Excuse me! Where can I buy stamps?
  B At a post office.
  A Is there a post office near here?
  B Yes, three hundred metres from here, next to the Internet café.

ADDITIONAL MATERIAL

Workbook Unit 12
Exercises 12 and 13 Further practice of the language used when shopping.

Don't forget!

Workbook Unit 12
Exercise 9 A pronunciation exercise to practise distinguishing vowel sounds.
Exercise 10 In this exercise students translate sentences containing the main grammar points presented in the unit.

Word list
Ask the students to turn to p136 and go through the words with them. Ask them to learn the words for homework, and test them on a few in the following lesson.

Video
Episode 5 *A night to remember*
David's date with Julia is common knowledge in the house – and the others enjoy teasing him about it. Unfortunately, his dream date has very expensive tastes which cause the miserly David a great deal of suffering. She eats and drinks her way through his wallet at an Italian restaurant. The journey home by taxi is no better. After saying goodbye to Julia, and with no spare cash, David has to go the long journey home on foot.

EXTRA IDEAS UNITS 9–12
On TB p117 there are additional photocopiable activities to review the language from Units 9–12. There is a reading text with tasks, a question formation exercise, and a matching activity on everyday English. You will need to pre-teach/check *wonderful, surprise, nothing, postman, envelope, suitcase,* and *keep a secret* for the reading text.

13

Colours and clothes • Present Continuous
Questions and negatives • What's the matter?

Introduction to the unit

This unit is called 'Here and now' and it introduces the Present Continuous in all forms. Students practise the tense in a range of contexts and it is contrasted with the Present Simple. The lexical set of clothes and colours is reviewed and extended, and this is a vehicle for further practice of the Present Continuous. Students also practise describing people with a focus on clothes, and colour of hair and eyes. There is a *Reading and speaking* section talking about what people usually do and what they are doing today. This consolidates the use of the two present tenses. The *Everyday English* section is called *What's the matter?* and it focuses on feelings such as *tired*, *hungry*, and suggestions with *Why don't you … ?*

Language aims

Grammar – Present Continuous In *New Headway Beginner*, students meet and practise the Present Simple relatively early in the course and this tense is consolidated across the units. This unit introduces the Present Continuous after students have had the opportunity for thorough practise of the Present Simple. The unit contrasts the use of the two tenses and gives students the opportunity to practise them in tandem. Despite presenting the Present Continuous later than the Present Simple, the two tenses can still cause confusion.

> **POSSIBLE PROBLEMS**
>
> Many other languages do not have the equivalent of the Present Continuous and they use a single present tense to express 'action which is true for a long time' and 'action happening now or around now'. This can lead students to use the Present Simple in English when they want to refer to action in progress:
>
> * *You wear a nice suit today.*
>
> Students also confuse the form of the two tenses. They are already familiar with *am/is/are* as parts of *be*, but they tend to start using them as the auxiliary with Present Simple, and using *do/does* as the auxiliary with Present Continuous. Common mistakes are:
>
> * *She's play tennis.*
> * *I'm coming from Spain.*
> * *You're go to work by bus.*
> * *What do you doing?*
> * *Do they working today?*
>
> The Present Continuous can also be used to refer to the future and this is covered in Unit 14 of the course.

Vocabulary Clothes and colours are reviewed and extended and students practise describing people's appearance.

Everyday English This section is called *What's the matter?* and it focuses on feelings, e.g. *tired*, *hungry*, etc. and suggestions to make people feel better.

> **POSSIBLE PROBLEMS**
>
> English uses *to be* with *hungry*, *thirsty*, *tired*, *cold*, and *hot*, whereas other languages express the same idea with the equivalent of *have*, e.g. Spanish: *Tengo sed*; French: *J'ai faim*. This can lead students to use *have* with the adjectives in English and make the following mistakes:
>
> * *I have hunger.*
> * *He has cold.*

Workbook Colours are reviewed and consolidated.

The Present Continuous is practised in all forms in a range of exercises.

The Present Simple and Present Continuous are reviewed in contrast.

Further reading practice is given with an exercise on a holiday postcard.

The lexical set of clothes and the function of describing people are consolidated in a range of exercises.

The language of talking about feelings and making suggestions from the *Everyday English* section is further practised.

Notes on the unit

STARTER (SB p96)

1   This *Starter* section reviews and extends the lexical set of colours and clothes. Focus attention on the colours and get students to find the colour black in the pictures as an example. Students continue finding the colours, working in pairs.

2   **T 13.1** Pre-teach/check *jacket, trousers, shirt,* and *shoes.* Focus attention on the example and then get students to complete the sentences. Play the recording and get students to check their answers.

> **Answers and tapescript**
> 1   George's jacket is **black**. Sadie's jacket is **red**.
> 2   His trousers are **grey**. Her trousers are **green**.
> 3   Her shirt is **yellow**. His shirt is **white**.
> 4   Her shoes are **blue**. His shoes are **brown**.

Play the recording again and get students to repeat the sentences. Students then practise the sentences in pairs. Monitor and check for correct pronunciation of the colours and clothes.

3   Demonstrate the activity by talking about the colours of your clothes. Use the model in exercise 2, e.g. *My shirt is blue*, etc. and do not use *I'm wearing* at this stage. Elicit examples from one or two students and then get them to continue in closed pairs. Monitor and check for correct pronunciation of the colours and clothes.

WORK AND HOLIDAYS (SB p97)

Present Continuous

1   This section reviews the Present Simple and introduces the positive forms of the Present Continuous. Exercise 1 highlights the use of Present Simple for facts and repeated actions.

Refer students back to the picture of George in the *Starter* section. Tell students they are going to read about his job. Pre-teach/check *wear* and *enjoy* and then focus attention on the example. Ask students to complete the rest of the text with the verbs.

Ask students to check in pairs and then check with the whole class by getting students to say the sentences aloud.

> **Answers**
> George **works** in a bank. He **starts** work at 9.00 and he **leaves** work at 5.30. He always **wears** a black jacket and grey trousers. He **has** lunch at 1.00. He sometimes **goes** to the park and **reads** his newspaper. He **enjoys** his job.

2   **T 13.2** This exercise introduces the Present Continuous for actions happening now and around now. Focus attention on the picture of George and his wife. Establish that they are on holiday. Play the recording and get students to read the text. If students query the verb forms, tell them they are in the Present Continuous, but do not go into a full explanation at this stage.

3   **T 13.3** Play the recording and get students to repeat chorally and individually. Encourage students to reproduce the contracted forms and the linking between *-ing* and a vowel:

He's wearing a T-shirt.

Check students understand that *'s* is the contracted form of *is*, and *'re* the contracted form of *are*.

4   Briefly review the use of *is* and *are* by getting students to say which verb can go with which subject (*is* – *George, His wife; are* – *We, Four people, Two people,* and *They*). Demonstrate the activity by eliciting the answer for George (*George is reading the menu.*) Students continue making sentences, working individually.

Get students to check in pairs before checking with the whole class.

> **Answers**
> George is reading the menu.
> His wife is wearing a blue T-shirt.
> Four people are swimming.
> Two people are playing tennis.
> We are enjoying our holiday.
> They are having lunch.

GRAMMAR SPOT

1   Focus attention on the examples and read the notes with the whole class. Ask students to underline the Present Continuous forms in the text in exercise 2. Highlight the full and short forms, e.g. *He's wearing … , His wife is reading … .*

2   Read the notes with the whole class. Remind students of the *-ing* form by giving students the infinitive and

eliciting the -ing form, e.g. go – going, eat – eating, swim – swimming, etc.

3 Focus attention on the sentences. Complete the first one with the whole class as an example (am studying). Then ask students to complete the other sentences.

Answers
I **am studying** English.
You **are wearing** jeans.
She **is reading** a book.
We **are working** in class.
They **are having** lunch.

Highlight that the Present Continuous can be used for actions happening now, e.g. *You're wearing jeans*, and around now, e.g. *I am studying English*.

Read Grammar Reference 13.1 on p127 together in class, and/or ask students to read it at home. Encourage them to ask you questions about it.

PRACTICE (SB p97)

Speaking

1 This exercise gives practice in the *he/she* and *they* forms of Present Continuous positive. Focus attention on the silhouettes and briefly review the verbs students will need to use (*cook, drive, have a shower, write, ski, eat an ice-cream, run, dance,* and *play football.*) With a weaker group, you could write the verbs on the board.

Focus attention on the example and highlight the use of the contracted form. Elicit one or two more examples and then get students to continue making sentences, working in pairs. Monitor and check for correct formation of the Present Continuous.

T 13.4 Play the recording and get students to check their answers. If students had problems during the task, play the recording again and get students to repeat.

Answers and tapescript
1 He's cooking.
2 He's driving.
3 He's having a shower.
4 She's writing.
5 She's skiing.
6 She's eating an ice-cream.
7 They're running.
8 They're dancing.
9 They're playing football.

2 Demonstrate the meaning of *mime*. Focus attention on the examples in the speech bubbles and drill the language. Choose an activity that you can mime for the

students and get them to guess what you are doing. Encourage them to give sentences in the Present Continuous rather than just call out the infinitive verb forms. Divide the students into pairs and get them to continue miming and guessing. Get them to change roles after each mime. Monitor and check for correct formation of the Present Continuous.

SUGGESTION
You can provide further practice of Present Continuous positive forms by getting students to think about what their family and friends are doing. Write the following questions on the board:
• *What are you doing now?*
• *What are your parents/friends/brothers and sisters/children doing now?*

Demonstrate the activity by giving your own answers, e.g.
I'm teaching English. I'm working in Room … with Class …
My mother's working at home.

Elicit some more examples from one or two students, e.g.
I'm studying English. I'm sitting in Room … next to …
My parents are having dinner.

Divide the class into pairs and get students to continue exchanging examples. Monitor and check for correct formation of the Present Continuous. Feed back on any common errors with the tense, and if necessary drill the corrected forms.

ADDITIONAL MATERIAL

Workbook Unit 13
Exercise 1 A review of colours.
Exercise 2 An exercise to consolidate the formation of the -ing form.
Exercise 3 An exercise to consolidate the positive form of the Present Continuous.

I'M WORKING (SB p98)

Questions and negatives

1 **T 13.5** This section introduces Present Continuous question forms (*wh-* and *Yes/No* questions) and negatives. Pre-teach/check *model, fashion show, listener, special,* and *talk* (verb). Focus attention on the photo and ask *What's her name?* (Sadie) and *What's her job?* (She's a model.) Play the recording and get students to read and listen to the interview. Check students understand what *it* in *I'm enjoying it very much* refers to (being in Milan). Ask students to underline the Present Continuous questions in the interview.

2 This is a transformation exercise to practise Present Continuous questions with *she*. Write the question and answer *What are you doing in Milan?* and *I'm working.* on the board, underlining the subject and auxiliary. Elicit the changes needed to make the question and answer about Sadie: *What is she doing in Milan? She's working.*

Drill the language in the speech bubbles chorally and individually. Get students to continue asking and answering about Sadie, working in closed pairs. (With a weaker group, you could elicit and drill the questions and answers first, and then get students to work in closed pairs.) Monitor and check for correct formation of Present Continuous third person singular questions and answers.

Check the answers with the whole class.

> **Answers**
> 1 What's she doing in Milan?
>   She's working.
> 2 Where is she staying?
>   She's staying with friends.
> 3 Is she having a good time?
>   Yes, she is.
> 4 What is she wearing?
>   She's wearing jeans and a T-shirt.

GRAMMAR SPOT

1 Focus attention on the questions and read the notes with the whole class. Highlight the full and short forms used.

2 Focus attention on the negatives and read the notes with the whole class. Highlight that short forms are usually used in the negatives. Ask students to underline the negative form in the interview in exercise 1.

3 Focus attention on the short answers and read the notes with the whole class. Highlight the full and short forms used. Ask students to underline the short answers in the interview in exercise 1.

Read Grammar Reference 13.2 and 13.3 on p127 together in class, and/or ask students to read it at home. Encourage them to ask you questions about it.

ADDITIONAL MATERIAL

Workbook Unit 13
Exercise 4 An exercise to consolidate the positive and negative forms of the Present Continuous.

PRACTICE (SB p99)

Asking questions

1 This exercise reviews *wh-* question words and practises Present Continuous question formation. Focus attention on the cartoons and check comprehension of all the verbs and answers given. Focus attention on the example and then elicit the question words and nouns that the students need to use:
2 what?
3 where?
4 why/three jumpers?
5 what?
6 how many?
7 who?

T 13.6 Get students to write the questions using the verbs in brackets, working individually. Play the recording and get students to check their answers.

> **Answers and tapescript**
> 1 A **What are you reading?**
>   B A love story.
> 2 A **What are you watching?**
>   B The news.
> 3 A **Where are you going?**
>   B To my bedroom.
> 4 A **Why are you wearing three jumpers?**
>   B Because I'm cold.
> 5 A **What are you eating?**
>   B Chocolate.
> 6 A **How many cakes are you making?**
>   B Five.
> 7 A **Who are you talking to?**
>   B My girlfriend.

If you feel students need more question and answer practice, play the recording again and get students to repeat. Encourage them to reproduce the falling intonation of the *wh-* questions. Students then practise the questions and answers in closed pairs.

2 This exercise practises *Yes/No* question formation in the Present Continuous. Focus attention on the cues and the example questions and short answers. Highlight that the question form is an inversion of the statement form. Get students to write the question forms for the exercise, working individually.

Check the answers with the whole class.

> **Answers**
> 1 Are you wearing a new jumper?
> 2 Are we learning Chinese?
> 3 Are we sitting in our classroom?
> 4 Are you wearing new shoes?
> 5 Is the teacher wearing blue trousers?

6 Is it raining?
7 Are all the students speaking English?
8 Are you learning a lot of English?

Model and drill the examples in the speech bubbles. Encourage students to reproduce the rising intonation of the *Yes/No* questions. Tell students that they have to stand up and ask the questions in a 'mingle' activity and that they should give true short answers. Get students to do the activity and monitor and check for correct question formation, intonation, and short answers.

Check it

3 Focus attention on the first pair of sentences as an example. Students continue working individually to choose the correct sentence.

Get students to check their answers in pairs before checking with the whole class.

Answers
1 I'm wearing a blue shirt today.
2 Where are you going?
3 Peter isn't working this week.
4 That's Peter over there. He's talking to the teacher.
5 Heidi is German. She comes from Berlin.

ADDITIONAL MATERIAL

Workbook Unit 13
Exercise 5 An exercise to consolidate questions and short answers in the Present Continuous.

READING AND SPEAKING (SB p100)

Today's different

NOTES
This is the first 'jigsaw' reading in the course. It is a technique which integrates reading and speaking skills. Students read one of four texts and they then work in groups and exchange information about their text in a speaking phase. It's important to remind students to read only their text and to get information about the other texts via speaking.

In the lesson before the *A photo of me* stage, ask students to bring in a photograph of themselves to talk about in class. Tell them that the photo needs to be an 'action shot' and show:
- where you are
- what you're doing
- who you're with
- what you're wearing

Get students to look up any useful words they need to talk about the picture. Also bring in a photo of yourself so that you can demonstrate the activity.

1 This section provides skills practice in reading and speaking, and also highlights the difference between the Present Simple and Present Continuous. Students also review the Past Simple in each reading text and in the questions.

Exercise 1 is a warm-up activity for the reading stage. It reviews the use of Present Simple for routines. Pre-teach/check *Christmas Day*. Give brief examples of what you do on each of the days and then elicit two or three more examples from the class. Students then continue asking and answering in closed pairs. Go round and help. Monitor and check but do not focus too heavily on errors as this activity is to raise interest in the topic, rather than to test accuracy.

2 Pre-teach/check the following new words from the texts: *meet* (friends), *get married*, *stand* (state verb), *adult* (noun), *have a barbecue*, *swimsuit*, *pack your bags*, and *ski clothes*. Also review the irregular past forms in the texts:
get up – got up
get (receive) *– got*
go – went
find – found

Assign a role and a text to each student and remind them to read only their text:

Student A – Isabel
Student B – Leo
Student C – Mark
Student D – Becca

Get students to read their text quickly and match the text to the correct photo. Briefly check the answers.

Answers
Isabel – photo 3
Leo – photo 4
Mark – photo 1
Becca – photo 2

3 Focus attention on the questions. Pre-teach/check *What happened … ?* in question 4. Get students to work individually and answer the questions about their text. Ask them to note down the answers to their questions. (With a weaker group, you could put all the A, B, C, and D students in separate groups so that they help each other answer the questions.) Go round and help as necessary.

SUGGESTION
You might want to feed in the language students can use for the information exchange, e.g.
Do you want to start?
You next.
Sorry, I don't understand.
Can you repeat, please?

4 Divide the class into groups of four. Make sure there is an A, B, C, and D student in each group. Demonstrate the activity by getting a couple of students from one group to talk about their text. Students continue exchanging the information about their text. Monitor and check for correct use of the Present Simple, Present Continuous, and Past Simple. Conduct a short follow-up phase by asking general questions, e.g.
Who has a similar routine to you?
Who is having the most interesting day?
Who would you most like to be?

Finally, feed back on any common errors from the information exchange and review the use of the tenses as necessary.

A photo of me

Demonstrate the activity by talking about a photo of yourself. Then elicit one or two more examples from students in the class. Get students to continue working in pairs and talking about their photo. Monitor and check for correct use of *be* and of the Present Continuous.

ADDITIONAL MATERIAL

Workbook Unit 13
Exercises 6 and 7 Exercises to consolidate the Present Simple and Present Continuous.
Exercise 9 Further reading practice and consolidation of the Present Simple and Present Continuous.

VOCABULARY AND SPEAKING (SB p102)

Clothes

1 This section reviews and extends the lexical set of clothes, introduces language for describing colour of hair and eyes, and recycles the Present Continuous in the context of describing people. Focus attention on the pictures of the models and on the example. Students continue labelling the clothes, working individually. Check the answers with the whole class.

Answers		
2 a tie	9	socks
3 trousers	10	a coat
4 shorts	11	sandals
5 a shirt	12	shoes
6 a dress	13	a jacket
7 trainers	14	a skirt
8 a hat	15	boots

T 13.7 Play the recording and get students to repeat chorally and individually. Check students can distinguish *shirt* and *skirt* and that they pronounce *trousers* correctly – /ˈtraʊzəz/. Elicit which items are for women (a skirt and a dress). Highlight the use of *a* with the singular items, e.g. *a jumper*, and that the plural items do not need *a*, e.g. *boots*. Highlight that the word *trousers* is plural in English, as this is different in other languages.

2 Briefly review the colours presented in the *Starter* section. Focus attention on the example in the speech bubble. Drill the language chorally and individually. Elicit one or two more examples from the class and then get students to continue in closed pairs. Monitor and check for correct use of clothes, colours, and the Present Continuous.

3 Focus attention on the example in the speech bubbles. Drill the language chorally and individually. Encourage students to reproduce the rising intonation on the *Yes/No* questions. Demonstrate the activity by standing back to back with a student and asking about his/her clothes. Divide the students into pairs, asking students to work with a different partner from another part of the room. Monitor and check for correct use of Present Continuous questions and short answers, names of clothes, and colours.

4 This exercise consolidates names of clothes and colours, and also recycles the Present Simple for talking about routines. Get students to ask you the questions and give true answers. Divide the class into pairs and get them to continue asking and answering. Monitor and check for correct use of Present Simple, names of clothes, and colours.

5 **T 13.8** This exercise presents the language used for describing hair and eyes. Play the first line of the recording and elicit the word to complete sentence 1 (*fair*). Play the rest of the recording and get students to complete the sentences. Check the answers with the whole class.

Answers and tapescript
1 She has long, **fair** hair.
2 He has **short**, black hair.
3 She has blue **eyes**.
4 He has **brown** eyes.

6 Focus attention on the example in the speech bubble. Demonstrate the activity by describing a student and getting the others to guess who it is. Elicit one or two more examples from the class and then get students to continue in closed pairs or small groups. Monitor and check for correct use of the Present Continuous, names of clothes, and language of describing people.

1 You can also do a 'describe and guess' activity based on pictures from magazines or students' own photographs. Student A describes a person in the picture or photo and Student B guesses who is it. Students then change roles.

2 You can review the Present Continuous and the language of describing with the photocopiable activity on TB p118. This is an information gap using different pictures. Photocopy enough pages for your students to work in pairs. Tell them that they are going to work with a partner and ask questions to find six differences between two similar pictures of a family. Divide the class into pairs. Give Student A and Student B their respective pictures. Remind them they shouldn't look at each other's picture. Drill the type of questions students can ask: *What is (the father) wearing? Is (the mother) listening to music?* etc.

   Tell students to circle the part of their picture when they find a difference. Students work in pairs to find all six differences. Monitor and check.

   Students compare their pictures to check they have found the differences.

ADDITIONAL MATERIAL

Workbook Unit 13

Exercises 10–13 A range of exercises to review clothes and the language of describing people.

EVERYDAY ENGLISH (SB p103)

What's the matter?

1 This section presents the language of talking about feelings and offering suggestions. Establish that the people in the cartoons all have problems, and pre-teach/check the question *What's the matter?* Focus attention on the cartoons and elicit the answer for sentence 1 (*She's cold.*) Students continue completing the sentences, working individually.

   T 13.9 Play the recording through once and get students to check their answers.

Answers and tapescript	
1 She's **cold**.	4 He's **thirsty**.
2 He's **hungry**.	5 They're **hot**.
3 They're **tired**.	6 She's **bored**.

   Play the recording again and get students to repeat chorally and individually. Make sure they pronounce *tired* and *bored* as one syllable – /taɪəd/, /bɔːd/ rather than */taɪred/, */bɔːred/. Get students to work in pairs.

Student A points to a cartoon and Student B says the corresponding sentence.

2 **T 13.10** Focus attention on the conversation. Play the recording and get students to read and listen. Play the recording again and get students to repeat. Highlight the use of *Why don't you ... ?* for making suggestions.

3 Check comprehension of the ideas in the lists. Elicit one or two more conversations from the class and then get students to continue in closed pairs, using the words from exercise 1. Monitor and check for correct use of the adjectives and *Why don't you ... ?*

SUGGESTION

Try to integrate language from the *Everyday English* sections in your lessons and encourage students to do the same. There is a big range of language that can be used quite naturally in the classroom context to reinforce the communicative value of what the students are learning. This includes:
What's the matter? I'm ...
Why don't you ... ?
Pardon?
All right.
Excuse me.
Sorry.
I don't know.
I don't understand.
Please./Thank you.
How do you spell ... ?
Can I ... ?

ADDITIONAL MATERIAL

Workbook Unit 13

Exercises 14 and 15 Further practice of the language of feelings and suggestions from the *Everyday English* section.

Don't forget!

Workbook Unit 13

Exercise 8 In this exercise students translate sentences containing the main grammar points presented in the unit.

Word list

Ask the students to turn to p137 and go through the words with them. Ask them to learn the words for homework, and test them on a few in the following lesson.

14

Present Continuous for future
Question word revision
Travel and transport • Going sightseeing

Introduction to the unit

This unit is called 'It's time to go!' and its theme is travel, transport, and sightseeing. The use of Present Continuous for future plans is presented, building on students' knowledge of the form of this tense from Unit 13. *Wh-* question words are reviewed as part of the practice of asking about plans with the Present Continuous. Students also get listening and speaking practice with a section on holiday plans, using the Present Continuous for future. The lexical set of transport and travel is reviewed and extended, and there is a *Reading* section on an amazing journey by car. The travel theme is carried through in the *Everyday English* section with a focus on sightseeing.

Language aims

Grammar – Present Continuous for future plans Students will be familiar with the form of the Present Continuous, having practised it for talking about actions happening now or around now in Unit 13. This unit presents and practises its other use – talking about future plans.

> **POSSIBLE PROBLEMS**
> The use of a present tense to refer to future plans may seem strange to students at first, but they soon become accustomed to it with practice. In the presentation and practice, ask a simple concept question – *Now or future?* about the use of the tense to make sure students are clear about the time reference.

Question words The questions words students have met in previous units are reviewed as part of the practice of the Present Continuous questions for future plans.

Vocabulary The lexical set of travel and transport is reviewed and extended. Students focus on forms of transport and collocations, e.g. *book a hotel*, *catch a plane*, etc. The travel theme is carried through in the *Reading* section with a text on an amazing journey in a Mini car!

Everyday English This highlights and practises the language used when talking about places you have visited and also practises conversations in a tourist office.

Workbook The Present Continuous for future plans is consolidated in the positive and question forms. Students also focus on the time reference in different Present Continuous sentences, and get further practice in understanding plans in a listening task.

There is a pronunciation exercise to practise shifting sentence stress.

The lexical set of travel and transport is consolidated.

Further reading and listening practice is given with another text on an eventful journey.

The language of going sightseeing from the *Everyday English* section is further practised.

Notes on the unit

STARTER (SB p104)

1   This *Starter* section reviews days, months, and how we say years in English. It also establishes the concepts of 'now' and 'future' as preparation for talking about future plans in the next section. Focus attention on the questions and elicit the answers from the class. Make sure students use *and* correctly when they say the year: 2002 – *two thousand and two*. Also check

for correct pronunciation and word stress in the months and days.

2 Get students to say the months round the class. If students have problems remembering the months, or pronouncing them, drill the words chorally and individually and then get students to repeat the task. Repeat the above procedure for the days of the week.

HOLIDAY PLANS (SB p104)

Present Continuous for future

1 **T 14.1** Focus attention on the photo and ask *What's her name?* (*Ellie.*) Focus attention on her diary and explain that it shows her plans for next week. Pre-teach/check *collect tickets*, *pack bags*, and *fly* from the diary. Play the recording and get students to listen and read Ellie's diary. Elicit why Ellie is excited (She's going on holiday to Mexico.)

> **Tapescript**
> I'm going on holiday to Mexico next Friday, so next week's very busy. On Monday I'm collecting my tickets from the travel agent. I'm going on holiday with my friends Ed and Lucy, so on Tuesday I'm meeting them after work and we're going shopping. On Wednesday I'm seeing the doctor at eleven o'clock, then I'm having lunch with mum. On Thursday I'm leaving work early and I'm packing. I'm taking just a bag and a rucksack. Then it's Friday. Friday's the big day! At six thirty in the morning I'm going by taxi to the airport. I'm meeting Ed and Lucy there and at nine thirty we're flying to Mexico City. I'm very excited!

2 This exercise presents the use of the Present Continuous for future plans, but treat it initially as an information gap-fill and leave the explanation of the tense use until you focus on the *Grammar Spot* section. Focus attention on sentence 1 as an example. Also elicit the answer to the second gap in sentence 3 (*having*) to alert students to the need for the *-ing* form in some sentences.

Get students to complete the sentences, working individually. Get them to check in pairs before checking with the whole class.

> **Answers**
> 1 On Monday she's collecting her **tickets** from the travel agent.
> 2 On Tuesday she's meeting Ed and Lucy after **work** and they're going **shopping**.
> 3 On Wednesday she's seeing the **doctor** at 11 o'clock, then she's **having** lunch with her mother.
> 4 On Thursday she's **leaving** work early and she's **packing** her bags.
> 5 On Friday at 6.30 in the morning she's going by **taxi** to the airport and she's **meeting** Ed and Lucy there. At 9.30 they're **flying** to Mexico.

> **GRAMMAR SPOT**
>
> 1 Read the notes as a class. Focus attention on the examples and ask *Now or future?* about each one (future). Establish that the form is the same as the tense students used in Unit 13 to talk about actions happening now, but that these sentences refer to future time.
>
> 2 Ask students to underline the examples of the Present Continuous in the sentences in exercise 1 of *Grammar Spot*.
>
> Read Grammar Reference 14.1 on p127 together in class, and/or ask students to read it at home. Encourage them to ask you questions about it.

ADDITIONAL MATERIAL

Workbook Unit 14
Exercises 1 and 2 Exercises to consolidate the form and concept of the Present Continuous for future.

Questions

3 **T 14.2** This section focuses on *wh-* questions with the Present Continuous for future plans. Focus attention on the question and answer and refer students back to Ellie's diary. Play the recording and get students to repeat chorally and individually. Encourage them to reproduce the falling intonation on the *wh-* question. Focus attention on the speech bubbles and elicit the answer (*She's meeting Ed and Lucy. They're going shopping.*) Get students to practise the exchange in open pairs. Students then continue in closed pairs, asking and answering the questions about the other days of the week. Monitor and check for correct question formation and intonation.

Check the answers by getting students to ask and answer across the class.

> **Answers**
> What's she doing on Wednesday? She's seeing the doctor at 11 o'clock. Then she's having lunch with her mother.
> What's she doing on Thursday? She's leaving work early and she's packing her bags.
> What's she doing on Friday? She's going by taxi to the airport and she's meeting Ed and Lucy there. They're flying to Mexico at 9.30 a.m.

4 Write your own diary for the next four days on the board. Give true examples if the language generated is within the students' range. If not, modify the examples so that they contain language students will recognize, e.g.

> *Tuesday – 6.30 p.m. play tennis with Dave*
> *Wednesday – 7.30 p.m. meet Helen and Jim in the pub*
> *Thursday – collect theatre tickets*
> *Friday – go swimming*

Revise *tomorrow* and *on* with days of the week. Elicit the question *What are you doing tomorrow?* from a student and reply with the information in your diary. Ask the question *What are you doing?* and highlight the shift in stress:

●　　　　●　　　　　●
S: *What are you doing tomorrow?*

●　　　●　　●
T: *What are you doing?*

Get students to ask you about the other three days and ask them the question back, highlighting the stress each time.

Ask students to write notes about their plans for the next four days. Elicit two or three examples of the exchange in open pairs. Then ask students to continue in closed pairs, finding out about each other's plans for the rest of the week. Monitor and check for correct question formation, intonation, and change in stress.

5 This exercise consolidates question formation with the Present Continuous and reviews *wh-* question words from previous units. Focus attention on the picture of Ellie and on the first two lines of the conversation. Ask *Where is Ellie?* (*She's at work.*) Ask *What is she doing?* (*She's reading about Mexico and talking to a friend.*)

Pre-teach/check *lucky*. Focus attention on the example and then get students to complete the conversation with the question words.

T 14.3 Get students to check in pairs before playing the recording. Check the answers with the whole class.

> **Answers and tapescript**
> A **What** are you doing?
> E I'm reading about Mexico.
> A **Why?**
> E Because I'm going there on holiday soon.
> A Oh lovely! **When** are you leaving?
> E We're leaving next Friday.
> A **Who** are you going with?
> E My friends Ed and Lucy.
> A **How** are you travelling?
> E We're travelling by plane to Mexico City, then by bus and train around the country.
> A **Where** are you staying?
> E We're staying in small hotels and hostels.
> A You're so lucky! Have a good time!
> E Thanks very much.

Get students to practise the conversation in closed pairs. If students have problems with pronunciation, drill key sections of the conversations and get students to practise again in closed pairs.

GRAMMAR SPOT

1 This exercise highlights the question form in all persons. Focus attention on the examples and then get students to form the question with *When* and *he*, *she*, *we*, and *they*. Check the answers by getting students to say the questions aloud. Check for the correct intonation (falling).

> **Answers**
> When is he leaving?
> When is she leaving?
> When are we leaving?
> When are they leaving?

Get students to underline the question forms in the conversation in exercise 5.

2 This exercise highlights the present and future uses of the Present Continuous. Ask students to answer the questions in pairs and then check with the whole class.

> **Answers**
> I'm reading about Mexico. (now)
> I'm leaving next Friday. (future)

Refer students back to Grammar Reference 14.1 on p127.

ADDITIONAL MATERIAL

Workbook Unit 14
Exercise 3 An exercise to practise *wh-* questions with the Present Continuous for future.

PRACTICE (SB p106)

Listening and speaking

1 This section consolidates the Present Continuous for future with a listening task and information gap activity on holiday plans. Students are also given the opportunity to personalize the language by talking about their own holiday plans.

Focus attention on the photos of the places and ask students to guess where they are. Tell students they are going to find out about the holiday plans of the people in the photos. Check the pronunciation of the names Marco /ˈmɑːkeʊ/, Rachel and Lara, /ˈreɪtʃl ən ˈlɑːrə/, and Didier /ˈdidiei/.

Exercise 1 consolidates the use of *wh-* questions with the Present Continuous for future. Briefly review the question words by putting a list of very short answers about your own holidays on the board and elicit the correct question word, e.g.

France (where?)
In August (when?)
For three weeks (how long?)
In a hotel (where?)
By plane (how?)
Because I want to relax on the beach (why?)

Focus attention on the cues in the chart and the example questions. Highlight the use of the Present Continuous by asking *Now or future?* (future). Then get students to write the other questions, using the cues in the chart.

T 14.4 Tell students they are going to listen to people talking about Marco's holiday plans and they have to check the questions and also complete the missing information. (With a weaker group, you could play the recording through once first and get students to check the questions, and then play it again for students to complete the missing information.) Play the recording and get students to complete the task. If necessary, play the recording again to allow students to complete their answers. Check the answers with the whole class, highlighting the use of *the* in the date.

Answers and tapescript
A Marco's going on holiday.
B Oh, **where's he going**?
A To Banff, in Canada.
B **Why is he going** there?
A Because it's good for skiing and he wants to go skiing.
B **When is he leaving**?
A Next week on the third of March.
B **How is he travelling**?
A By plane to Vancouver and then by train to Banff.
B **Where is he staying**?
A In the Banff Springs Hotel.
B And **how long is he staying**?
A Just ten days.

Chart

When/leave?	3 March
How/travel?	by plane and train
How long/stay?	10 days

2 Focus attention on the examples in the speech bubbles. Drill the language, highlighting the falling intonation on the *wh-* question. Then elicit one or two more exchanges in open pairs. Students continue in closed pairs. Monitor and check for correct use of the Present Continuous for future, and for intonation in the questions.

3 This is an information gap activity based on Rachel and Lara's, and Didier's holiday plans. Pre-teach *uncle* and *youth hostel* from the charts on p139 and p140 of their books. Check the pronunciation of the places Whangaparada /ˌwæŋɡəpəˈrɑːdə/, New Zealand /njuːˈziːlənd/, Paris /ˈpærɪs/, and Edinburgh /ˈedɪnbrə/. Remind students of the question to ask to check spelling

– *How do you spell … ?* Divide the class into pairs and assign a role, Student A or Student B, to each student. Refer all the Student As to p139 and all the Student Bs to p140. Explain that students have to ask and answer questions and get the information to complete their chart. Remind them not to show each other their chart but to exchange the information through speaking.

Focus attention on the examples in the speech bubbles and drill the language. Students continue asking and answering in closed pairs. (With a weaker group, you could elicit all the questions from the cues in the chart as a class activity and then get students to do the information exchange.) Monitor and check for correct use of the Present Continuous, intonation on the *wh-* questions, and use of the alphabet. Get students to check their answers by comparing their completed charts. Feed back on any common errors in a brief follow-up session.

4 This exercise gives students the opportunity to talk about their own holiday plans. Focus attention on the examples in the speech bubbles. Drill the language and then get students to ask you the questions. Elicit one or two more exchanges in open pairs and then get students to continue in closed pairs. Monitor and check for correct use of Present Continuous.

The second phase of this exercise practises the third person singular form. Focus attention on the example in the speech bubble and highlight the third person forms in the verbs. Elicit more examples from the class.

ADDITIONAL MATERIAL

Workbook Unit 14
Exercise 4 Further listening practice based on a diary activity of future plans.

Talking about you

5 This section reviews the Past Simple with both regular and irregular verbs and gives practice of *Yes/No* questions with the Present Continuous for future plans. It also highlights the intonation of the *Yes/No* question forms.

Read through the list of sentences about yesterday and ask *Now or past?* (past). Briefly review the verbs forms by eliciting the corresponding infinitive, e.g. *got up – get up, went – go, walked – walk*, etc. Focus attention on the example for number 1 and ask *Now or future?* (future). Elicit the questions for numbers 2 and 3 (*Are you going swimming tomorrow? Are you walking to work tomorrow?*) Get students to write the questions, working individually.

T 14.5 Play the recording through once and ask students to check they have formed the questions correctly. Play the recording again and get students to repeat chorally and individually. Encourage them to reproduce the rising intonation on the *Yes/No* questions.

Review the formation of short answers by getting students to ask you questions 1, 2, 6, and 7. (These are the questions that students can apply to all students.) Reply *Yes, I am./No, I'm not.* And then get students to ask and answer in open pairs. Check for intonation and drill the questions again if necessary. Students then ask and answer in closed pairs.

> **Answers and tapescript**
> 1 I got up early.
>   **Are you getting up early tomorrow?**
> 2 I went swimming.
>   **Are you going swimming tomorrow?**
> 3 I walked to work.
>   **Are you walking to work tomorrow?**
> 4 I had lunch in my office.
>   **Are you having lunch in your office tomorrow?**
> 5 I left work late.
>   **Are you leaving work late tomorrow?**
> 6 I met a friend.
>   **Are you meeting a friend tomorrow?**
> 7 We had dinner in a restaurant.
>   **Are you having dinner in a restaurant tomorrow?**

6 This exercise gives students the opportunity to use the Past Simple and the Present Continuous for future to talk about themselves. Demonstrate the activity by writing five things that you did yesterday on the board, e.g. *I went to the cinema.* Elicit the question about tomorrow and give an answer, e.g. *Are you going to the cinema tomorrow? No, I'm not. I'm playing squash.* Drill the examples in the speech bubbles and then get students to continue in closed pairs. Monitor and check for correct use of the Past Simple and the Present Continuous for future, and for correct intonation. Feed back on any common errors with the whole class.

> **SUGGESTION**
> Try to review the Past Simple and the Present Continuous for future by talking about what students did/are going to do at different times, e.g. last/next weekend, during the last/next holidays, on their last/next birthday, etc. You can set up short pair or group work activities as 'warm-up' stages at the start of a class, or as 'fillers' for students who finish a task before the others.

Check it

7 Focus attention on the first pair of sentences as an example. Students continue working individually to choose the correct sentence.

Get students to check their answers in pairs before checking with the whole class.

> **Answers**
> 1 I'm leaving tomorrow.
> 2 We're going to the cinema this evening.
> 3 Where are they going on holiday?
> 4 What are you doing on Saturday evening?
> 5 What are you doing tomorrow?

READING (SB p108)

An amazing journey

1 Check comprehension of the title of the text *To Australia and back in a Mini.* Tell students they are going to read about an amazing journey in a car. Focus attention on the questions. Get students to ask you the questions and give true answers. Get the students to ask and answer the questions in closed pairs.

2 Focus attention on the photo and caption, and the map. Elicit the answers to the questions (*John and Carys Pollard. Their car is about 40 years old. It's a Mini.*) Ask students to predict what happens on the amazing journey.

3 Pre-teach/check *cost* (verb), *later*, *still* (adverb), *Moscow, Finland, the Arctic Circle, via, return* (verb), *ship* (noun), *give something a rest.* Tell students that the text contains a lot of numbers and dates. Get students to read the text through quickly and underline each one. Briefly elicit if students predictions about the text were correct. Then elicit how we say each number and date. Check students understand what each number and date refers to:

1964 – the year Mr Pollard bought the Mini
£505 – the price of the Mini
250,000 – the number of miles the Mini has done
59 – Mr Pollard's age
1966 – the year Mr Pollard drove to Moscow, Finland, and the Arctic Circle
1967 – the year Mr Pollard married his wife
30 – the number of years Mr Pollard and Mrs Pollard stayed in Australia

The questions test comprehension of the details in the text and consolidate the Past Simple and Present Continuous for future. Pre-teach *twice* for the answer to number 5. Focus attention on the examples and check students understand the convention of ticking (✔) true information and crossing (✘) false information. Remind them they need to correct the false sentences. Get students to read the text more slowly and complete the task.

Get students to check the answers in pairs before checking with the whole class. Highlight the use of contrastive stress in the sentences that needed correcting.

Answers
1 He didn't buy a VW. He bought a Mini.
2 ✔
3 ✔
4 He didn't pay £250,000 for it. He paid £505 for it.
5 He didn't go to Russia three times in his old Mini. He went to Russia twice.
6 ✔
7 John and his wife didn't stay in Australia because they had no money. They stayed in Australia because John found a job.
8 They aren't buying a new Mini soon. They don't want to sell their old Mini.
9 They aren't returning to Australia by ship. They're returning to Australia by plane.
10 ✔

4 Focus attention on the interview. Check students understand the abbreviations of the speakers (I = Interviewer, JP = John Pollard). Elicit the words to complete the first gap (*In 1964*). Tell students to complete the rest of the interview, using the information in the text.

T 14.6 Play the recording and get students to check their answers.

Answers and tapescript
I This is an amazing car, John. When did you buy it?
JP **In 1964**, when I was a student.
I And how much did it cost?
JP **£505.**
I Why did you buy it?
JP Because I **wanted** to travel. In 1966 **I drove to** Moscow, Finland, and the Arctic Circle.
I Does your wife like the Mini?
JP Oh, yes. She loves it. We **married** in 1967 and we **drove to** Australia via India. We stayed in Australia **for thirty** years.
I When did you come back to England?
JP **Last month.**
I Are you going back to Australia?
JP Yes, we are. We**'re flying back** next month.
I Are you leaving the Mini in England?
JP No, we aren't. The Mini **is travelling** by ship.

Get students to practise the conversation in closed pairs. If students have problems with pronunciation, drill key sections of the conversation and get students to practise again in closed pairs.

ADDITIONAL MATERIAL

Workbook Unit 14
Exercises 10 and 11 Further reading and listening practice.

Transport and travel

1 This section reviews and extends the lexical set of transport and travel, and also gives further practice of the Past Simple. Focus attention on the words in the box and the pictures. Elicit the answer for number 1 (*bicycle*) and get students to continue matching, working in pairs. Check the answers with the whole class, making sure students can pronounce the words correctly.

Answers
1 bicycle
2 motorbike
3 ship
4 the Underground

2 Elicit one or two more examples of forms of transport from the class, e.g. *car*, *bus*, and then get students to continue working in groups of three. Elicit the answers, checking the spelling and the pronunciation, and write them on the board in groups: *by road/rail*, *by air*, *by sea*.

Possible answers

By road/rail	By air	By sea
car	plane	ferry
bus	helicopter	boat
coach		
lorry		
van		
train		
tram		

3 This is a collocation exercise with common travel words. Focus attention on the example and then get students to continue matching, working in pairs. Check the answers with the whole class.

Answers
pack your bags
book a hotel
catch a plane
have a great time
arrive in Rome
go sightseeing

4 This exercise consolidates the collocations presented in exercise 3. Focus attention on the first and last sentences given as examples and then elicit the second sentence (*We booked the hotel and the flight.*) Get students to write 2 in the correct box. Students continue ordering sentences, working individually.

T 14.7 Get students to check in pairs before playing the recording and getting students to check against the tape.

5   This exercise gives further practice in the Past Simple and the language of transport and travel. Demonstrate the activity by talking about a journey you went on. Say where you went, how you travelled, and how long the journey was. Elicit another example from a confident student and then get students to continue in closed pairs or groups of three, taking it in turns to ask and answer about a journey in the past. Monitor and check for correct use of the Past Simple and names of transport.

ADDITIONAL MATERIAL

Workbook Unit 14
Exercises 8 and 9 Exercises to practise the lexical set of travel and transport.

EVERYDAY ENGLISH (SB p111)

Going sightseeing

1   This sections focuses on the topic of sightseeing. Focus attention on the names of the cities and the dates. Elicit sentences by asking *Where and when?* (*I went to London in July 1999. I went to Paris in April 2001.*) Ask *What did you see?* and *What did you buy?* and elicit possible information about sights and souvenirs, e.g. *We saw Buckingham Palace. We bought some clothes. We saw the Eiffel Tower. We bought some wine.*

Review the question *Did you have a good time?* Get students to write down two cities and dates when they were a tourist. Students talk about the cities in the closed pairs, using the ideas in the Student's Book. Encourage them to ask *Did you have a good time?* about each trip.

2   This section practises typical conversations in a tourist office and reviews *would like* from Unit 12. Focus attention on the photos and ask *Where are the people?* (*In a tourist office.*) and *What are they asking about?* (*A map, a bus tour, and a museum.*) Pre-teach/check *take* (verb to show length of time). Make sure students understand that there are a different number of words in each gap each time.

T 14.8   Play the first line of the conversation and elicit the words for the first gap (*help you*). Play the rest of the recording and get students to complete the conversations. If necessary, play the recording again and allow students to complete any missing answers. Then check the answers with the whole class.

Get students to practise the conversations in closed pairs. If students have problems with pronunciation, drill key sections of the conversation and get students to practise again in closed pairs.

3   This exercise gives students the opportunity to talk about sights in their town or city, and also to roleplay conversations in a tourist office. Focus attention on the examples in the speech bubbles. Check comprehension of *market*. Give an example of places to visit in your town and elicit more examples from the class about places where they live. Students continue in closed pairs.

Write key words from the students' examples on the board to help them during the roleplay, e.g.
Nouns: *cathedral, museum, art gallery, square, monument, college, theatre, palace*
Verbs: *go on a tour, see, visit, buy, go to, take a photo of*

Divide the class into pairs and get them to make up conversations, using the conversations in exercise 2 as a model. Let students write their conversations down in the initial stage and go round monitoring and helping. Give students time to rehearse their conversations a few times but then encourage them not to refer to the text when they act out the roleplays. (With a weaker group, you could draft the conversations as a class activity and write them up on the board. Students rehearse from the text on the board. Then rub off some of the words from the board so that there are just key words left and get students to act out the conversations.)

SUGGESTION

You can give students further practice in talking about sightseeing with the photocopiable activity on TB p119. This is an information gap activity – Student A has information about Emma and Student B has information about Nick. There is also space for students to exchange information about a trip they went on. Photocopy enough pages for students to work in pairs and cut each page in half. Pre-teach/check *souvenir* from both charts, *square*, *modern art museum*, *canals*, and *boat trip* from Student A's chart, and *Scandinavian*, *jazz club*, *national museum*, and *royal palace* from Student B's. Divide the class into pairs and assign a role, A or B, to each student. Hand out the relevant chart to each student and check they recognize Emma as a woman's name and Nick as a man's name. Focus attention on the categories on the left-hand side. Elicit the questions students will need to ask about Emma and Nick:

Place	Where did he/she go?
Time	When did he/she go there?
Travel	How did he/she travel?
Activities	What did he/she do?
Sightseeing	What did he/she visit?
Souvenirs	What did he/she buy?
Opinion	What did he/she think of the place?
Like to go again?	Would he/she like to go again?

Tell students they might have to ask for the spelling of different places and review the question *How do you spell … ?* Remind students not to show each other their chart, but to exchange the information through speaking. Demonstrate the activity by getting one Student A to ask the first two questions about Nick and for his/her partner to give the answers. Students continue, working in closed pairs. Monitor and check for correct use of the Past Simple and *would like*. Ask students to check their answers by comparing the information in their completed charts.

Ask students to complete the *You* column with information about a trip they went on. Elicit one or two question and answer exchanges with the *you* form, e.g. *Where did you go? I went to … .* Students then continue, working in closed pairs. Monitor and check as before. Ask students to check their answers by comparing the information in their completed charts. Feed back on any common errors.

ADDITIONAL MATERIAL

Workbook Unit 14
Exercises 12 and 13 Further practice of the language used when sightseeing.

Don't forget!

Workbook Unit 14
Exercises 5 and 6 Pronunciation exercises to practise shifting sentence stress.
Exercise 7 In this exercise students translate sentences containing the main grammar points presented in the unit.

Word list
Ask the students to turn to p137 and go through the words with them. Ask them to learn the words for homework, and test them on a few in the following lesson.

Video
Episode 6 *Close encounters*
Alison, Jane's student sister, is coming to stay, so the housemates are cleaning the house. However, Ali arrives two and a half hours early and Jane is unable to meet her in town. Matt volunteers to go to the café rendezvous. Unfortunately, his car gets a flat tyre on the way and he arrives late – only to greet the wrong person. After some confusion, Ali and Matt set off home – with Matt holding the other woman's bag. They finally get home after talking to the police.

> **EXTRA IDEAS UNITS 13 AND 14**
> On TB p120 there are additional photocopiable activities to review the language from Units 13 and 14. There is a reading text with tasks, a question formation exercise, and a matching activity on everyday English. You will need to pre-teach/check *suit*, *without*, *glove*, *formal/informal*, *pink*, *popular*, *fashionable*, *pub*, *designer labels*, and *spend* for the reading text.

Stop and check 4 for Units 11–14 (TB p139).
Progress test 3 for Units 11–14 (TB p127).

Photocopiable material

The following material may be photocopied freely for classroom use. It may not be adapted, printed, or sold without the permission of Oxford University Press.

Extra ideas, suggestions, and practice pp 106–120

Progress tests pp 121–9

Stop and checks pp 130–141

Photocopiable material

Unit 2 **Suggestion** (TB p15)

Name Yoshi	**Name** Brian
Kumiko	Liz
Country Japan	**Country** Canada

Name Fernando	**Name** Kevin
Marta	Margaret
Country Spain	**Country** Northern Ireland

Name Mike	**Name** Michel
Carol	Marie
Country England	**Country** France

Name Robert	**Name** Marco
Britney	Sara
Country The United States	**Country** Italy

Name Gareth	**Name** Luis
Morgan	Ana
Country Wales	**Country** Brazil

Name Calum	**Name** Paul
Fiona	Kim
Country Scotland	**Country** Australia

Unit 3 Suggestion (TB p23)

Role cards for female students

Name	Françoise Monet
Country	France
Phone number	33 57 45 89
Age	28
Job	shop assistant
Married?	Yes

Name	Rosa Sanchez
Country	Spain
Phone number	386 91 45
Age	28
Job	doctor
Married?	Yes

Name	Mary Macdonald
Country	Scotland
Phone number	553 6316
Age	26
Job	teacher
Married?	Yes

Name	Sally Porter
Country	Canada
Phone number	514 499 6021
Age	25
Job	taxi driver
Married?	No

Role cards for male students

Name	Jim Scott
Country	Australia
Phone number	9422 0573
Age	30
Job	businessman
Married?	No

Name	Fernando Ramos
Country	Brazil
Phone number	237 5441
Age	27
Job	police officer
Married?	No

Name	David Evans
Country	Wales
Phone number	437791
Age	23
Job	nurse
Married?	Yes

Name	Yoshi Suzuki
Country	Japan
Phone number	5995 2702
Age	19
Job	student
Married?	Yes

Extra ideas Units 1–4 Revision

Reading

1 Look at the texts about people in London. Read them quickly and answer the questions.

1 Is Lucia from London?
2 How old is Daniel?
3 Where is Todd from?
4 Who is from Japan?
5 Two people have children. Who?
6 Who isn't married?

Hi! Welcome to London ...

My name's **LUCIA CLARKE**. I'm from Brescia in Italy. I'm married. My husband's name is James. He's from London. We have a son, Daniel, and a daughter, Teresa. Daniel is twelve and Teresa is eight. James and I are both teachers at the same school. It isn't in the centre of London but it's near our house.

- -

I'm **TODD HADDING** from Seattle in the United States. I'm in London with my rock group, *The Drivers*. We're on tour in England, France, and Spain. I'm not married but I have a girlfriend here in London. She's a student and her name's Laura. She's beautiful!

- -

My name's **SUMIO TANAKA**. I'm a businessman from Japan. My company has an office in Tokyo and in London, too. I'm married and I have two daughters. They are students at a school in the centre of London. They are very happy here.

---

2 Read the interviews again. Are these sentences true (✓) or false (✗)?

1 Lucia has two daughters.
2 Lucia is a teacher.
3 James's school is in the centre of London.
4 Todd is a taxi driver.
5 Laura is Todd's girlfriend.
6 Sumio's company has two offices.
7 Sumio's children aren't happy in London.

Language work

1 Write questions for these answers.

1 **What's your name?**
  My name's Elena Majewska.
2 _____ ?
  M – A – J – E – W – S – K – A.
3 _____ ?
  I'm from Warsaw in Poland.
4 _____ ?
  I'm 35.
5 _____ ?
  No, I'm divorced.
6 _____ ?
  I'm a bank manager.
7 _____ ?
  It's in the centre of town.
8 _____ ?
  My favourite music is jazz.

2 Practise the questions and answers with a partner.

Everyday English

Match the lines (1–5) with the answers (a–e).

1 ☐ What's this in English?
2 ☐ Have a good journey!
3 ☐ Good night.
4 ☐ How are you?
5 ☐ Are you all right?

a Fine, thanks.
b Sleep well!
c Thank you.
d I don't know. Sorry.
e Yes, I'm fine.

Unit 5 Practice 5 (SB p35)

Role cards for Student A

Role cards for Student B

Student A

NAME	Isabella Ponti
TOWN / COUNTRY	Milan, Italy
A HOUSE OR A FLAT	flat
JOB	doctor
PLACE OF WORK	hospital
LANGUAGES	3 – Italian, French, and a little English
SPORTS	skiing and tennis

Student B

NAME	Monique Duval
TOWN / COUNTRY	Carnac, France
A HOUSE OR A FLAT	house
JOB	teacher
PLACE OF WORK	school in the town centre
LANGUAGES	2 – French and English
SPORTS	football and swimming

Student A

NAME	Mario Bellini
TOWN / COUNTRY	Milan, Italy
A HOUSE OR A FLAT	flat
JOB	doctor
PLACE OF WORK	hospital
LANGUAGES	3 – Italian, French, and a little English
SPORTS	skiing and tennis

Student B

NAME	Alain Gaultier
TOWN / COUNTRY	Carnac, France
A HOUSE OR A FLAT	house
JOB	teacher
PLACE OF WORK	school in the town centre
LANGUAGES	2 – French and English
SPORTS	football and swimming

Student A

NAME	Isabella Ponti
TOWN / COUNTRY	Milan, Italy
A HOUSE OR A FLAT	flat
JOB	doctor
PLACE OF WORK	hospital
LANGUAGES	3 – Italian, French, and a little English
SPORTS	skiing and tennis

Student B

NAME	Monique Duval
TOWN / COUNTRY	Carnac, France
A HOUSE OR A FLAT	house
JOB	teacher
PLACE OF WORK	school in the town centre
LANGUAGES	2 – French and English
SPORTS	football and swimming

Student A

NAME	Mario Bellini
TOWN / COUNTRY	Milan, Italy
A HOUSE OR A FLAT	flat
JOB	doctor
PLACE OF WORK	hospital
LANGUAGES	3 – Italian, French, and a little English
SPORTS	skiing and tennis

Student B

NAME	Alain Gaultier
TOWN / COUNTRY	Carnac, France
A HOUSE OR A FLAT	house
JOB	teacher
PLACE OF WORK	school in the town centre
LANGUAGES	2 – French and English
SPORTS	football and swimming

Student A What time is it, please?

Student B What time is it, please?

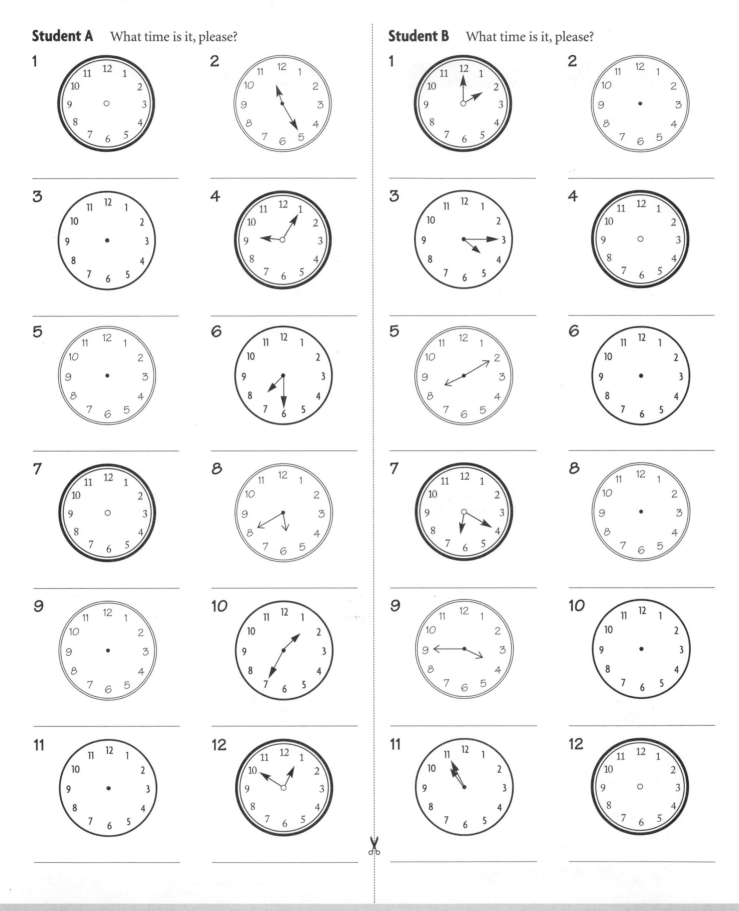

Adjectives

big	new	horrible	cold
lovely	small	hot	old

Nouns

bag	book	camera	computer
hamburger	sandwich	television	bus
dog	coffee	tea	mobile phone
radio	CD player	clock	glass

Extra ideas Units 5–8 Revision

Reading

1 Read the text quickly and answer these questions.

 1 What's Nicola's job?
 2 Where does she live?
 3 What's her favourite room?
 4 What does she do there?

Writer, **Nicola Carlton,** *describes her favourite room ...*

My house is in the centre of Manchester and it's about 90 years old. I work from home and my favourite room is my office. It's a beautiful room with big windows and I love **it**! In the office, I have my computer, two comfortable armchairs, a CD player, and a small fridge! There are photos of my three children on the walls. They're at university and I only see **them** in the holidays.

I get up at about 7 a.m. every morning and have a shower. I have breakfast in the office and I work at my computer all day. I don't usually go out of the office because it has everything I want – my work, music, food, and coffee! I don't have a telephone but I have email. My mother has a computer and I send messages to **her** every day – **she** loves **them**!

In the evening, I listen to music in the office and eat my dinner. My friends sometimes visit **me** and we have a glass of wine or two. I go to bed at about 11.30 p.m. – but in my bedroom, not in the office!

---

2 Read the text again. Are these sentences true (✓) or false (✗)?

 1 Nicola doesn't go out to work.
 2 Nicola's office is very light.
 3 Nicola's children don't visit her in the holidays.
 4 Nicola doesn't telephone her mother.
 5 Nicola sleeps in her office.

3 Look at the words in **bold** in the text. What or who do they refer to?

Language work

1 Write questions for these answers.

 1 **Do you live in a flat?**
 Yes, I do. I live in a flat in the centre.

 2 _____?
 My favourite room is the living room.

 3 _____?
 No, I work in an office.

 4 _____?
 Yes, I sometimes work late.

 5 _____?
 No, I don't. I want to be a writer.

 6 _____?
 No, but I speak French and Italian.

 7 _____?
 Because English is important for my job.

 8 _____?
 I like red wine and beer.

 9 _____?
 I watch TV in the evening.

 10 _____?
 I have two sisters and a brother.

2 Practise the questions and answers with a partner.

Everyday English

Match the questions (1–5) with the answers (a–e).

 1 ☐ What time is it, please?
 2 ☐ Can I try on this jacket, please?
 3 ☐ How much is that?
 4 ☐ Is there a bank near here?
 5 ☐ Is it far to the station?

 a Twelve ninety-nine, please.
 b About fifteen minutes.
 c Yes. Go down King's Road and turn right.
 d It's five thirty.
 e Yes, the changing rooms are over there.

Unit 9 **Suggestion** (TB p64)

Student A *Who was … ?*

1
Name: _____
Job: _____
Born: _____
Country: _____

4
Name: **Bob Marley**
Job: **singer and musician**
Born: **1945**
Country: **Jamaica**

2
Name: **James Dean**
Job: **actor**
Born: **1931**
Country: **the United States**

5
Name: _____
Job: _____
Born: _____
Country: _____

3
Name: _____
Job: _____
Born: _____
Country: _____

6
Name: **Anna Pavlova**
Job: **dancer**
Born: **1881**
Country: **Russia**

Student B *Who was … ?*

1
Name: **Albert Einstein**
Job: **scientist**
Born: **1879**
Country: **Germany**

4
Name: _____
Job: _____
Born: _____
Country: _____

2
Name: _____
Job: _____
Born: _____
Country: _____

5
Name: **John F. Kennedy**
Job: **politician**
Born: **1917**
Country: **the United States**

3
Name: **Agatha Christie**
Job: **writer**
Born: **1890**
Country: **England**

6
Name: _____
Job: _____
Born: _____
Country: _____

Unit 10 **Suggestion** (TB p71)

Student A   Jane's flat

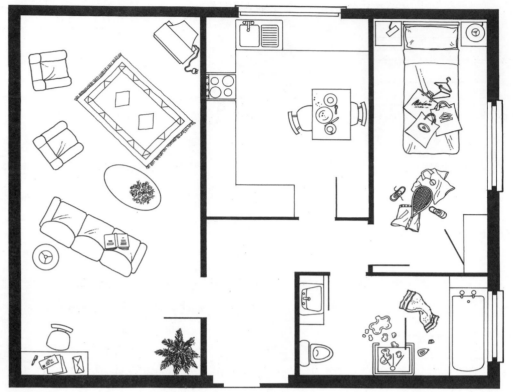

Student A's question

What did Paul do yesterday?

What sport/Paul/play/yesterday?
What/he/read?
Where/he/play the guitar?

Paul/cook a meal?
He/watch a video?
He/have a bath?
He/work at his computer?

Student B   Paul's flat

Student B's questions

What did Jane do yesterday?

Where/Jane/go/yesterday?
What/she/read?
What/sport/she/play?

Jane/have breakfast?
She/write a letter?
She/have a bath?
She/watch TV?

Unit 11 Suggestion (TB p81)

LISTEN TO	PLAY	BOOK	WATCH	READ
the news	computer games	a book	a room	basketball
the piano	a magazine	a ticket	cards	a newspaper
a table	music	a CD	TV	a hotel
chess	a holiday	a video	tennis	music
a letter	a film	the news	a cassette	the guitar

1 Complete the dialogue with the correct form of *listen to*, *play*, *book*, *watch*, or *read*. Use the Present Simple and Past Simple.

A Did you have a good weekend?

B Yes, I ___played___ tennis with my brother on Saturday and yesterday I (1) _____ my favourite films on video. What about you?

A I (2) _____ my summer holiday on the Internet – two weeks in Portugal.

B Really? That's interesting. Do you use your computer a lot?

A Oh yes, every day. I (3) _____ computer games, (4) _____ music and (5) _____ newspapers.

B Can you (6) _____ theatre tickets on the Internet? I want to see a new play in London.

A Yes, of course. It's easy. I can show you.

B OK. Thanks.

2 Practise the dialogue in pairs.

1 Complete the dialogue with the correct form of *listen to*, *play*, *book*, *watch*, or *read*. Use the Present Simple and Past Simple.

A Did you have a good weekend?

B Yes, I ___played___ tennis with my brother on Saturday and yesterday I (1) _____ my favourite films on video. What about you?

A I (2) _____ my summer holiday on the Internet – two weeks in Portugal.

B Really? That's interesting. Do you use your computer a lot?

A Oh yes, every day. I (3) _____ computer games, (4) _____ music and (5) _____ newspapers.

B Can you (6) _____ theatre tickets on the Internet? I want to see a new play in London.

A Yes, of course. It's easy. I can show you.

B OK. Thanks.

2 Practise the dialogue in pairs.

Unit 12 **Suggestion** (TB p89)

1 There are three dialogues on this page. Put the lines in the correct order.

B At a post office.	**B** OK. The changing rooms are over there.
A Medium, I think.	**A** Excuse me! Do you sell *Le Monde*?
A Excuse me! Where can I buy stamps?	**B** Sure. What size are you?
B No, I'm sorry. We don't.	**A** Is there a post office near here?
A I'd like to try on this shirt, please.	**A** Where can I buy French newspapers?
B Try the railway station.	**B** Yes, three hundred metres from here, next to the Internet café.

2 Where are the people in each dialogue?
3 Practise the dialogues with a partner.

Extra Ideas Units 9–12 Revision

Reading

1 Work in groups and answer the questions.
   1 Do you like surprises?
   2 Did you have a surprise on your last birthday?
   3 Did you organize a surprise for a friend's birthday?

> ## .....*A wonderful surprise*.................
>
> Last Saturday was my fortieth birthday. I got up early but my husband and children stayed in bed. I thought, 'That's OK. I can open my birthday cards now.' I looked in every room in the house, but nothing – no cards, presents, flowers, or chocolates. I was upset but I thought, 'It doesn't matter. I can wait.'
>
> An hour later the postman arrived and gave me lots of envelopes. 'Fantastic – my cards!' I said, and then I saw that the letters were not for me. My husband and children got up and said, 'Happy Birthday!' but didn't give me a card or present.
>
> Then at twelve o'clock a taxi arrived at the house. I thought it was a mistake but my husband said, 'Get in the taxi. I've got your jacket and suitcase.' We went to the airport and arrived in Paris that afternoon. We went shopping for my birthday present – a beautiful painting of the city. In the evening we had a delicious dinner – champagne, seafood, steak, and French cheese.
>
> On Sunday we had breakfast in the oldest café in Paris, went on a boat on the River Seine, and walked along the famous streets. We arrived home on Sunday evening after a perfect weekend. The next day I asked my husband, 'How did you keep the holiday a secret?' 'I booked it on the Internet,' he answered, 'because I know you never use the computer!'

2 Read the text. Are these sentences true (✓) or false (✗)?
   1 The writer didn't receive any presents on the morning of her birthday.
   2 The postman gave the writer some birthday cards.
   3 The writer didn't think the taxi was for her.
   4 The writer and her husband stayed two nights in Paris.
   5 The writer didn't know about the holiday because her husband booked it on the Internet.

Language work

1 Write questions about your partner's last holiday.
   1 Where/go?
      Where did you go?
   2 go/in summer?
      Did you go in summer?
   3 Who/with?
      _____?
   4 travel/by plane?
      _____?
   5 Where/stay?
      _____?
   6 What/eat?
      _____?
   7 weather/good?
      _____?
   8 have/a good time?
      _____?

2 Ask and answer the questions with a partner.

Everyday English

1 Match the lines (1–5) with the answers (a–e).
   1 ☐ I'm sorry. I forgot your birthday.
   2 ☐ Can you help me? I'm lost!
   3 ☐ It's time to go to the station.
   4 ☐ What would you like?
   5 ☐ I can't understand this word.

   a Where do you want to go?
   b You can check it in my dictionary.
   c Black coffee, please.
   d It doesn't matter.
   e But I can't find my ticket.

Unit 13 Suggestion (TB p96)

Student A

Student B

Unit 14 Suggestion (TB p104)

Student A

	EMMA	NICK	YOU
Place	Amsterdam		
Time	November 2000		
Travel	plane and train		
Activities	sightseeing, shopping		
Sightseeing	Dam Square, the Modern Art Museum, the canals on a boat trip		
Souvenirs	chocolate, cheese		
Opinion	fantastic for a short break		
Like to go again ?	Yes		

Student B

	EMMA	NICK	YOU
Place		Stockholm	
Time		August 1998	
Travel		plane and bus	
Activities		tried Scandinavian food, jazz clubs	
Sightseeing		the Old Town, National Museum of Art, Royal Palace	
Souvenirs		—	
Opinion		OK, but quite expensive	
Like to go again ?		No	

Extra Ideas Units 13–14 Revision

Reading

1 Read the text quickly and make a list of clothes and colours.

Clothes	Colours
suit	blue

What are you wearing?

The world of clothes and fashion is changing. In the 1950s, men wore a suit for work and women never went out without a hat and gloves. Today, people can wear jeans and a T-shirt in the office and young men only wear a suit for interviews or weddings. Colours are also different today. People wear blue, green, yellow, and red as well as more formal colours like black, grey, and brown. My boyfriend works in an office and today he's wearing jeans and a pink shirt!

Sports clothes are very popular today. I'm wearing jogging trousers, a T-shirt, and trainers today, but I don't go jogging! I wear them because they are fashionable and comfortable. People sometimes wear ski jackets and walking boots or trainers when they go to the pub!

Children are also very interested in fashion. In the past, parents chose and bought clothes for children and teenagers. Now, children choose their own clothes and often like to have designer labels. My sister's children are wearing Paul Smith jeans, Donna Karan T-shirts and Nike trainers at the moment. I think she spends more money on clothes for them than I spend on my clothes!

I like today's fashions because they are more informal and men and women can wear the same things. I often borrow my boyfriend's trousers, shirts, and T-shirts—but he doesn't borrow my clothes!

2 Read the text again and answer these questions.
1 How is today's fashion different from in the 1950s?
2 What clothes and colours can people wear for work?
3 Does the writer wear sports clothes to go jogging?
4 Do parents choose clothes for today's teenagers?
5 Why are children's clothes expensive?
6 Why does the writer like today's fashions?

Language work

1 Write questions for your partner.
1 How often/go shopping for clothes?
   How often do you go shopping for clothes?
2 like/today's fashions?
   Do you like today's fashions?
3 What/favourite clothes shops?
   _____ ?
4 buy clothes/on the Internet?
   _____ ?
5 How much/spend on clothes?
   _____ ?
6 buy/designer labels?
   _____ ?
7 What/wear for work/school/university?
   _____ ?
8 What/wear/now?
   _____ ?
9 What/favourite colours?
   _____ ?
10 borrow/other people's clothes?
   _____ ?

2 Ask and answer the questions with a partner.

Everyday English

Match the lines (1–6) with the answers (a–f).
1 ☐ I'm bored.
2 ☐ I'd like to go on a tour of the city.
3 ☐ I'm hungry.
4 ☐ When is the museum open?
5 ☐ How much is it to get in to the museum?
6 ☐ I'm thirsty.

a Why don't you have a banana?
b Five pounds for adults.
c From ten until five thirty.
d Why don't you have a glass of water?
e That's fine. The next bus leaves at 11.30.
f Why don't you read a book?

Progress test 1

UNITS 1–5

Exercise 1 The present tense of *to be*

Complete the table with the present tense of *to be*.

		Positive	Negative
1	I	am	'm not
2	You	_____	_____
3	He/She/It	_____	_____
4	We	_____	_____
5	They	_____	_____

8

Exercise 2 *to be* – positive, negative, and questions

Complete the sentences with the correct form of *to be*.

1 I **'m** from Manchester in England.

2 _____ you a student?

3 My brother _____ a doctor.

4 My parents _____ from London. They're from Brighton.

5 Are you married? No, I _____ .

6 My sister and I _____ from Japan.

7 _____ your parents from the United States?

8 Jane _____ a doctor. She's a teacher.

9 Is he a taxi driver? Yes, he _____ .

10 The wine _____ from Spain. It's from Portugal.

11 _____ your teacher from England?

10

Exercise 3 Questions

Match a line in A with a line in B to make a question. Then find an answer in C.

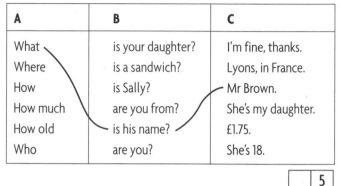

A	B	C
What	is your daughter?	I'm fine, thanks.
Where	is a sandwich?	Lyons, in France.
How	is Sally?	Mr Brown.
How much	are you from?	She's my daughter.
How old	is his name?	£1.75.
Who	are you?	She's 18.

5

Exercise 4 Word order

Write the words in the correct order.

1 English / is / What / this / in / ?
   What is this in English?

2 wife / is / This / Peter's

   _____

3 phone / is / What / their / number / ?

   _____

4 the / house / have / We / a / in / country

   _____

5 your / you / do / How / spell / surname / ?

   _____

6 you / Do / Spanish / like / wine / ?

   _____

7 well / I / speak / French / don't / very

   _____

8 car / don't / a / We / have / German

   _____

9 Chinese / they / Do / eat / food / ?

   _____

8

Exercise 5 *a* or *an*?

Complete the sentences with *a* or *an*.

1 It's __an__ American city.

2 He's _____ actor.

3 Are you _____ teacher?

4 I have _____ Italian car.

5 We don't have _____ big house.

6 I have _____ English friend.

7 She's _____ student.

8 They don't have _____ computer.

9 She's _____ Australian doctor.

10 Is he _____ businessman?

	9

Exercise 6 *has/have*

Complete the sentences with the correct form of *have*.

1 I __have__ a brother and a sister.

2 He _____ a small farm in Wales.

3 I like Chinese food but we _____ a Chinese restaurant in town.

4 They _____ a flat in London.

5 I'm not married but I _____ a lot of friends.

6 John _____ a new computer.

7 _____ they _____ a big family?

8 My sister _____ a dog and a cat.

9 _____ you _____ a dictionary?

	8

Exercise 7 Present Simple

Complete the sentences with the correct form of the verb in brackets.

1 My husband and I __live__ (live) in the country.

2 I _____ (not like) swimming.

3 They _____ (drink) French wine.

4 What sports _____ the children _____ (like)?

5 We _____ (work) in a hospital.

6 You _____ (not like) hamburgers.

7 How many languages _____ you _____ (speak)?

8 _____ your and your family _____ (speak) German?

9 Helen and Dave _____ (not work) in London.

10 Where _____ you _____ (live)?

11 _____ you _____ (eat) Chinese or Italian food?

	10

Exercise 8 Subject pronouns and possessive adjectives

Choose the correct word.

1 *My / (I)*'m from Italy.

2 Is this *you / your* dictionary?

3 My brother is a doctor. *His / He*'s 27.

4 This is my mother. *He / She*'s a teacher.

5 Do you like *we / our* house?

6 I'm Anna and this is *my / I* husband.

7 Is this your daughter? What's *her / his* name?

8 My father is from Poland. *His / Her* name's Arek.

9 What are *they / their* names?

	8

Exercise 9 Possessive *'s*

Tick (✓) the correct sentence.

1 a ☐ This is Davids car.
   b ☑ This is David's car.

2 a ☐ Peter's wife is American.
   b ☐ Peter is wife is American.

3 a ☐ What's your teacher name?
   b ☐ What's your teacher's name?

4 a ☐ The children's names are Emma and Simon.
   b ☐ The childrens names are Emma and Simon.

5 a ☐ Mr Browns car is American.
   b ☐ Mr Brown's car is American.

6 a ☐ Her husband name is Paolo.
   b ☐ Her husband's name is Paolo.

	5

Exercise 10 Numbers

Write the numbers in words.

1 17 _seventeen_ _____
2 29 _____
3 37 _____
4 43 _____
5 59 _____
6 62 _____
7 74 _____
8 88 _____
9 91 _____
10 100 _____

☐ 9

Exercise 11 Word groups

1 Put the words in the correct column.

> ~~teacher~~ parent sandwich actor beer sister
> hamburger bank manager daughter wine son
> chocolate shop assistant ice-cream police officer
> coffee orange tea Coca-Cola husband waiter

Jobs	Family	Food	Drinks
teacher	_____	_____	_____
_____	_____	_____	_____
_____	_____	_____	_____
_____	_____	_____	_____
_____	_____	_____	_____

☐ 20

TOTAL ☐ 100

Progress test 2

Exercise 1 Present Simple and frequency adverbs

Write complete sentences with the words in brackets.

1 I / go to bed late (usually)
   I usually go to bed late.

2 He / work late (never)

   _____

3 I / go to work by car (sometimes)

   _____

4 My son / have lunch at school (always)

   _____

5 She / see her friends after school (usually)

   _____

6 I / buy a newspaper (never)

   _____

7 Helen / go windsurfing (sometimes)

   _____

   [6]

Exercise 2 Object pronouns

Choose the correct word.

1 My daughter visited (me) / my last month.

2 My son lives near you. Do you know he / him?

3 We bought a video but we didn't watch it / them.

4 My daughter is a doctor. This is a photo of him / her.

5 Our homework is very difficult. Can you help we / us?

6 We phoned Mum and Dad last week but we didn't see them / they.

7 You are very nice. I like you / your.

   [6]

Exercise 3 *there is/are* and prepositions of place

Write sentences about the picture.

1 a TV / the room
   There's a TV in the room.

2 two books / the table

   _____

3 a lamp / the sofa

   _____

4 three pictures / the walls

   _____

5 a cat / the table

   _____

6 a magazine / the bag

   _____

   [10]

Exercise 4 The past tense of *to be*

Complete the table with the past tense of *to be*.

		Positive	Negative
1	I	was	wasn't
2	You	_____	_____
3	He/She/It	_____	_____
4	We	_____	_____
5	They	_____	_____

[8]

Exercise 5 *do*, *was*, and *did*

Complete the sentences with the verbs in the box.

do / does	was / were	did

1 Where __*does*__ he work?

2 _____ you like French food?

3 Where _____ you last night?

4 What _____ you do last weekend?

5 _____ she live in New York now?

6 _____ you go skiing last year?

7 When _____ he born?

8 We _____ at home yesterday.

9 How many children _____ they have now?

[8]

Exercise 6 Past Simple

Complete the sentences with the Past Simple of the verbs in brackets. There are regular and irregular verbs.

1 She ___*played*___ (play) tennis yesterday.

2 I _____ (not work) at my computer yesterday.

3 We _____ (buy) a new video recorder last month.

4 Where _____ you _____ (go) on holiday last year?

5 They _____ (stay) at home last weekend.

6 He _____ (see) his friends last night.

7 You _____ (not take) the painting to an expert.

8 _____ you _____ (eat) in the hotel?

9 The children _____ (do) their homework on their computer.

[8]

Exercise 7 Negatives

Write the sentences in the negative.

1 I work in an office.
   I don't work in an office.

2 The film is very good.
   _____

3 There's a CD player in the car.
   _____

4 She goes to work by car.
   _____

5 We go shopping in town.
   _____

6 There are a lot of hotels in this area.
   _____

7 The weather was very hot.
   _____

8 My children were born in the US.
   _____

9 I was born in 1989.
   _____

10 David played baseball at school.
    _____

11 I had a big lunch.
    _____

[10]

Exercise 8 Days of the week

Complete the days in order.

Days: __Monday__ , _____ , _____ , _____ , _____ , _____ , _____

[6]

Exercise 9 Dates

Write the dates in words.

1 5 / 5   _the fifth of May_
2 1 / 2   _____
3 19 / 6   _____
4 3 / 8   _____
5 31 / 12 _____
6 12 / 10 _____
7 17 / 4   _____
8 5 / 1   _____
9 7 / 7   _____

8

Exercise 10 Prepositions of time

Write the correct preposition, *in*, *on*, or *at*.

1 **in**_____ the evening
2 _____ Monday
3 _____ seven o'clock
4 _____ Sunday morning
5 _____ the afternoon
6 _____ five thirty
7 _____ the weekend

6

Exercise 11 Words that go together

Match a verb in A with a line in B.

A	B
get up	in a chalet
go	cards
watch	beer
listen to	a good time
play	a CD
stay	in a hospital
work	sailing
cook	a meal
eat	in restaurants
have	early
drink	a video

10

Exercise 12 Which one is different?

(Circle) the different word.

1 newsagent supermarket (park) chemist
2 France German Italy Portugal
3 shower CD player TV video recorder
4 ice hockey swimming sailing skiing
5 twenty-second twenty-nine thirteenth ninth
6 writer painter footballer singer
7 watched ate got took
8 swimming windsurfing sailing walking
9 floor kitchen wall window

8

Exercise 13 Adjectives

Match the opposites.

A	B
new	big
early	old
small	horrible
expensive	slow
fast	hot
cold	late
lovely	cheap

6

TOTAL 100

Progress test 3

Exercise 1 Word order

Put the words in the correct order.

1 fast / you / Can / swim / ?
   Can you swim fast?

2 She / long / hair / fair / has

   _____

3 tour / the / long / How / does / bus / last / ?

   _____

4 radio / listen / to / like / you / Would / to / the / ?

   _____

5 Can / tell / please / you / me / the / time / ?

   _____

6 car / want / They / to / a / buy / new

   _____

7 like / would / to / What / you / drink / ?

   _____

8 and / a / is / He / wearing / jeans / T-shirt

   _____

9 weekend / going / are / Where / you / next?

   _____

10 bed / you / Why / don't / go / early / to / ?

   _____

11 agent / collected / We / our / the / tickets / travel /
    from

   _____

   | 10 |

Exercise 2 can and can't

Look at the information in the table and complete the sentences with *can* or *can't* and a verb.

	use a computer	ride a horse	play the guitar	cook
James	✓	✗	✗	✓
Helen	✓	✓	✗	✗
Sue	✓	✗	✓	✗

1 Helen ___can ride a horse___ but James and Sue can't.

2 James and Helen _____
   but Sue can.

3 James can use a computer, but he _____
   _____ and he _____ .

4 Everybody _____ .

5 _____ Helen and Sue _____ ? No,
   they can't.

6 Who _____ ? Only Helen
   can.

   | 6 |

Exercise 3 want, like, and would like

Tick (✓) the correct sentence.

1 A ☑ What would you like for dessert?
       ☐ What do you like for dessert?

   B Ice-cream, please.

2 A ☐ Would you like a glass of wine?
       ☐ Do you like wine?

   B Yes, I love it.

3 A ☐ I want to send an email, please.
       ☐ I'd want to send an email, please.

   B That's fine. Try computer number 3.

4 A ☐ Would you like to listen to some music?
       ☐ Do you like listening to music?

   B That's a nice idea.

5 A ☐ I like to buy these postcards, please.
       ☐ I'd like to buy these postcards, please.

   B Two pounds fifty, please.

6 A ☐ What sports do you like doing?
       ☐ What sports would you like doing?

   B I love football and squash.

   | 5 |

Exercise 4 Present Continuous

Complete the sentences with the Present Continuous form of the verbs in the box.

| read write wear rain have work enjoy leave drive |

1 What __are__ you __reading__ ? It's a love story.

2 He can't go to the cinema because he _____ late.

3 I _____ work early because I don't feel well.

4 In this photo she _____ shorts and a T-shirt.

5 I can't talk to you now. I _____ the car.

6 _____ it _____ ? No, the weather is lovely today.

7 Where's Liz? She _____ a shower.

8 _____ you _____ your holiday? Yes, everything is great.

9 The children _____ a letter to their grandparents.

[8]

Exercise 5 Present Simple and Continuous

Complete the sentences with the Present Simple or the Present Continuous form of the verbs in brackets.

1 I usually __walk__ (walk) to work but this morning I __'m driving__ (drive) to my office.

2 I _____ (not see) my parents very often but they _____ (stay) with me at the moment.

3 We usually _____ (have) lunch at home but today we _____ (eat) in a nice restaurant.

4 Why _____ you _____ (wear) jeans for work today? You usually _____ (wear) more formal clothes.

5 My friends and I _____ (learn) French at the moment. We _____ (like) it very much.

6 My sister _____ (live) in a flat in London but she _____ (travel) in Europe at the moment.

[10]

Exercise 6 Past Simple and Present Continuous for future

Write positive and negative sentences, using the verbs.

1 I / get up early

__I got up early__ _____ yesterday.

__I'm not getting up early__ _____ tomorrow.

2 she / cook dinner

_____ yesterday.

_____ tomorrow.

3 we / work late

_____ yesterday.

_____ tomorrow.

4 they / leave home early

_____ yesterday.

_____ tomorrow.

5 I / go to bed late

_____ yesterday.

_____ tomorrow.

6 you / stay at home

_____ yesterday.

_____ tomorrow.

7 Richard / see his doctor

_____ yesterday.

_____ tomorrow.

[12]

Exercise 7 Negatives

1 I can draw well.

__I can't draw well.__ _____

2 She wants to sell her house.

_____

3 They like sightseeing.

_____

4 He can swim.

_____

5 He works in a bank.

_____

6 We walk to work every day.

_____

7   I'm watching this film.

_____

8   The children are doing their homework.

_____

9   You are playing very well.

_____

10 We're staying in the hotel for a week.

_____

11 We had a nice meal at the restaurant.

_____

12 You collected the tickets yesterday.

_____

13 Angela saw her family last week.

_____

⬚ 12

Exercise 8 *am / is / are , do / does / did*

Complete the sentences with a verb from the box.

am/'m not   is/isn't   are/aren't   does/doesn't
do/don't   did/didn't

1 I **am** watching TV.
2 My husband _____ going skiing next month.
3 Where _____ the bus tour leave from?
4 How often _____ you travel by plane?
5 They usually go to Italy on holiday but they _____ going there this year.
6 We had lunch in a restaurant but we _____ enjoy it.
7 Why don't we go out? It _____ raining now.
8 Are you using your computer? No, I _____ .
9 They live in Spain but they _____ speak Spanish very well.
10 I _____ catching the plane at seven thirty.
11 Does Paula like skiing? No, she _____ .
12 _____ you have a good weekend?
13 _____ you enjoying the party?

⬚ 12

Exercise 9 Which one is different?

Circle the different word.

1 (bank) chemist newsagent supermarket
2 wine coffee mineral water cake
3 cheese ham meal vegetables
4 soup chocolate cake ice-cream apple pie
5 plane airport ferry train
6 farmer grandmother interpreter architect
7 passport ticket travel agent stamp
8 shoes shorts jeans trousers
9 T-shirt dress jacket coat
10 black red grey long
11 dessert waiter main course side order
12 film photo interview camera
13 post office stamp letter email

⬚ 12

Exercise 10 Words that go together

Match a verb in A with a line in B.

A	B
listen to	a friend
watch	a plane
read	chess
chat to	in Paris
wear	sightseeing
play	shorts
book	a good time
catch	a cake
change	your bags
go	a video
have	a CD
pack	a magazine
arrive	money
make	a holiday

⬚ 13

TOTAL ⬚ 100

Stop and check 1

Correct the mistakes

Each sentence has a mistake. Find it and correct it.

1   Hello, ╪ John.
    Hello, I'm John. _____

2   What's you name?
    _____

3   My name are Ana.
    _____

4   This Helen Smith.
    _____

5   Is a book.
    _____

6   Where you are from?
    _____

7   I'm am from Spain.
    _____

8   He's a businessman. Her name's James.
    _____

9   What's she job? She's a doctor.
    _____

10 He no is a teacher. He's a student.
    _____

11 How old you?
    _____

12 Is she from London? Yes, she's.
    _____

13 Is he a shop assistant? No, he not.
    _____

14 Are you from France? No, I amn't.
    _____

15 He's phone number is 772541.
    _____

16 My teacher and I is 30.
    _____

    [15]

my / your, he / she / they, his / her

(Circle) the correct word.

1   (My)/ I name's Karen.

2   He's from Japan. *His / Her* name's Hiro.

3   Helen and Sally are in a pop group. *They / She* are on tour.

4   What's *you / your* address?

5   This is Linda. *Her / She*'s from Manchester.

6   Where are the students? *They're / You're* in London.

7   Mr Evans is from London. *She's / He's* a businessman.

    [6]

Questions and answers

1   Match the questions (1–8) and the answers (a–h).

    1 [f] What's your job?
    2 [ ] Where's he from?
    3 [ ] Is she a shop assistant?
    4 [ ] What's his name?
    5 [ ] How old are you?
    6 [ ] How are you?
    7 [ ] Are you married?
    8 [ ] What's this is English?

    a No, she isn't.
    b Mr Brown.
    c Glasgow, in Scotland.
    d I'm 27.
    e No, we aren't.
    f I'm a student.
    g Fine, thanks.
    h It's a camera.

    [7]

2 Look at the identity card and write the questions.

NAME:	Emma Cartwright
CITY:	Liverpool, England
JOB:	Police officer
AGE:	29
PHONE NUMBER:	0151 876 1290
MARRIED?:	Yes

1 **What's her name?**

Her name's Emma Cartwright.

2 _____

She's from Liverpool in England.

3 _____

She's a police officer.

4 _____

She's 29.

5 _____

It's 0151 876 1290.

6 _____

Yes, she is.

☐ 10

Negatives

Write the sentences in the negative.

1 It's from Spain.

It isn't from Spain.

2 She's a nurse.

_____

3 Karl is from Canada.

_____

4 Julie is 29.

_____

5 I'm married.

_____

6 Jim and Sue are students.

_____

7 They are in New York.

_____ ☐ 12

Plurals

Write the sentences in the plural.

1 It's a book.

They're books.

2 I'm English.

_____

3 It's a sandwich.

_____

4 He's a student.

_____

5 She's from the United States.

_____

6 I'm not on tour.

_____

7 Is she a doctor?

_____ ☐ 12

Numbers

1 Match the numbers in A with the words in B.

A	B
6	five
1	two
2	seven
5	six
8	nine
4	eight
9	one
3	four
10	three
7	ten

☐ 9

2 Write the numbers in words.

1 12 _twelve_   5 14 _____

2 11 _____   6 30 _____

3 28 _____   7 13 _____

4 20 _____   8 15 _____

[ ] 7

Vocabulary

1 Put the words in the correct column.

doctor photograph nurse sandwich student book
teacher television businessman shop assistant camera
taxi driver bag police officer computer hamburger

Jobs	Everyday things
doctor	photograph
_____	_____
_____	_____
_____	_____
_____	_____
_____	_____
_____	_____

[ ] 14

2 Write the countries.

1 aclodstn   _Scotland_

2 ajpna   _____

3 auitasarl   _____

4 rcafne   _____

5 apnsi   _____

6 lnaegnd   _____

7 ltyia   _____

8 het tduine tesats _____

9 libarz   _____

[ ] 8

TRANSLATE

Translate the sentences into your language. Translate the _ideas_, not word by word.

1 What's your name?

_____

2 How are you?

_____

3 I'm fine, thanks.

_____

4 What's this in English?

_____

5 He's a taxi driver.

_____

6 His name's John. Her name's Karen.

_____

7 How old are you?

_____

8 I'm twenty-six.

_____

9 They aren't married.

_____

10 Is she from Spain? Yes, she is.

_____

TOTAL [ ] 100

Stop and check 2

Correct the mistakes

Each sentence has a mistake. Find it and correct it.

1 ~~They~~ teacher is from Wales.
   Their teacher is from Wales.

2 My sisters husband is a doctor.
   _____

3 The childrens live in London.
   _____

4 He have a new car.
   _____

5 We car is Italian.
   _____

6 How old have you?
   _____

7 I am like tennis.
   _____

8 I no speak German very well.
   _____

9 She live in Tokyo.
   _____

10 We have a house big.
   _____

11 They not like Chinese food.
   _____

12 Where she work?
   _____

13 My husband don't work in an office.
   _____

14 Does they speak French?
   _____

15 What sports do she like?
   _____

16 We don't never drink wine.
   _____

15

Questions and negatives

1 Write questions.

   1 Where / you / live?
      Where do you live?

   2 How / you / spell / your name?
      _____

   3 How many / sisters / he / have?
      _____

   4 What / food / she / like?
      _____

   5 Where / you / have lunch?
      _____

   6 What / music / you / like?
      _____

   7 How many / languages / they / speak?
      _____

   8 What time / you / get up?
      _____

   9 What / drinks / the children / like?
      _____

   10 What time / Helen / go to bed?
      _____

   11 Where / your teacher / come from?
      _____

10

2 Write the statements as questions and negatives.

   1 Julie is Richard's sister.
      Is Julie Richard's sister?
      Julie isn't Richard's sister.

   2 They have a house in the centre.
      _____ ?
      _____ .

3 He speaks three languages.

_____?

_____.

4 You get up early.

_____?

_____.

5 Victoria has lunch in her office.

_____?

_____.

6 He goes to bed late.

_____?

_____.

7 We have lessons at 7.30.

_____?

_____.

8 Your parents drink wine.

_____?

_____.

9 She speaks English well.

_____?

_____.

10 He cooks lunch.

_____?

_____.

18

Prepositions

Complete the sentences with the prepositions in the box.

| in   on   by   at |

1 We live __in__ the city centre.

2 I go to work _____ 8.30.

3 Do you work _____ the evening?

4 The children go to school _____ bus.

5 He works _____ a hospital.

6 We don't get up early _____ the weekend.

7 My parents eat in a restaurant _____ Friday evening.

8 I don't go to school _____ Saturday.

9 We don't watch TV _____ the afternoon.

10 They have lunch _____ one o'clock.

11 I sometimes go to work _____ taxi.

10

Times and prices

Write the times and prices.

1

It's one ten.

2

29p

It's twenty-nine p.

3

_____

4

_____

5

_____

6

_____

7

_____

8

95p

_____

9

£1.35

_____

10

£12.72

_____

11

£68.41

_____

12

£99.99

_____

10

© Oxford University Press   **Photocopiable**

Vocabulary – countries and nationalities

Complete the table.

Country	Nationality
England	**English**
Portugal	
_____	Spanish
France	
_____	German
Italy	_____
Brazil	_____
_____	American
Japan	_____

8

Vocabulary – words that go together

Match a line in A with a line in B.

A	B
watch	late
listen to	coffee
get up	shopping
drink	music
work	the piano
stay	a shower
go	in an office
have	to work
walk	at home
play	TV

9

Vocabulary – word groups

Put the words in the correct column. Each column has a different number of words.

~~good~~ studio beautiful skiing college big office
funny classroom favourite tennis nice flat
swimming farm small school great restaurant
football university

Adjectives	Places	Sports
good		

20

TOTAL 100

TRANSLATE

Translate the sentences into your language. Translate the *ideas*, not word by word.

1 John is Diana's husband.

_____

2 What's your friend's address?

_____

3 My wife has a good job.

_____

4 We have two children.

_____

5 I like swimming.

_____

6 We don't like Chinese food.

_____

7 'Do you live in the country?' 'Yes, I do.'

_____

8 He leaves school at four thirty.

_____

9 'Does Graham walk to work?' 'No, he doesn't.'

_____

10 We never go out in the evening.

_____

Stop and check 3

Correct the mistakes

Each sentence has a mistake. Find it and correct it.

1 Do you like dogs? Yes, I love ~~it~~.
   Do you like dogs? Yes, I love them.

2 My son is a student and I don't see her very often.
   _____

3 That's a photo of my children and my.
   _____

4 She lives in a old house.
   _____

5 There is three magazines on the table.
   _____

6 There aren't some good restaurants in this area.
   _____

7 There aren't a computer in the living room.
   _____

8 Are there a nice shops in the city centre?
   _____

9 I am born in 1985.
   _____

10 Where was you born?
   _____

11 The weather isn't very good yesterday.
   _____

12 She play tennis yesterday morning.
   _____

13 She goed on holiday last week.
   _____

14 Where did you go ski?
   _____

15 What did you had for breakfast?
   _____

16 Did you buyed a newspaper yesterday?
   _____

[15]

Questions and answers

Match the questions (1–11) with the answers (a–k).

1 [b] How are you?
2 [ ] What did you have for lunch?
3 [ ] Where are my keys?
4 [ ] What time did you get up?
5 [ ] How old are your children?
6 [ ] How many children do you have?
7 [ ] How much was your camera?
8 [ ] Why do you want to learn English?
9 [ ] Do you like jazz?
10 [ ] How do you travel to work?
11 [ ] Who was Agatha Christie?

a At about seven thirty.
b Fine, thanks.
c About a hundred pounds.
d Yes, I love it.
e By car.
f They're on the table.
g She was an English writer.
h Because I need it for my job.
i Two – a boy and a girl.
j Twelve and fifteen.
k Pizza and salad.

[10]

there is / are

Complete the sentences with the correct form of *there is / are*.

1 <u>There</u> <u>is</u> a new computer in my school.

2 _____ _____ a Thai restaurant near here.

3 _____ _____ twenty students in my group.

4 There's a TV, but _____ _____ a video recorder.

5 _____ _____ a new cooker in the kitchen?

6 _____ _____ any pictures on the walls?

7 There are some nice shops, but _____ _____ any supermarkets.

[6]

Past Simple

Complete the text with the Past Simple form of the verbs in brackets. There are regular and irregular verbs.

Elvis Presley (1) __was__ (be) born on 8 January 1935. He (2) _____ (live) with his parents in Tupelo, Mississippi for the first thirteen years of his life. In 1948, they (3) _____ (go) to Memphis because his father (4) _____ (want) to find a job. Elvis (5) _____ (not like) his new home or school, but he (6) _____ (love) music. He (7) _____ (leave) school in 1953 and (8) _____ (work) in different jobs. Two years later, Elvis (9) _____ (join) RCA Records and in very little time he (10) _____ (be) famous for his music, dancing and films. He (11) _____ (have) hundreds of hits including 'Love me Tender', 'Hound Dog', 'Blue Suede Shoes', and 'Jailhouse Rock'.

☐ 20

Irregular verbs

Write the Past Simple form of these irregular verbs.

1 go   __went__   5 buy _____
2 see _____   6 take _____
3 get _____   7 say _____
4 do   _____   8 eat _____

☐ 7

was / were / did / didn't

Complete the sentences with the verbs in the box.

was	wasn't	were	weren't	did	didn't

1 I __was__ 25 on my last birthday.
2 The weather _____ cold and wet last week.
3 '_____ you on holiday last week?' 'Yes, I was.'
4 _____ you get up early yesterday?
5 We _____ at work yesterday. It was a holiday.
6 I love holidays, but I _____ have a good time last year.
7 I went to see my friend but she _____ at home.
8 'Were they at the party?' 'No, they _____.'
9 'Did he go swimming yesterday?' 'No, he _____.'

☐ 8

Questions and negatives

Write the statements as questions and negatives.

1 He's a doctor.
   Is he a doctor?
   He isn't a doctor.

2 There's a CD player in the living room.
   _____ ?
   _____ .

3 She was born in 1980.
   _____ ?
   _____ .

4 He was a good student.
   _____ ?
   _____ .

5 We stayed at home last weekend.
   _____ ?
   _____ .

6 You went to bed early last night.
   _____ ?
   _____ .

☐ 10

Vocabulary

Put the words in the correct column.

~~good~~ sailing painter lamp cheap princess baseball
kitchen new writer hot dancing shower musician skiing
cooker singer tennis bed delicious fast president
armchair cards lovely

Adjectives	Rooms and furniture	People and jobs	Sports and activities
good			

24

TOTAL ▮ 100

Translate the sentences into your language. Translate the *ideas*, not word by word.

1 'Why do you want to leave your job?' 'Because I don't like it.'

_____

2 How many brothers and sister do you have?

_____

3 'What's this?' 'It's my new English book.'

_____

4 There aren't any Spanish restaurants in my town.

_____

5 Where were you born?

_____

6 She was a singer.

_____

7 I went swimming yesterday morning.

_____

8 We saw our friends last week.

_____

9 What did you do yesterday?

_____

10 He didn't have a good time on holiday.

_____

Stop and check 4

Correct the mistakes

Each sentence has a mistake. Find it and correct it.

1 He ~~haves~~ lunch at home.
   He has lunch at home.

2 I can speaking French.
   _____

3 She want to send an email.
   _____

4 'I like a coffee, please.' 'Here you are.'
   _____

5 'Do you like to come to my party?' 'Yes, please.'
   _____

6 I'd like shopping.
   _____

7 We learning English.
   _____

8 What do you wearing?
   _____

9 He no working today.
   _____

10 I'm do my homework now.
    _____

11 That's my father over there. He wears a black hat.
    _____

12 Where are you coming from?
    _____

13 We go on holiday next month.
    _____

14 Do you work tomorrow?
    _____

15 We had a good time last weekend.
    _____

16 How much did you stay in Spain?
    _____

|15|

Questions and answers

1 Match the questions (1–9) with the answers (a–i).

1 [f] Do you sell computer magazines?
2 [ ] What would you like to start?
3 [ ] Can you tell me the time, please?
4 [ ] Why don't you sit down and relax?
5 [ ] What's the problem?
6 [ ] Where can I buy a phone card?
7 [ ] How long does the bus tour take?
8 [ ] Can I help you?
9 [ ] When is the tourist office open?

a I'm lost.
b Try the newsagent.
c From nine o'clock to seven o'clock every day.
d It's two fifteen.
e The soup, please.
f No, I'm sorry, we don't.
g I'm just looking, thanks.
h About an hour.
i That's a good idea.

|8|

2 Complete the questions with a question word or words.

1 **What** 's your name?
   My name's Victoria Simpson.

2 _____ are you doing?
   I'm writing to my friend.

3 _____ are you going on holiday?
   We're going to Italy.

4 _____ did you travel?
   We travelled by train and bus.

5 _____ did you return early?
   Because the weather was bad.

6 _____ did you go on holiday with?
   I went with my parents.

7 _____ do you get up?
   At seven thirty.

8 _____ did your car cost?
   About £5,000.

9 _____ brothers and sisters do you have?
Two brothers and a sister.

10 _____ is your daughter?
She's 15. Her birthday is in June.

11 _____ is your party?
It's on Saturday 20th of July.

☐ 10

can / want / like / would like

Choose the correct word.

1 '(Do)/ Would you want a drink?' 'Yes, please.'

2 'Do you like Italian food?' 'Yes, I like / do.'

3 'Do / Would you like to watch a video?' 'That's a good idea.'

4 I'd like / I like to buy a computer, please.

5 My father wants / want to learn English.

6 You can buying / buy stamps in a post office.

7 She doesn't / don't like dogs.

8 I cant / can't speak German very well.

9 Do they like sail / sailing?

10 He can / cans use a computer.

11 We like / We'd like our new house.

☐ 10

Present Simple and Continuous

Complete the sentences with the correct form of the verb in brackets.

1 He usually __goes__ (go) to work by bus.

2 We __'re having__ (have) lunch at the moment.

3 She _____ (phone) her parents every day.

4 She's on the beach and she _____ (wear) a swimsuit.

5 _____ you usually _____ (get up) late at weekends?

6 John _____ (have) a birthday party every year.

7 Don't talk to Linda. She _____ (do) her homework at the moment.

8 Where are Mum and Dad? They _____ (sit) in the garden.

9 The children always _____ (watch) TV in the evening.

10 _____ they _____ (work) at home today?

11 Put your jacket on. It _____ (rain).

12 How often _____ you _____ (go) to the theatre?

☐ 10

Present Continuous for future

Complete the sentences with a verb and a noun from the boxes. Use the Present Continuous.

> **Verbs:**
> ~~stay~~ travel collect get married meet go have
>
> **Nouns:**
> ~~hotel~~ restaurant cinema friends church train tickets

1 We __'re staying__ in a __hotel__ in Edinburgh next month.

2 My boyfriend and I _____ in a beautiful _____ next month.

3 _____ you _____ the _____ from the travel agent tomorrow morning?

4 Tomorrow is Saturday. I _____ my _____ in town.

5 They _____ dinner in a new _____ tomorrow.

6 She _____ to France by _____ next week.

7 We _____ to the _____ next weekend to see the new Brad Pitt film.

☐ 12

Past, present, and future

Complete the dialogue with the correct form of the verbs in brackets. Use the Present Simple, Present Continuous, Present Continuous for future, and Past Simple.

A What (1) __are__ you __doing__ (do) tomorrow?

B I (2) _____ (play) tennis with my brother.

A Really? (3) _____ you _____ (play) every week?

B Only in the summer. But my brother (4) _____ (play) two or three times every week – he's very good. He (5) _____ (start) when he was a child, but (6) I _____ (not like) sport very much then. (7) _____ you _____ in sport?

A Well, I (8) _____ (go) swimming every week, and windsurfing in the summer. I (9) _____ (go) to Australia last year.

B (10) _____ you _____ (have) a good time?

A Yes, it was fantastic. I was with some friends and we (11) _____ (travel) to different places. We (12) _____ (visit) Sydney and Melbourne.

B (13) _____ you _____ (go) to Australia for your next holiday?

A No, we (14) _____ (go) to the US. My sister (15) _____ (live) in Florida and we (16) _____ (stay) with her for two weeks in August.

B That's great! Have a good time!

A Thanks very much.

[ ] 15

Vocabulary – word groups

Put the words in the correct column.

~~hamburger~~ red fish bicycle jeans fries yellow jacket ham plane grey jumper underground cheese steak train white T-shirt trousers brown ship

Food	Clothes	Colours	Transport
hamburger			

[ ] 20

TOTAL [100]

TRANSLATE

Translate the sentences into your language. Translate the *ideas*, not word by word.

1 I can't play the guitar.

   _____

2 Can I help you?

   _____

3 'Would you like a sandwich?' 'No, thank you.'

   _____

4 I'd like to go to the theatre this evening.

   _____

5 We're learning English.

   _____

6 What are you reading?

   _____

7 Do you read the newspaper every day?

   _____

8 We're flying to New York tomorrow.

   _____

9 What are you doing next weekend?

   _____

Answer keys

Extra ideas Units 1–4

Reading

1 1 No, she isn't.
   2 He's 12.
   3 He's from the United States.
   4 Sumio
   5 Lucia and Sumio
   6 Todd

2 1 false   4 false   7 false
   2 true   5 true
   3 false   6 true

Language work

1 2 How do you spell your surname?
   3 Where are you from?
   4 How old are you?
   5 Are you married?
   6 What's your job?
   7 Where's your bank?
   8 What's your favourite music?

Everyday English

1 d   2 c   3 b   4 a   5 e

Extra ideas Units 5–8

Reading

1 1 She's a writer.
   2 She lives in Manchester.
   3 Her favourite room is her office.
   4 She has breakfast, works, listens to music, and eats her dinner in her office.

2 1 true   3 false   5 false
   2 true   4 true

3 it – Nicola's room
   them – Nicola's children
   her – Nicola's mother
   she – Nicola's mother
   them – email messages
   me – Nicola

Language work

1 Possible answers:
   2 What's your favourite room?
   3 Do you work from home?
   4 Do you work late?
   5 Do you like your job?
   6 Do you speak German?
   7 Why do you want to learn English?
   8 What drinks do you like?
   9 What do you do in the evening?
   10 How many brothers and sisters do you have?

Everyday English

1 d   2 e   3 a   4 c   5 b

Extra ideas Units 9–12

Reading

1 Students' own answers.

2 1 true   3 true   5 true
   2 false   4 false

Language work

1 3 Who did you go with?
   4 Did you travel by plane?
   5 Where did you stay?
   6 What did you eat?
   7 Was the weather good?
   8 Did you have a good time?

Everyday English

1 d   2 a   3 e   4 c   5 b

Extra ideas Units 13–14

Reading

1

Clothes	Colours
suit	blue
hat	green
gloves	yellow
jeans	red
T-shirt	black
shirt	grey
sports clothes	brown
jogging trousers	pink
trainers	
ski jacket	
walking boots	
trousers	

2 1 People wear informal clothes and colours today.
   2 People can wear jeans and T-shirts for work. They can wear blue, red, yellow, red and pink.
   3 No, she doesn't. She wears sports clothes because they are fashionable and comfortable.
   4 No, they don't. Children choose their own clothes.
   5 Children's clothes are expensive because they like to have designer labels.
   6 She likes today's fashions because they are more informal and men and women can wear the same things.

Language work

3 What are your favourite clothes shops?
4 Do you buy clothes on the Internet?
5 How much do you spend on clothes?
6 Do you buy designer labels?
7 What do you wear for work/school/ university?
8 What are you wearing now?
9 What are your favourite colours?
10 Do you borrow other people's clothes?

Everyday English

1 f   2 e   3 a   4 c   5 b   6 d

Progress test 1

Exercise 1

2 are   aren't
3 is   isn't
4 are   aren't
5 are   aren't

Exercise 2

2 Are   7 Are
3 is   8 isn't
4 aren't   9 is
5 'm not   10 isn't
6 are   11 Is

Exercise 3

'Where are you from?' 'Lyons, in France.'
'How are you?' 'I'm fine, thanks.'
'How much is a sandwich?' '£1.75.'
'How old is your daughter?' 'She's 18.'
'Who is Sally?' 'She's my daughter.'

Exercise 4

2 This is Peter's wife.
3 What is their phone number?
4 We have a house in the country.
5 How do you spell your surname?
6 Do you like Spanish wine?
7 I don't speak French very well.
8 We don't have a German car.
9 Do they eat Chinese food?

Exercise 5

2 an   5 a   8 a
3 a   6 an   9 an
4 an   7 a   10 a

Exercise 6

2 has   6 has
3 don't have   7 Do … have
4 have   8 has
5 have   9 Do … have

Exercise 7

2 don't like   7 do … speak
3 drink   8 Do … speak
4 do … like   9 don't work
5 work   10 do … live
6 don't like   11 Do … eat

Exercise 8

2 your   6 my
3 He's   7 her
4 She   8 His
5 our   9 their

Exercise 9

2a   3b   4a   5b   6b

Exercise 10

2 twenty-nine   7 seventy-four
3 thirty-seven   8 eighty-eight
4 forty-three   9 ninety-one
5 fifty-nine   10 one hundred
6 sixty-two

Exercise 11

Jobs	Family	Food	Drinks
actor	parent	sandwich	beer
bank manager	sister	hamburger	wine
shop assistant	daughter	chocolate	coffee
police officer	son	ice-cream	tea
waiter	husband	orange	Coca-Cola

Progress test 2

Exercise 1

2 He never works late.
3 I sometimes go to work by car.
4 My son always has lunch at school.
5 She usually sees her friends after school.
6 I never buy a newspaper.
7 Helen sometimes goes windsurfing.

Exercise 2

2 him   5 us
3 it   6 them
4 her   7 you

Exercise 3

2 There are two books on the table.
3 There's a lamp next to the sofa.
4 There are three pictures on the walls.
5 There's a cat under the table.
6 There's a magazine in the bag.

Exercise 4

2 were   weren't
3 was   wasn't
4 were   weren't
5 were   weren't

Exercise 5

2 Do   6 Did
3 were   7 was
4 did   8 were
5 Does   9 do

Exercise 6

2 didn't work   6 saw
3 bought   7 didn't take
4 did … go   8 Did … eat
5 stayed   9 did

Exercise 7

2 The film isn't very good.
3 There isn't a CD player in the car.
4 She doesn't go to work by car.
5 We don't go shopping in town.
6 There aren't a lot of hotels in this area.
7 The weather wasn't very hot.
8 My children weren't born in the US.
9 I wasn't born in 1989.
10 David didn't play baseball at school.
11 I didn't have a big lunch.

Exercise 8

Tuesday, Wednesday, Thursday, Friday, Saturday, Sunday

Exercise 9

2 the first of February
3 the nineteenth of June
4 the third of August
5 the thirty-first of December
6 the twelfth of October
7 the seventeenth of April
8 the fifth of January
9 the seventh of July

Exercise 10

2 on		4 on		6 at	
3 at		5 in		7 at	

Exercise 11

go sailing
watch a video
listen to a CD
play cards
stay in a chalet
work in a hospital
cook a meal
eat in restaurants
have a good time
drink beer

Exercise 12

2 German (The others are countries.)
3 shower (The others are electrical appliances.)
4 ice hockey (The others go with *go*, not *play*.)
5 twenty-nine (The others are ordinals.)
6 footballer (The others are jobs in the Arts.)
7 watched (The others are irregular.)
8 walking (The others are water sports.)
9 kitchen (The others are parts of a room.)

Exercise 13

early – late
small – big
expensive – cheap
fast – slow
cold – hot
lovely – horrible

Progress test 3

Exercise 1

2 She has long, fair hair.
3 How long does the bus tour last?
4 Would you like to listen to the radio?
5 Can you tell me the time, please?
6 They want to buy a new car.
7 What would you like to drink?
8 He is wearing jeans and a T-shirt. *or* He is wearing a T-shirt and jeans.
9 Where are you going next weekend?
10 Why don't you go to bed early?
11 We collected our tickets from the travel agent.

Exercise 2

2 can't play the guitar
3 can't ride a horse   can't play the guitar
4 can use a computer
5 Can … cook
6 can ride a horse

Exercise 3

2 Do you like wine?
3 I want to send an email, please.
4 Would you like to listen to some music?
5 I'd like to buy these postcards, please.
6 What sports do you like doing?

Exercise 4

2 's working	6 Is … raining
3 'm leaving	7 's having
4 's wearing	8 Are … enjoying
5 'm driving	9 are writing

Exercise 5

2 don't see   are staying
3 have   are eating
4 are … wearing   wear
5 are learning   like
6 lives   's travelling

Exercise 6

2 She cooked dinner yesterday. She isn't cooking dinner tomorrow.
3 We worked late yesterday. We aren't working late tomorrow.
4 They left home early yesterday. They aren't leaving home early tomorrow.
5 I went to bed late yesterday. I'm not going to bed late tomorrow.
6 You stayed at home yesterday. You aren't staying at home tomorrow.
7 Richard saw his doctor yesterday. He isn't seeing his doctor tomorrow.

Exercise 7

2 She doesn't want to sell her house.
3 They don't like sightseeing.
4 He can't swim.
5 He doesn't work in a bank.
6 We don't walk to work every day.
7 I'm not watching this film.
8 The children aren't doing their homework.
9 You aren't playing very well.
10 We aren't staying in the hotel for a week.
11 We didn't have a nice meal at the restaurant.
12 You didn't collect the tickets yesterday.
13 Angela didn't see her family last week.

Exercise 8

2 is	6 didn't	10 am			
3 does	7 isn't	11 doesn't			
4 do	8 'm not	12 Did			
5 aren't	9 don't	13 Are			

Exercise 9

2 cake (The others are drinks.)
3 meal (The others are types of food.)
4 soup (The others are desserts.)
5 airport (The others are forms of transport.)
6 grandmother (The others are jobs.)
7 stamp (The others are to do with travelling.)
8 shoes (The others are worn on the legs.)
9 dress (The others are items of clothing for both men and women.)
10 long (The others are colours.)
11 waiter (The others are parts of a meal.)
12 interview (The others are to do with taking photos.)
13 email (The others are to do with sending letters.)

Exercise 10

watch a video
read a magazine
chat to a friend
wear shorts
play chess
book a holiday
catch a plane
change money
go sightseeing
have a good time
pack your bags
arrive in Paris
make a cake

Stop and check 1

Correct the mistakes

2 What's your name?
3 My name is Ana.
4 This is Helen Smith.
5 It's a book.
6 Where are you from?
7 I'm from Spain. / I am from Spain.
8 He's a businessman. His name's James.
9 What's her job? She's a doctor.
10 He isn't a teacher. He's a student.
11 How old are you?
12 Is she from London? Yes, she is.
13 Is he a shop assistant? No, he isn't.
14 Are you from France? No, I'm not.
15 His phone number is 772541.
16 My teacher and I are 30.

my/your, he/she/they, his/her

2 His
3 They
4 your
5 She's
6 They're
7 He's

Questions and answers

1 2 c   3 a   4 b   5 d   6 g   7 e   8 h

2 2 Where's she from?
   3 What's her job?
   4 How old is she?
   5 What's her phone number?
   6 Is she married?

Negatives

2 She isn't a nurse.
3 Karl isn't from Canada.
4 Julie isn't 29.
5 I'm not married.
6 Jim and Sue aren't students.
7 They aren't in New York.

Plurals

2 We're English.
3 They're sandwiches.
4 They're students.
5 They're from the United States.
6 We aren't on tour.
7 Are they doctors?

Numbers

1 6 six   8 eight   10 ten
   1 one   4 four   7 seven
   2 two   9 nine
   5 five   3 three

2 2 eleven   6 thirty
   3 twenty-eight   7 thirteen
   4 twenty   8 fifteen
   5 fourteen

Vocabulary

1

Jobs	Everyday things
nurse	sandwich
student	book
teacher	television
businessman	camera
shop assistant	bag
taxi driver	computer
police officer	hamburger

2 2 Japan   6 England
   3 Australia   7 Italy
   4 France   8 the United States
   5 Spain   9 Brazil

Translate

The idea behind this is that students begin to be aware of the similarities and differences between English and L1. Emphasize that they must not translate word by word. Obviously it will only be possible to check their answers in a monolingual class but even in a multilingual class students can discuss their answers in nationality groups.

Stop and check 2

Correct the mistakes

2 My sister's husband is a doctor.
3 The children live in London.
4 He has a new car.
5 Our car is Italian.
6 How old are you?
7 I like tennis.
8 I don't speak German very well.
9 She lives in Tokyo.
10 We have a big house.
11 They don't like Chinese food.
12 Where does she work?
13 My husband doesn't work in an office.
14 Do they speak French?
15 What sports does she like?
16 We never drink wine.

Questions and negatives

1 2 How do you spell your name?
   3 How many sisters does he have?
   4 What food does she like?
   5 Where do you have lunch?
   6 What music do you like?
   7 How many languages do they speak?
   8 What time do you get up?
   9 What drinks do the children like?
   10 What time does Helen go to bed?
   11 Where does your teacher come from?

2 1 Do they have a house in the centre?
      They don't have a house in the centre.
   2 Does he speak three languages?
      He doesn't speak three languages.
   3 Do you get up early?
      You don't get up early.
   4 Does Victoria have lunch in her office?
      Victoria doesn't have lunch in her office.
   5 Does he go to bed late?
      He doesn't go to bed late.
   6 Do we have lessons at 7.30?
      We don't have lessons at 7.30.
   7 Do your parents drink wine?
      Your parents don't drink wine.
   8 Does she speak English well?
      She doesn't speak English well.
   9 Does he cook lunch?
      He doesn't cook lunch.

Prepositions

2 at
3 in
4 by
5 in
6 at
7 on
8 on
9 in
10 at
11 by

Times and prices

3 It's twelve o'clock.
4 It's eleven thirty.
5 It's nine forty-five.
6 It's two twenty.
7 It's four fifty-five.
8 It's ninety-five p.
9 It's one pound thirty-five.
10 It's twelve pounds seventy-two.
11 It's sixty-eight pounds forty-one.
12 It's ninety-nine pounds ninety-nine.

Vocabulary – countries and nationalities

Country	Nationality
England	**English**
Portugal	**Portuguese**
Spain	Spanish
France	**French**
Germany	German
Italy	**Italian**
Brazil	**Brazilian**
the United States	American
Japan	**Japanese**

Vocabulary – words that go together

listen to music
get up late
drink coffee
work in an office
stay at home
go shopping
have a shower
walk to work
play the piano

Vocabulary – word groups

Adjectives	Places	Sports
beautiful	studio	skiing
big	college	tennis
funny	office	swimming
favourite	classroom	football
nice	flat	
small	farm	
great	school	
	restaurant	
	university	

Translate

See note about translation on p145.

Stop and check 3

Correct the mistakes

2 My son is a student and I don't see him very often.
3 That's a photo of my children and me.
4 She lives in an old house.
5 There are three magazines on the table.
6 There aren't any good restaurants in this area.
7 There isn't a computer in the living room.
8 Are there any nice shops in the city centre?
9 I was born in 1985.
10 Where were you born?
11 The weather wasn't very good yesterday.
12 She played tennis yesterday morning.
13 She went on holiday last week.
14 Where did you go skiing?
15 What did you have for breakfast?
16 Did you buy a newspaper yesterday?

Questions and answers

2k 3f 4a 5j 6i 7c 8h 9d 10e 11g

there is/are

2 There is
3 There are
4 there isn't
5 Is there
6 Are there
7 there aren't

Past Simple

2 lived
3 went
4 wanted
5 didn't like
6 loved
7 left
8 worked
9 joined
10 was
11 had

Irregular verbs

2 saw
3 got
4 did
5 bought
6 took
7 said
8 ate

was/were/did/didn't

2 was
3 Were
4 Did
5 weren't
6 didn't
7 wasn't
8 weren't
9 didn't

Questions and negatives

2 Is there a CD player in the living room?
  There isn't a CD player in the living room.

3 Was she born in 1980?
  She wasn't born in 1980.

4 Was he a good student?
  He wasn't a good student.

5 Did we stay at home last weekend?
  We didn't stay at home last weekend.

6 Did you go to bed early last night?
  You didn't go to bed early last night.

Vocabulary

Adjectives	Rooms and furniture	People and jobs	Sports and activities
cheap	lamp	painter	sailing
new	kitchen	princess	baseball
hot	shower	writer	dancing
delicious	cooker	musician	skiing
fast	bed	singer	tennis
lovely	armchair	president	cards

Translate

See note about translation on p145.

Stop and check 4

Correct the mistakes

2 I can speak French.
3 She wants to send an email.
4 'I'd like a coffee, please.' 'Here you are.'
5 'Would you like to come to my party?' 'Yes, please.'
6 I like shopping.
7 We are learning English.
8 What are you wearing?
9 He isn't working today.
10 I'm doing my homework now.
11 That's my father over there. He's wearing a black hat.
12 Where do you come from?
13 We're going on holiday next month.
14 Are you working tomorrow?
15 We had a good time last weekend.
16 How long did you stay in Spain?

Questions and answers

1 2e 3d 4i 5a 6b 7h 8g 9c

2 2 What   7 What time
   3 Where   8 How much
   4 How   9 How many
   5 Why   10 How old
   6 Who   11 When

can / want / like / would like

2 do   7 doesn't
3 Would   8 can't
4 I'd like   9 sailing
5 wants   10 can
6 buy   11 We like

Present Simple and Continuous

3 phones   8 are sitting
4 's wearing   9 watch
5 Do…get up   10 Are … working
6 has   11 's raining
7 is doing   12 do … go

Present Continuous for future

2 are getting married / church
3 Are … collecting / tickets
4 am meeting / friends
5 are having / restaurant
6 is travelling / train
7 are going / cinema

Past, present, and future

2 am playing
3 Do … play
4 plays
5 started
6 didn't like
7 Are … interested
8 go
9 went
10 Did … have
11 travelled
12 visited
13 Are … going
14 are going
15 lives
16 are staying

Vocabulary – word groups

Food	Clothes	Colours	Transport
fish	jeans	red	bicycle
fries	jacket	yellow	plane
ham	jumper	grey	underground
cheese	T-shirt	white	train
steak	trousers	brown	ship

Translate

See note about translation on p145.